PN
3433.8
.F8

Future females.

A

y

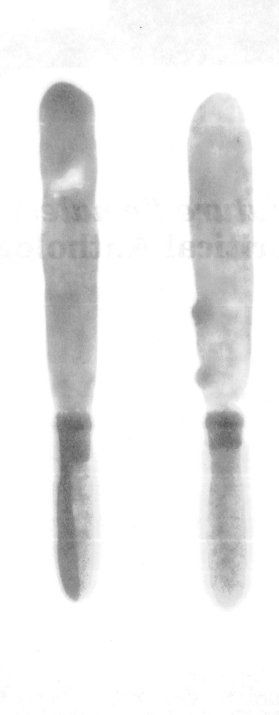

Future Females:
A Critical Anthology

Marleen S. Barr

Virginia Polytechnic Institute and State University

Bowling Green State University Popular Press
Bowling Green, Ohio 43403

For
Roslyn [H.] Barr and George [E.] Barr
Stella Diamond and Samuel Diamond
May Barr and Harry Barr

(I believe they *all* know...)

With love and appreciation

Acknowledgements

Pat Browne made this book possible. Her patience and understanding are greatly appreciated.

It was a pleasure to work with all of the contributors. I thank them for allowing me to include their work.

Norman N. Holland, Jeffrey Berman, and Eric S. Rabkin read and commented upon "Charles Bronson, Samurai, and Other Feminine Images." Any remaining errors are, of course, my own.

Lyman Tower Sargent's "An Ambiguous Legacy" first appeared in *Extrapolation*. Thomas Clareson generously permitted me to reprint it.

Contents

*Susan Janice Anderson used this expression in her introduction to *Aurora: Beyond Equality*.

Marlene S. Barr

Preface

"A JUSTIFICATION FOR PAYING SERIOUS attention to science fiction may by now be necessary only for other literary critics and scholars. Still, the question of why a book addressing itself to science fiction...has to be faced briefly."[1] This comment, the opening statement of Darko Suvin's recent book, concerns me since *Future Females* addresses itself to *women* in science fiction. After all, metaphorically speaking, if the mere mention of this genre causes a ruffling of academic feathers, then, relating it to women is analogous to placing all those simply ruffled feathers in front of a wind machine.

Unfortunately, Pamela Sargent reminds us that such an attitude toward women-related topics would not be limited to the academic community's mainstream:

[Russ'] 'When It Changed' won the Nebula Award....Yet it was also severely criticized in some science fiction publications. It is a bit odd that readers should feel threatened by a story in which well-characterized, likeable women can get along without men, when there is such an abundance of science fiction in which well-characterized, likeable men get along without women.[2]

This reaction exemplifies my belief that everyone will not welcome the creation of a book-length critical space where science fiction is viewed in terms of women. This anthology was compiled to provide such a space.

As Roger Schlobin's bibliography indicates, women are certainly contributing to the science fiction field. Anthologies of fiction have called attention to these contributions by introducing new female artists, illustrating the history of women's input into the genre, and reminding readers that science fiction is especially suited for speculation about women's future roles.[3] We have collections of fiction devoted to women and science fiction; we need collections of critical essays which illuminate this fiction. The time for *Future Females* has come.

Of course, this proper moment owes its existence to the efforts of feminists. Minda Rae Amiran's *College English* article which questions the validity of "women's literature," helps to focus the anthology in light of feminist criticism. She states:

1

I am well aware that many feminists today are not concerned with women's literature as literature. They wish us to reconsider our values and assumptions, or to rediscover forgotten books by women...or they wish to use literary materials to document the sufferings of womankind; or they wish to expose the conflicts of female authors, or to learn ways of coping from female protagonists. Their interest is political, broadly defined....However, the issues are not always so clear cut.[4]

Since the contributions do fall into Amiran's categories, according to her viewpoint, the essay collection is clear cut and broadly political. At the beginning of any venture, the presence of directness and relevancy are necessary and positive.

*   *   *

Joanna Russ, Carol Pearson and Lyman Tower Sargent have written articles about utopia, literature which shares generic boundaries with science fiction[5] and comments upon reality by asking readers to reconsider their values and assumptions; these essays also acquaint us with the work of women—and men—which might have been either forgotten or overlooked. The reconsideration of proper feminine roles is the subject of Edward J. Whetmore's analysis of the *Star Trek* episode in which it was appropriate to change "Ms." with "Captain." And, Scott Sanders shows how science fiction has reinforced stereotypic ideas by equating women with nature. All these essays heighten our understanding of restrictions women have faced: utopias point to conditions which should be improved; nature, or biology, must not be seen as destiny; and, the female captain gave up the ship.

The contributions of Jeffrey Berman, Eric S. Rabkin, and Norman N. Holland also generate the rethinking of some assumptions. This time, however, instead of pondering social roles, readers might reexamine their expectations of the critical essays they expect to find in a book about women and science fiction. For example, it seems reasonable to assume that every article in this volume would stress science fiction's depiction of women as insignificant helpmates or sex objects. No so. Rabkin illuminates the genre's positive portrayals of women. Nor is Berman complaining. His "Where's All the Fiction in Science Fiction?" relies upon women-centered texts to discuss science fiction's visions of future artists. And, Holland's presence in a science fiction anthology is quite unexpected.

Just as unexpectedly, when James D. Merritt cites examples of Milton's Eve in twentieth century science fiction, a scholar of the Victorian period has his say about contemporary literature in terms of a seventeenth century masterpiece. Of course, Eve caused all the sufferings of mankind—and womankind. Two essays in this volume point out that, like Eve, female science fiction writers also face conflicts of interest: Susan Kress' article analyzes the logic behind Marge Piercy's use of science fiction, and Suzy McKee Charnas discusses her experiences as a woman who creates female characters. A female writer's work helped me describe how I have coped with the consequences of gender in our society.

After summarizing these essays I must say that I feel more responsible for the presence of specific critical voices rather than for the subject matter of those voices. I chose the contributors; they chose their topics. While making those choices, I was attempting to find a satisfactory reply to a specific question: What should an anthology of critical essays about women and science fiction look like? A concern I share with Sandra M. Gilbert guided me toward my version of the answer:

While it is obviously important for women of letters to talk with passion and conviction to and about each other, I think it is just as important for us to talk to—and be heard by—our male colleagues...the dangers of separatism are real and great. Lately, alas, it has seemed to me that by and large we feminist critics talk only to each other and to a few other literary women who define themselves as potential converts to our creed...feminist criticism is and should be a major current in the mainstream of contemporary thought.[6]

I tried to avoid the dangers of limiting the book to one perspective by including the work of men and women with diversified interests: feminists, those who would not call themselves feminists, science fiction writers, a media specialist, a political scientist, established scholars and younger scholars. Despite my efforts to present a broad range of background and opinion, in a single volume, diversity must, of course, have restrictions.

The differing viewpoints which are a part of the book enabled me to ponder, to use Ursula Le Guin's term, some "thought experiments."[7] I wondered: What would result when a female critic and a male critic both re-created a novel about the eradication of gender? What would an author/critic, a women's studies professor, and a scholar whose training was not in literature conclude about the female citizens of utopian societies? Would a woman be more scrupulous in her use of the word "non-sexist" than a man? What happens when the relationship between women and science fiction is discussed in terms of more than one art form? How does a female critic's analysis of a woman writer's work differ from a woman writer's discussion of her own creative process? Is it an accident that two male critics allude to a man's masterpiece as they argue that science fiction's portrayal of women is less than fair?

I do not desire to analyze the analyses. However, I will say that I hope this essay collection evokes some thoughts which range beyond science fiction's relationship to sexism. Although sexism cannot be entirely dismissed from the discussion, the book also considers women science fiction writers, female science fiction characters, male science fiction writers whose tales involve women, and expectations of critical essays about women in the genre. These categories reflect my desire to give "women and science fiction" wide definition and scope, even though they do not exhaust all possible ways of speaking about the term.

Responses to some of the essays appear within the volume. They create a feeling of dialogue and thereby form another aspect of the answer to my question about the appearance of this anthology. Annette Kolodny explains:

> ...perhaps we can ... disagree without rancor and without personal anger. For, in truth, our enterprise is *communal* to the extent that it is cumulative and aggregative, and, simultaneously, *individual* to the extent that each critical work is authored and unique. In short, what I am proposing is a kind of communal frame of mind which encourages debate and dialogue among individuals—but among individuals who are, first and foremost, committed to the validity of the shared effort...we can and must develop not only new critical methodologies but new and different critical voices as well.[8]

I think these responses do point toward a formulation of new and different critical voices: Whetmore read Arthur Asa Berger's comments without personal anger; Robert Scholes rejected the judgmental voice of a respondent and acted as a disseminator of further information; Anne Hudson Jones expanded upon one of Rabkin's points without attacking his conclusion. These attitudes are possible positive examples of Kolodny's call for a communal frame of mind among committed individuals.

Finally, this community of essays illustrates my notion that in addition to recovering the work of women who wrote during a bygone era, scholars who are interested in women and literature should devote more attention to science fiction's future visions. Consider: societies where women do not suffer from gender-based disadvantages may only emerge in science fiction's pages. More optimistically, even if future generations enjoy an equitable society, unlike Arthur C. Clarke's Stormgren,[9] we cannot witness something which occurs after our lifetime.

Science fiction, the realm of bulging blobs who devour partially undressed, distressed damsels, is also the home of speculations about future females. Science fiction should form a major current in the contemporary stream of feminist thought.

*   *   *

The book's title alludes to women, science fiction, and criticism. Its preface refers to feminist criticism to focus these three categories in terms of one another. This focal point is logical since women, science fiction and the criticism of women's literature fall into a common niche: they are all struggling to achieve recognition and respect. Of course, as a female, feminist critic who thinks seriously about science fiction, I have a strong response to the necessity of such struggles. Yet I hope these efforts are successfully achieved with the least amount of rancor and anger. Or, may these goals be reached without windblown feathers!

Notes

[1] Darko Suvin, *Metamorphoses of Science Fiction* (New Haven: Yale Univ. Press, 1979), p. vii.

[2] Pamela Sargent, "Introduction: Women of Wonder," in *Women of Wonder*, ed. Pamela Sargent (New York: Vintage Books, 1975), p. liii.

[3] In addition to the three Sargent anthologies, see Susan Janice Anderson and Vonda N. McIntyre, *Aurora: Beyond Equality* (New York: Fawcett, 1976).

[4] Minda Rae Amiran, "What Women's Literature?" *College English*, 39 (1978), 654.

[5] Eric S. Rabkin, *The Fantastic In Literature* (Princeton: Princeton Univ. Press, 1976), pp. 138-50.

[6] Sandra M. Gilbert, "Life Studies, or, Speech After Long Silence: Feminist Critics Today," *College English*, 40 (1979), 862-63.

[7] Ursula K. Le Guin, "Is Gender Necessary?" in *Aurora: Beyond Equality,* ed. Susan Janice Anderson and Vonda N. McIntyre (New York: Fawcett, 1976), p. 132.

[8] Annette Kolodny, "Some Notes on Defining A Feminist Literary Criticism" *Critical Inquiry*, 2 (1975), 91-92.

[9] Arthur C. Clarke, *Childhood's End* (New York: Ballantine Books, 1953), p. 64.

I Beyond BEMS and Boobs

Eric S. Rabkin

Science Fiction Women
Before Liberation

SCIENCE FICTION is and has been roundly, hotly, passionately and sometimes even fairly criticized for treating its female characters with lust, disdain, hostility, smarm and ever-present narrow-mindedness of both the ignorant and willful varieties. There is no denying that woman has been exploited as a sex object by science fiction publishers and cover illustrators who seem to hold to the tantalizing credo that half a garment is better than none. Authors, both female and male, have trivialized women characters starting even with the melodramatically long-suffering Elizabeth Lavenza, fiancée of the title scientist in *Frankenstein* (1818) by Mary Shelley, the grandmother of science fiction. It is true: science fiction needed, and may well still need, liberation. An honest effort at reformation of attitudes, however, depends less on slogans and outrage than on intelligent analysis and depth of commitment. For the newly guilt-ridden, it is easier to excoriate the genre than to examine it. Exactly how bad has science fiction been?

Science fiction has in a sense maltreated women by ignoring them. Thomas D. Clareson's pioneering anthology of science fiction criticism, *SF: The Other Side of Realism* (1971), includes essays on individual novels, individual authors and such general topics as "Robots in Science Fiction" (by Stanislaw Lem), but there is nothing on women in science fiction. One can hardly blame Clareson, of course; the essays to be reprinted had not yet been written. There were, of course, scattered observations. Sam J. Lundwall, for example, writing of modern science fiction, asserts that

> The woman in science fiction remains what she was, a compulsory appendage....
> even though women usually are present in the space ships, they are generally treated
> like some kind of inferior creature.... By her obvious ignorance ... she would give
> the hero the opportunity to launch into long explanations ... [and] she should be
> abducted by some horrible green monster with lots of fangs, which lovingly wound its
> tentacles around her appetizing form...(*Science Fiction: What It's All About*, 1971,
> ch. 7).

Anne McCaffrey has judiciously qualified such criticism in part by centering it on literature before our current political era:

9

Prior to the '60s ... in many stories ... the girl was still a "thing," to be "used" to perpetuate the hero's magnificent chromosomes. Or perhaps, to prove that the guy wasn't "queer." I mean, all those men locked away on a spaceship ... ('Hitch Your Dragon to a Star: Romance and Glamour in Science Fiction' in Reginald Bretnor, ed., *Science Fiction: Today and Tomorrow,* 1974).

Once upon a time, at least, something certainly seems to have been wrong.

To give science fiction its due, what might once have been so egregiously male-centered has not remained so. Pamela Sargent has edited an excellent series of anthologies of stories (*Women of Wonder,* 1974; *More Women of Wonder,* 1976; *The New Women of Wonder,* 1977) both by and about women that demonstrates through artistic achievement and sheer volume that a countervailing beachhead has now been permanently won on what once might have been considered exclusively male territory. These female writers, of course, are no more homogeneous in their writerly aims and political attitudes than are the male writers with whom they share the shelves of the local bookstore. Ursula K. Le Guin, for example, wrote an elegiac story ("The Day Before the Revolution," 1974) about the peaceful, nostalgic death of Odo, the woman who founded the anti-possessive philosophy of an "ambiguously utopian" world presented in Le Guin's widely-honored novel *The Dispossessed* (1974). Odo, on her dying day, thinks back to the man who in part inspired her, the man she likes to speak of "as 'my husband.' ... The word she should use as a good Odonian, of course, was 'partner.' But why the hell did she have to be a good Odonian?" Le Guin is gentle in her treatment of a good person grown old in striving to forge a new philosophy for others while never fully escaping the philosophy under which she was herself raised. *We Who Are About To* ... by Joanna Russ (1977) brutally contrasts Le Guin's work in both plot and attitude. In this novel of a group accidentally stranded on an uninhabited planet, the protagonist-narrator is so resentful of the possibility that human life will be established there by the expedient of breeding children among the surviving females, herself included, that she murders all her fellow reluctant colonists and commits suicide herself. Her bitterness extends even to the reader, as we see in this passage dictated into a tape recorder by the protagonist after she has taken the drugs which will turn out to be fatal:

I'm going to do a joke; I will put as the last words on this, Oh I see people in uniforms coming through the brush downstream; someone's coming to rescue me, Goddam.
    And there they are! Coming through the brush—almost at the horizon, I think, but in white—people in white, as if they were the survey team for this tagged,

unfurnished house—and they're following the line of the river. Six of them. Coming this way. What a damned nuisance, I will have to be alive again, how exasperating.
   Bet you believed it.
   Told you, joke.

A fledgling movement might need to be doctrinaire in its attitudes, but the movement of women writers and their concerns into this field is anything but doctrinaire. Such diversity argues that women today do feel themselves to have a secure place in science fiction, even if too small a place. Granted this present security and its future promise, perhaps we ought not to spend too many hours in frothing about the past.

   A further telling index of the present expansion and maturity of science fiction is the fact that even male writers are paying more attention to their female characters, often to quite good effect, sometimes using them even as that rare bird, the female protagonist. Such is obviously the case in Samuel R. Delany's award-winning *Babel-17* (1966) in which Rydra Wong, a poet/linguist/rocket captain, cracks the code that is destroying our galactic defenses, develops a new way of guiding ships in cosmic combat, and rehabilitates the man who will finally become her lover. Most important for this discussion, that lover, although an impressive individual, remains a less creative and energetic character than Rydra herself. In *A Very Private Life* (1968), Michael Frayn has created a delightful picaresque satire in which we follow not a lad's episodic adventures in the past but a girl's episodic adventures in the future. "Once upon a time there will be a little girl called Uncumber." By the end of this innovative, future tense narration, Uncumber is no girl, and quite a full person. Another notable science fiction novel of education is Alexei Panshin's *Rite of Passage* (1968). Mia Havero and Jimmy Dentremont are childhood puppy lovers and two of a group of children of a roving space colony who are dropped individually on a hostile planet for their citizenship trial by endurance. Mia and Jimmy manage to find each other, mostly through Mia's skill (although Jimmy is quite formidable); they undergo a further and more adult sexual initiation together thanks largely to Mia's stability; and both undergo vocational readjustments, both deciding privately that should they survive, they will adopt the vocation they had thought best suited for their lover. Panshin tells this award-winning tale by using Mia as his first person narrator. That male writers have come around so far suggests forcefully that the problem of androcentrism is perhaps not so pressing today as it once was.

   Panshin's novel is peculiarly important as a sign of change because Panshin is so strongly associated with Robert A. Heinlein, often thought of as the Papa Hemingway of science fiction. In *The*

Puppet Masters (1951), for example, Heinlein's first person narrator at one point "felt warm and relaxed, as if I had just killed a man or had a woman" (ch. 10). Panshin has studied Heinlein thoroughly and admiringly, as the younger writer makes clear in his criticism (see Alexei Panshin, *Heinlein in Dimension*, 1968). *Rite of Passage* itself is a very close reworking, this time with a female protagonist, of a plot Heinlein used for *Tunnel in the Sky* (1955), a novel of "stereotyped and sexist characterization" (Francis J. Molson, in Neil Barron, ed., *Anatomy of Wonder*, 1976). But even in *The Puppet Masters,* Heinlein is trying to give women more status than that of futuristic housewife dully pushing buttons on cleaning and cooking machines. Unfortunately, Heinlein's attempts at liberation are circumscribed by the ideas available to him. About the best he can do with Mary, the woman our hero will ultimately marry, is make her too a secret agent and have her described through the lens of romanticism. As the protagonist's father, head of the agency, explains,

most women are damn fools and children. But they've got more range than we've got. The brave ones are braver, the good ones better—and the vile ones viler (ch. 11).

Earlier in the novel, in order to find out who might be infested by an alien, mind-controlling leech, the secret agents have to undergo a body search together.

When Mary's turn came, she took her clothes off quickly and without a fuss. She made nothing of it, and wore her skin with quiet dignity. She added considerably to the pile of hardware. I decided she just plain liked guns (ch.6).

The Freudian implications here are too obvious to need explication. With Professor Higgins, Heinlein tries to make his "woman be more like a man." In fairness to Heinlein, one must note that he does *not* make marriage the end of Mary's swashbuckling career; as the novel closes, the protagonist is about to depart Earth, leading a twelve year extermination expedition to the "nest" of the alien leeches and Mary is on board. Although " 'she is a hero' " which the progatonist " 'miss[es] by a couple of points' " (ch. 11), it is the man who leads the expedition. But at least Mary isn't running the galley. Heinlein *is* trying. Bear with him, please; he has most of Western culture to overcome.

If we recognize how hard some science fiction writers have tried to imagine women more fully than melodrama allows or more diversely than their culture has encouraged, and if we recognize that these authors, men as well as women, have made notable progress, perhaps we can without polemic or spleen look back through science fiction in order to take the true measure of its male chauvinism. There are bad cases to be examined, no doubt. Only having examined them can we understand how hard some science fiction writers worked, even before the '60s, to do right by women.

The oldest, most consistent and most profound difficulty women had to overcome in their presentations in science fiction was getting presented in science fiction at all. Even when the story might seem today to cry out for a woman's point of view, that point of view was—at least in the worst cases—absent. C.I. Defontenay creates one of these grotesque omissions in *Star* (1854). Here is the narrator's meditation on a race which is not only hermaphroditic but uniformly self-impregnating:

Parental love is the life and joy of that race. How could it be otherwise? Free from the cares of conjugal love, all the desires of their hearts are poured out upon their children. Never, as among human males, does a gnawing doubt come to trouble their parental quietude. Besides, their children are engendered of their blood; each child is of the flesh of one alone; each is maintained in one's bowels and never was carried and nursed by a wife become indifferent or hateful. Among a human race provided with two sexes, the child, completely the woman's, is linked to its father only by an extremely fragile bond, which doubt sometimes breaks in his eyes as in the eyes of the world. How many fathers, having a profound and necessary desire for paternity, have regretted not being, like women, more competely participants in the procreations of an individual of their blood? (bk. 3, ch. 1; P.J. Sokolowski, trans).

It is not bad enough that Defontenay should view woman as faithless, stupid and fit only for the work of a brood mare; in addition, having the need of but one sex, he flies in the face of all biological fact and insists that the single sex that bears the children be considered the fathers rather than the mothers. From this benighted vantage in the mid-nineteenth century, Gloria Steinem and Robert Heinlein must appear nearly indistinguishable. Fortunately, Defontenay represents a fairly isolated extreme, one that was bound to grow ever more archaic as the political climate changed and as technology mitigated the biological differences between the sexes by providing first tools to increase human power, mobility and endurance and then tools to assist or restrain procreation.

Those science fiction writers who tried to get beyond the stereotypes offered them by their culture still often came smack athwart biology. In H.G. Wells' *A Modern Utopia* (1905), the state pays women on the birth of each child and supports mother and child financially not at a flat rate but by giving higher sums if the children achieve higher levels of excellence and lower sums if the children falter. This system is intended to foster the creation of the best possible citizens in the narrative world and intended by Wells to demonstrate to his Victorian audience his belief that all good work was equally respectable, including the work of motherhood. Since gestation has seemed until quite recently to be necessarily a female duty and since in Western culture child-rearing has been almost universally dominated by those who do the childbearing, it is small wonder that Wells could think as far as freeing woman's economic role but not as far as freeing her vocational role. In most of his novels, as is well known, there are no female characters of consequence; this is not unusual if one considers the nature of Wells' culture. But when he does turn his mind toward woman's roles, although he cannot see beyond her entrapment by one of her biological functions, he should be credited with at least working toward liberation from that functional constraint: that child-bearing is necessary for human survival need not mean that it is to be classed as one of the distasteful but unavoidable "natural functions." Wells' work, although it assumed women still constrained by function, represents a decided attack on the prejudices that led to the comparatively benign omission of women in Victorian works like Verne's and certainly an improvement over the malignant omissions in works like Defontenay's.

Some male science fiction writers have honestly tried to overcome the pitfalls of omission and functional determinism of women by imbuing their female characters with what they believed to be truly admirable traits alternative to those in their male characters. Today we believe that the very idea that a whole range of personality features is inherently feminine (selflessness and stability, for example) while a mutually exclusive range is inherently masculine (selfishness and adventurousness, for instance) is a silly if not pernicious result of acculturation. However, we should remember that the process of acculturation is not a conscious and malicious evil perpetrated by men on women but rather a process that characterizes the whole culture. Indeed, the women who raise boys mold the men of tomorrow. From our vantage, the traditional attitudes seem chains that bind women to often false ideals of helplessness and men to often false ideals of physical bravery. Further, the balance of these evils has usually tipped more heavily against the woman. Still, we should recognize that before Women's Liberation most traditionalists held their attitudes unconsciously and often used them not for exploitation but for cooperation, forging functional lives by using the obviously workable principle of the division of labor.

Nonetheless, an honest historian of science fiction must recognize that most science fiction still winds up depicting woman exploited. The first dominant image is that of woman exploited through her selflessness. As the ambient culture accepts a progressively clearer recognition that women focus their attention not only on children but on the man with whom those children are begotten, selflessness takes on another face, that of the lovestruck female. This image, a perverse hypertrophy of the Victorian ideal of uncorrupted female sensibility, leads especially in our time of reliable female contraceptives to a recognition of female sexuality, the act of love divorced from begetting. For some, the effort to imagine new roles for women sadly reduces to aggrandizing this sexuality, in effect expressing hostility against women for sharing with men a certain animal spirit and so casting woman back into pornography and the status of sex object. Science fiction has done all this.

The trammeling of woman by enlarging her presumptive selflessness has led to a number of grotesqueries. In "Helen O'Loy" (1938), Lester del Rey has two male friends create a perfect woman. That she is a robot must indicate something about the characters' views of women, if not del Rey's. Dave marries her and he; she and Phil keep forever the secret of the nature of Dave's wife. When Dave dies, Helen throws away her immortality in order to "cross this last bridge side by side." She sends a deathbed note to Phil asking him to burn her metal body with acid, protect the secret from the morticians, and have her buried with Dave. The story ends with Phil musing to himself:

I'm an old man now, and can view things more sanely; I should have married and raised a family, I suppose. But ... [sic] there was only one Helen O'Loy.

As Beverly Friend has written, "Frankly, one in sf is too many" ("Virgin Territory: Women and Sex in Science Fiction," quoted in Pamela Sargent's "Introduction" to *Women of Wonder*). As a portrayal of woman, Helen is clearly indefensible. Today's readers, sensitized as we are, may well bridle at this characterization and reject the story as a whole. But such a reaction would be wasteful; the story would not have struck its contemporary audience as exploitative in part because that audience, both male and female, largely held traditional attitudes unconsciously. Still, it was an era in which women were breaking out of the roles assigned by tradition; they were beginning to work outside the home, to vote, to smoke and to "flap." No one in that period could fairly expect a real woman to fulfill the criteria of femininity that had been instilled in men as boys. Instead of asking that of woman, the science fiction male turned to technology, just as utopian writers of the nineteenth century had attempted to obviate the ancient problem of slave labor by relying on the labor of machines. The story is really not about Helen, after all, although she reincarnates a male ideal of female perfection that goes back to Helen O'Troy, but about Phil, the faithful and quiet friend who has the grace to accept the fact that his creation has a right to choose a life of its own. Fidelity and grace are not laughable qualities in Phil and they are narratively the result of his relationship with Helen. She does make a human contribution and one could as well see machines humanized by this character as see women mechanized by it. Certainly Helen's example of the presumably feminine virtue of selflessness has been compelling enough to make the masculine Phil act selflessly as well. Phil's actions toward his creation, granting it marriage and life, contrast markedly with Victor Frankenstein's refusal to grant a bride to his creation, the demon. Taking Mary Shelley's early novel as part of del Rey's literary context, we can see that in some measure his story that shamelessly employs standard sexual stereotypes ends by transcending them.

Selflessness rears its head most strangely in Philip Jose Farmer's *The Lovers* (novel, 1961; shorter version, 1952) in which a human falls in love with a beautiful woman only to discover that she is an insect-like creature highly adapted to attracting humans as part of the alien reproductive cycle. Reproduction among these creatures involves the gestation of young within the mother and their consumption of her flesh. When they are born, she is revealed as a hollow shell. Farmer's hero is so imbued with love of her and is so affected by her willingness to die for her children that instead of rejecting the maggots in disgust, he decides to remain on the alien world and raise them as his true heirs. This is the last image of the novel:

Black hair cascaded from beneath the sheet and fell over the pillow.
    Hal did not rise. He sat in the chair, and he moaned, "Jeanette! Jeanette! If you had only loved me enough to tell me...".

As Phil has been made to see beyond physical differences (human v. machine), Hal has been made to see beyond racial differences. We have no trouble reading Wells' *The War of the Worlds* (1898) as a racial allegory in which the Martian invaders are to the conquered English as the real-life conquering English are to the natives of Africa and Asia. If the presence of a female character motivates us to take a modern and strongly feminist point of view, we may well read Farmer's Jeanette as a neurotic projection of a belief in female hostility toward men; but if we read *The Lovers* as a racial allegory of the '50s, we find that the narrow stereotypes of the times serve to fashion a story that tries to promote not only the presumably feminine virtue of selflessness but the unsexed virtue of tolerance.

Despite the fact that some of the stories that seem to reveal science fiction's male chauvinism are susceptible to the softening light of historical imagination and the intellectual strategy of reinterpretation, one still must admit, as we have throughout, that the genre has much to be embarrassed for. In *Ringworld* (1970), for example, Larry Niven makes his central plot device the fact that a young woman, Teela Brown, is genetically predisposed to have great good luck. Her presence alone, however, is all that the other adventurers (all male) seem to need to accomplish their mission and once accomplished they return to their home planets without Teela, who stays on Ringworld lovestruck by a macho type named Seeker. The lovestruck heroine, who fortunately grows rarer today, was a mainstay of science fiction before Women's Liberation. In *The Deep Range* (1957), for instance, Arthur C. Clarke creates a sexy, young marine biologist named Indra Langenburg. Her real role in this novel of the growth of sea-farming and the growth of Walter Franklin, its chief proponent, is not to learn about sea life but to provide home life. When she is first seen in the novel (ch. 3), she is busy disemboweling a shark as part of her research. She marries Walter and later (ch. 12) was "still doing part-time work at the Hawaii Aquarium when her household duties permitted." Later still (ch. 15) Indra muses on the possibility of getting some of her notes in shape for publication:

Even if nothing came of these dreams, it was pleasant to have them and to know you might make the best of both worlds. So Indra Franklin, housewife and ichthyologist, told herself as she went back into the kitchen to prepare lunch for her ever-hungry son.

And finally (ch. 16),

Anne Franklin arrived wide-eyed and wide-mouthed into the world and Indra began to have her first serious doubts of continuing her academic career.

Fortunately, Clarke, like all writers working today, has responded to Women's Liberation. In his later work, like *Rendezvous with Rama* (1973), he did much better. Other writers responded differently.

Some who have responded to the new female freedoms have apparently seen the liberation of woman as the unleashing of female hostility toward men. They dramatize this hostility in their stories and simultaneously pay that hostility back by using the hostile female character as a sex object. Robert Scheckley's comic "Can You Feel Anything When I Do This?" (first published in *Playboy* in August, 1969) inverts "Helen O'Loy" in almost every respect. Melisande is a bored woman married to a boring man in a boring and automated future. An omnifunctional home appliance (called Rom) sees her in a store one day, falls in love with her, and has a dispatching machine send him to her. To make a short story shorter, the machine brings Melisande to the best climax of her life and then fully expects to take up life as her lover, but she gets furious and, with obvious symbolism, rips his cord from his canister. The story ends with this paragraph:

> The Rom couldn't answer, of course. But maybe he knew—just before the end—that there wasn't anything personal in it. It wasn't that he was a metal cylinder colored orange and red. He should have known that it wouldn't have mattered if he had been a green plastic sphere, or a willow tree, or a beautiful young man.

A woman freed, apparently, becomes the worst exemplar of the presumably male trait of selfishness. Sheckley here is equipping Melisande with a true case of penis envy.

Pete Adams and Charles Nightingale have written "Planting Time" (1975), a story that combines some of the motifs of *The Lovers* with some of the attitudes of "Can You Feel Anything When I Do This?" Briefly, the story is an apparently omniscient narration in which Randy Richmond discovers an intelligent plant that responds to his thoughts and quickly grows to physically mimic gorgeous human females lying on couches. It attracts the man to itself by releasing sexually arousing aromas and he serves the alien plant as bees serve Earthly plants. The sex the plant offers is apparently out of this world. Randy (which as an adjective means "lecherous") barely manages to escape this seductive planet with a bunch of seed pods, knowing now that he can establish successful brothels wherever he wishes, so long as he doesn't become too addicted to the plant's exhausting allurements. In the last paragraph, the narration is revealed as being from the point of view of one of the plants:

> So that, girls, is the story of the famed horticulturist Randy Richmond... All strength to his compost, and may his flyspray never dwindle! Now, dig in. Another batch of conservationists just stopped by our greenhouse.

By using the term "compost," the author demonstrates that the females are reducing the male to mere object, and an object better dead than alive.

One can hardly help comparing the hostility toward men on the planet of seductive plants with the quietude Le Guin projects in "Vaster than Empires and More Slow" (1971). This story concerns the exploration of a completely forested planet that apparently has no animal life. All the members of the crew see the place simply as a forest with the exception of the team's "Sensor." He finally comes to learn that the "trees" of this whole world are rhizomatically interconnected to form a single world-sized sentience utterly alien to minds that have existed with "Others." He risks his selfhood by opening his mind to an understanding of the planet's vegetable consciousness and achieves a sufficiently good understanding that he decides to remain, as a "colonist" with this earth-mother, while the rest of the crew, respecting a knowledge they cannot share, leaves him and the planet in peace.

Work like Le Guin's should make more narrow-minded science fiction writers blush—and it sometimes does. At the same time that we have noted the historical depths of male chauvinism and admitted that it persists even today, we have noticed that after all much of what we condemn deserves better of us. Indeed, a fair assessment of the way science fiction has portrayed women requires that we understand how the works we have examined came to be and that we seek not only works that reveal narrow-mindedness but contrasting works that function without the exploitation of women.

The first criticism we raised of science fiction is that it ignored women or, when it portrayed them, drew them stereotypically. This is certainly true. However, in extenuation, one should note that the same can often be said of the way science fiction has treated men. This is not in and of itself a bad thing. As David Ketterer has written,

science fiction is often attacked because it characteristically lacks human interest and emotional involvement. But this seeming weakness can be regarded as a strength. The point is that, like St. John's Apocalypse, the cosmic scope of science fiction and the magnitude of the events or phenomena it treats causes the individual human being to shrink from view (*New Worlds For Old*, 1974, ch. 12).

Ketterer's argument surely has cogency in discussing many "cosmic" fictions, like Arthur C. Clarke's *2001* (1968). A feminist could rightly point out that there are only two consequential female characters, a stewardess and an astronaut's mother; but in fairness one should note that there are very few characters of any type and the reactions of readers of the book and viewers of the film version clearly show that the only *interesting* character is Hal the computer (who sometimes uses a female voice and sometimes a male voice). The astronauts, who are—perhaps regrettably—men, are absolutely forgettable as individuals. And so they should be. In this novel with its billion year time span, Clarke is not concerned with individuals.

Even in non-cosmic science fiction, characterization is often quite properly sketchy. The label "science fiction," after all, embraces diverse aims and diverse audiences. Sword-and-sorcery, futurology, technophobia and raw power fantasies surely require differing sorts of characterization. We need to understand that although this melange called science fiction contains some intellectually startling works and some very refined writing, the vast majority of science fiction is what John G. Cawelti has called "formula literature." Although he is writing in general, his generalities obviously apply to the elitist critical reception of science fiction:

> Two central aspects of formulaic structure have been generally condemned in the serious artistic thought of the last hundred years: their essential standardization and their primary relation to the needs of escape and relaxation (*Adventure, Mystery, and Romance*, 1976, p. 8).

Cawelti offers a convincing demonstration that such condemnation is near-sighted; he personally enjoys formula literature, often for its artistic achievement within its own limitations. But he does recognize that those limitations arise because formulas have certain uses, including the affirmation of "existing interests and attitudes by presenting an imaginary world that is aligned with these interests and attitudes" (p. 35). The great bulk of science fiction is formulaic and as such does and should rely on the stereotypes of men as well as women held by the ambient culture.

It has been argued, of course, that as a literature that imagines alternatives science fiction has a special obligation to imagine alternative roles for women. This position has merit. However, if a given work, like *The War of the Worlds,* happens to have colonial race relations as its main interest and happens to explore this interest by fantastic dramatization, the author who hopes to make his strange narrative world clear has an increased need to rely on the conventions of characterization to provide a firm narrative foundation. How much more so the need for conventions when the setting is in the future or on a thoroughly alien planet.

It could be argued, however, that science fiction *should* choose women's roles as its main interest. Today, of course, it often does. But we must remember, before we condemn writers of fifteen or more years ago, that writers need to eat and the market for science fiction was male in large measure because the culture associated males with science and females with the arts. Cawelti makes rough (too rough) and ready distinctions among a number of formulae. Of special interest in regard to markets is his contrast between "adventure" and "romance":

> The central fantasy of the adventure story is that of the hero ... overcoming obstacles and dangers and accomplishing some important and moral mission.... The feminine equivalent of the adventure story is the romance.... The crucial defining characteristic of romance is not that it stars a female but that its organizing action is the development of a love relationship, usually between a man and a woman. Because this is the central line of development, the romance differs from the adventure story... (pp. 39, 41).

Like it or not, this has been historically true of formulaic writing and thus of the vast majority of science fiction. Since science fiction has been for males, it has usually been written as stories of adventure. Verne, for example, writes adventures: women need not apply. Yet Verne is not anti-feminist; Nemo hates men every bit as much as he hates women. Women are just absent and absent not because, as in Defontenay's case, the author disparages them but because the requirements of this form, as directed to a particular expectable audience, make women characters almost unnecessary.

Edward Bellamy has been criticized because Edith Leete in *Looking Backward* (1888) is such a simp. And she truly is. But please note that the book's "hero," her lover Julian West, is an opinionated twerp. Bellamy's literary mistake was not that he relied on his culture's convention for characterization; his mistake was trying to write a romance at all. *Looking Backward* is, after all, a speculative essay only dressed out as a romance. As essay its institution of communal kitchens and automatic income to all citizens makes rather more allowance for female independence from domestic slavery than one would imagine under the administration of Grover Cleveland. Bellamy is able to smuggle Edith in only because the availability of formula conventions makes her inclusion economical—and hence not too distracting from the main argument. I rather believe that Bellamy included her not out of anti-feminism but out of feminism. His passion for a political alternative led him to create a literary mutant.

Formula literature, because it is buttressed by convention, is uniquely capable of presenting mutations—if they come in small enough doses. As Cawelti writes, "literary formulas assist in the process of assimilating changes in values to traditional imaginative constructs" (p. 36). Capitalizing on this, science fiction has in fact often given female characters much freer reign than they receive in any other formula literature (melodrama, for example) or in the highly-praised "realistic" novels which supposedly set our literary standards.

One branch of science fiction that habitually considers alternative roles for women is utopian fiction. Literature which takes as its major aim the exposition of a culture is able, even compelled, to treat its characters largely as representatives of social niches. Freed of the necessity of presenting a hero, as in adventure stories, the utopian writer can dwell on the general qualities of society. William Morris abhorred Bellamy's book and countered it with *News From Nowhere* (1890). It is true that all the cooks and waitresses we see in the book are female, but such work is radically reduced in time-consumption, much increased in public esteem, and represents only a tiny aspect of a woman's self-image. Women in Morris' society are free to chuck their work just as men are; they are free to terminate a marriage by walking out just as men are; they are free to take the necessities of life from society just as men are. This is rather remarkable in the writing of a Victorian; especially remarkable in the writing of a man enduring faithfully the adultery of his wife with his former best friend. The gentleness in Morris' pastoral future is a reproach to the hostility expressed in some of the stories that come after liberation.

The utopian penchant for offering alternatives to women has never flagged. In *Walden II* (1948) Skinner discusses female equality at great length and sometimes even dramatizes it (though his teachers and housekeepers are, unfortunately, all women). Rachel Meyerson, for whom the community's founder Frazier is lovestruck (a neat reversal of the conventions), is perhaps the strongest and most appealing character in the book. In *I, Robot* (1950), a composite novel in which benign robots finally assume perfect and benevolent control of the world, Isaac Asimov creates, really, only one character, the "robopsychologist" named Dr. Susan Calvin. Some have criticized her as spinsterish, anti-social and persnickety, but this is unfair. That she can live a fulfilled life without marriage ought to please feminists; that she prefers the necessarily good and intelligent robots to the intermittently nasty and stupid general run of humanity (of both sexes) is hardly unreasonable; and that the old woman reveals a stereotypical characteristic of old age hardly constitutes an affront to her femininity. After all, this forceful and far-sighted scientist who almost single-handedly brings mankind from an age of repeated war to an age of eternal peace, functions within the bounds of popular formulaic literature. In Eugene Zamiatin's *We* (1920), a dystopian work that risks breaking even further out of formulaic bounds, we find that the strongest character is the female I-330. Although the story is narrated by D-503, a man who either loves or lusts after her, she is the real driving force. It is her tenderness and sexuality that cause him to recognize his intellectual and political plight; it is her courage that offers him and the reader an example of resistance to government oppression; it is her complexity of mind (did she merely use D-503 or did she actually love him?) that shows the shallowness of the other mathematized citizens of the United State; it is her leadership that sparks the abortive revolution; and it is her commitment to her ideology above her personal attachments that strikes the strongest blow for liberation of women from the velvet cage of their traditional virtues.

These positive portrayals of women occur not in adventures or even romances but in works of social speculation. As we have seen, it is fitting that characterization function differently in different works. It seems unfair to tar "science fiction" with a chauvinist brush by concentrating on works which are almost necessarily without three dimensional female characters when the treatment of women in some science fictions of the speculative type has been so outstanding in imagining women in alternatives to their culturally approved roles. Beyond this, we should recognize that even in some of the more adventurous science fictions, male authors have managed to think usefully about women's roles. In *The Space Merchants* (1953), Frederik Pohl and C.M. Kornbluth presented a dreadful future dominated by advertizing cartels. The main character is a copywriter and the main development of the story is his recognition that his privileged position rests on gross social injustice, his enforced exile, his battle back to civilization and power and his eventual commitment to revolution. The novel is an amalgam of Bildungsroman, dystopia and above all, adventure. There are only three female characters of consequence in this novel: a demented sadist named Hedy, a lovestruck secretary named Hester and Dr. Kathy Nevin. Hedy embodies female hostility and symbolizes her penis envy by driving knitting needles up along the protagonist's nerves. We feel no remorse—but also no prurient pleasure—when he is able to kill her and escape. Hester throws over her whole life to aid the protagonist, first by abandoning her job and last by committing suicide. We feel no great remorse for the action of this minor character but we may be annoyed at the "hero" for not seeing that he has been exploiting her. Dr. Nevin, on the other hand, offers a successful integration of female independence and female sympathy. She has been, before the story begins, married to the protagonist but, try as she does, she cannot get around his egotism and has let their contract lapse. In the course of the novel she is revealed as both a competent practicing physician and a leader of the resistance forces. It turns out that, although she cannot abide living with the protagonist, she has silently used her underground connections to prevent his murder by his political foes. At the end, when the protagonist has seen the light and is leaving Earth with the other resisters to set up a superior society on Venus, she recognizes that he has truly changed and invites him to share her cabin. Hedy and Hester are both despicable; but their qualities, tempered and combined in an intelligent and full human being, can blossom into a truly liberated—and liberating—character like Dr. Nevin.

Science fiction speculation on ethics and religion has, like speculation on society and politics, often created a full range of female characters unbounded by convention. In David Lindsay's *A Voyage to Arcturus* (1920), a surrealistic novel populated by myriad strange creatures of at least three distinct sexes, we find female characters of great courage and moral strength, like Joiwind; of rapacious sexuality, like Oceaxe; of aggressive dominance, like

Tydomin; and of simple adventurousness, like Gleameil. The narrator of Olaf Stapledon's *Star Maker* (1937) is a human male granted a mystical journey through the cosmos and through the eons, learning ever more about the ways in which life can support other life in "community." But his interstellar search is based, he feels, on his fundamental earthly experience as part of

a long-married couple … like two close trees whose trunks have grown upwards together as a single shaft, mutually distorting, but mutually supporting … even the whole cosmos with all its inane immensities could not convince me that this our prized atom of community, imperfect as it was, short-lived as it must be, was not significant (pt. 1, ch. 1).

Stapledon, in *Sirius* (1944), creates in Plaxy a woman who demonstrates the independent and supportive nature he prizes in both women and men.

Ethically speculative science fiction may have a reason for valuing women even beyond those reasons it shares with socially speculative science fiction. Religion, in our culture, always calls Christianity to mind and Christianity is in part dominated by the revered image of Mary. Now, Mary's chastity and her primary role as bearer of the male Messiah certainly feed anti-feminist conceptions of the housebound woman; but her ethical superiority clearly deflects any attempt at male exploitation (unless one wants to accuse God the Father). In *A Canticle for Leibowitz* (1959), Walter M. Miller, Jr. shows us how men have made a botch of the world time and again. Civilization is shattered by atomic war; it builds back up; it repeats the annihilation. But just before that second annihilation we see three female figures (even though the main locale of the novel is a monastery). One is a mother of a mutant. This woman forcefully rejects the Abbot's arguments for the sanctity of all life; she reluctantly accepts the government's offer of euthanasia for her child. The second woman is Mrs. Grales (note the name) who is a long-suffering and obsessively pious woman, a "tomato seller" who cares for her mutant, a quiescent second head on her aged shoulders, while she maintains her independent life. The third woman, emerging under the influence of the rain of radiation, is Rachel (which means "patience"), the quiescent head now quickening as the old woman dies. Rachel is youth, a green-eyed sprite who rejects the Abbot's blessing because she does not need it: she is Eve returned at last, a human without Original Sin. Rachel is more perfect than ever a man has been since the Fall. The men in this highly compelex book may or may not have found a partial salvation in the rocket full of children they launch before the atomic fires, but the women are shown to make the hard decisions and to forge the continuity of humanity.

Science fiction has been lambasted for its treatment of women and, as we have seen, the anger expended on the genre has not been without its too frequent and barbaric sources. But we need to mitigate that criticism. First, science fiction today is not nearly so male-centered as it once was. This is true not only for the work of the female writers but for the work of the male writers. Second, many of the works from the past which at first strike us as unredeemably anti-feminist may on second reading reveal other features which justify them as art. Third, the unflattering roles women have taken in science fiction have often been a consequence of the nature of formula writing, the attitudes of the ambient culture and the expectations of the marketplace. Fourth, even within these constraints, science fiction has been bolder in imagining alternative roles for women than has any other formula literature. Fifth, the non-formulaic branches of science fiction have not in fact been peculiarly narrow-minded in the treatment of women but have, on the contrary, shown women in a wide diversity of roles, some representing human possibilities far more admirable than any we commonly find among women or men. Rather than continuing the cry of outrage over past failures, it is time to recognize that science fiction has been and continues to be a leading voice in the chorus for cultural change that has helped to make the present women's movement a political reality.

Anne Hudson Jones

Alexei Panshin's Almost Non-Sexist
Rite of Passage

AN INTERESTING CRITICAL discussion of female rites of passage in American literature is offered by Elaine Ginsberg in her article "The Female Initiation Theme in American Fiction."[1] She points out that although the initiation theme is one of the most pervasive in American fiction, it is seldom developed using a girl as the protagonist. She suggests this is because women have traditionally been expected to remain pure and innocent, to remain *un*initiated into knowledge, evil, or the world beyond the home. According to Ginsberg, in nineteenth-century American fiction, those female characters who do gain a wider knowledge of the world are portrayed as fallen women. In twentieth-century American fiction, Ginsberg notes, female initiation stories typically show a girl developing a sense of her sexuality and then confine her to home and woman's work: marriage and motherhood. This pattern should surprise no one. In literature as in life, rites of passage—especially when the passage is between childhood and adulthood—reflect the prevailing values of a culture by focusing attention on those qualities which are most important for adult success in that culture. To offer a convincing variation on the traditional American literary pattern of female initiation,[2] an author would have to posit an alternative society. Alexei Panshin does just that in his science fiction novel *Rite of Passage*.

Until recently, science fiction has been no more liberated in its presentation of female characters than traditional fiction. When *Rite of Passage* appeared in 1968, it was one of a very few science fiction novels to have a female protagonist, and it was one of the first science fiction works to present a relatively non-sexist future society. This is all the more remarkable because Panshin is male, despite his having a name many people mistake for a woman's. *Rite of Passage* is interesting because it so nearly succeeds in depicting a non-sexist society. It is instructive because it falls short: we can learn from its flaws. In his contribution to this volume, "Science Fiction Women Before Liberation," Eric Rabkin uses *Rite of*

Passage to exemplify how far male writers have come in their presentation of women characters. He suggests that "the problem of androcentrism is perhaps not so pressing today as it once was." However, the flaws in the novel result from residual androcentrism. They illustrate that male writers have not come far enough. The novel's importance lies in the questions it implicitly raises about rites of passage and sex roles in a sexist society; the novel's shortcomings show just how difficult it is for someone living in our society to envision a truly non-sexist one.

Rite of Passage presents a twenty-second-century community made up of survivors of the population wars that destroyed Earth in 2041. The society exists in a spaceship and carefully regulates itself to avoid repeating Earth's disaster. To help prevent overpopulation, the Ship's society has instituted an element of control, a rite of passage known as Trial, designed to eliminate the stupid, the foolish, the immature, and even the just plain unlucky. Fourteen-year-olds who have completed an eighteen-month survival class are dropped, individually, on a strange planet and are left to survive for thirty days. Everyone must undergo Trial and a "reasonably high percentage"[3] die. Those who survive come home and are considered adults.

Trial is not the society's only form of population control nor is it just a barbaric, atavistic rite. Birth control is practiced by all sexually active adults on the Ship. The Ship's children learn that "population pressure is the ultimate cause of every war" (p. 9), and they grow up thinking of Free Birthers as stupid and suicidal. But because the Ship offers a protected environment, there is little chance for natural selection of the sort that has historically determined the survival of the fittest—whatever that has meant from time to time, and culture to culture. To maintain some genetic selection, the Ship's Eugenist recommends certain pairings. Some people meet only to have a child and then go their separate ways. Trial offers another kind of selection, environmental selection. Children are not just left to die; they are trained to live. If they are physically and mentally adept and strong, they have a good chance of surviving. Trial "makes being an adult a meaningful sort of thing, because adulthood has been earned" (p. 107).

In preparation for Trial, all twelve-year-olds begin a survival class. They are trained in a variety of skills, among them needlepoint, dance, hand-to-hand combat, and the use of weapons. Girls and boys are tested in exactly the same way, and they receive the same training. Nothing inessential is taught; the aim is to develop the ability to "react smoothly and intelligently in difficult situations" (p. 119). The male instructor describes dancing as "deadly serious.... [Because] when you are in a position where you have to do the exact right thing in an instant, deft movement is the most important element" (p. 118). He proves to be right even before Trial. In a tiger hunt, the culmination of the survival class, the group stalks, stones, and stabs the animal to death. Those who don't move quickly enough are mauled.

The protagonist of the novel, the young girl whose rite of passage readers follow, is Mia Havero. Because she narrates her story from a retrospective point of view, there is never any question about Mia's survival. In the beginning Mia says that the changes in her are "the things to keep your eye on" (p. 7). They are. But the significant changes are different from those readers probably expect. At first, Mia looks and acts like a stereotypical tomboy. She has dark, short-cropped hair; she wears shorts, shirts, and sandals; and she gets into fights at soccer games. During the course of the novel, Mia develops into a sexually mature young woman. She begins menstruating, wearing a bra, dating, and having sexual intercourse. She also develops her taste in clothes to include more flattering garments. But these changes are not significant factors in Mia's life or in the novel. They are secondary to the more important change involved in becoming an adult: becoming mature as a person—not just as a woman.

In a society like that of the Ship, with a low, controlled birthrate and long adult life spans, women cannot devote their lives just to motherhood. Siblings on the Ship are often twenty years or more apart, and children often live away from their parents in communal dorms. The meaning of "motherhood" is different from what it is in our society. And identity defined by sex role—"I am a wife; I am a mother"—is just not sufficient. One must also have an identity as a person, defined by one's abilities or profession: "I am an artist; I am a teacher." Marriage and motherhood may accompany that professional identity, but they cannot replace it. Although Mia fully expects to be both a wife and mother, she does not expect to be *only* a wife and mother. Significantly, when Mia was four, her mother left home to study art with a well-known artist, leaving Mia to live with her father. Mia's parents' marriage is clearly not ended: her mother is doing what she wants and needs to do, just as her father is doing what he wants and needs to do.

When innate ability is more important than gender and when the societal rite of passage tests survival skills rather than sexual skills, sexual initiation—even for females—does not have the same significance that it has in sexist societies. Sexual aspects of growth are only incidental to Mia, as they are not to the girl in a typical initiation story. For example, about beginning to menstruate, Mia says only: "... during that summer, I had my first menstrual period—that's important insofar as I took it as a sign that I was

growing up, but that's about all you can say for it" (p. 118). The only
other time she mentions menstruation is her first night on Trial: "I
ached all over. If it weren't the wrong time of the month, I would
have thought I was having my period" (p. 188). Mia's reaction to her
first sexual experience—again during Trial—is equally matter-of-
fact:

> Sex in the Ship is for adults. We were not officially adults, but we needed each
> other then, and I was no longer quite the stickler for rules that I once had been. We
> needed each other then and it was the proper time. If we didn't make it back to the
> Ship, who would ever care? And if we made it back to the Ship, we would be officially
> adults and the question would be irrelevant.
>
> So we made love there in the dark with the rain falling outside, safe in each
> other's arms. Neither of us knew what we were doing, except theoretically, and we
> were as clumsy as kittens. It was something of a botch, too, in an extremely pleasant
> way. At the climax there was simply a hint of something we couldn't reach.
>
> We lay quietly and after a few minutes Jimmy said, "How was that?"
>
> I said, somewhat sleepily, "I think it takes practice."
>
> Just before I fell asleep, I said, "It was comforting, though." (pp. 225-6)

Unlike the typical female adolescent in American fiction, in neither
instance does Mia know the fear and turmoil that usually result
from these sexual experiences.

It is possible, of course, that Mia's reaction has more to do with
the male authorship of the novel than with the novel's non-sexist
society. Perhaps Panshin just didn't know how female authors
usually depict girls' reactions. Most of the twentieth-century female
initiation stories are by women writers.[4] Panshin may only be
presenting the reaction he would like a girl to have when she is
sexually initiated. I can't ignore this possibility. But the fact of the
fiction remains: survival is of paramount importance to Mia. Sex
can, at best, occupy second place in her priorities—and this is
because of the rules of her society.

Before Trial, Mia and her best friend, Jimmy Dentremont, had
planned to rejoin each other once they were on the ground but they
have a spat and Mia insists upon remaining alone. On Tintera, the
planet where Mia and her group are dropped, Mia thinks about
herself and her readiness for her ordeal. She calls herself "the
Compleat Young Girl, hell on wheels." She can "build one-fifteenth
of a log cabin, kill one-thirty-first of a tiger, kiss, do needlepoint,
pass through an obstacle course, and come pretty close (in theory) to
killing somebody with [her] bare hands" (p. 187). What she cannot
do is keep her mouth shut when she should: she calls a local Tinteran
ruffian a "big bastard," and he beats her senseless. Afterwards, she
is rescued by an old man who wants her to be his surrogate
daughter.

What follows resembles a role reversal western. Mia even thinks
of what she is doing in terms of cowboys and the west. Jimmy

Dentremont has been jailed for trespassing, and Mia breaks into the jail to free him. Thus far, the pattern is certainly not sexist. But after Jimmy is free, Mia takes him back to the house where she's been staying so that they can gather what they need to make their escape. A policeman comes to the door to arrest the old man, who is a political dissident. The old man resists and the policeman clubs him to death. Mia screams, the policeman raises his gun to shoot her, and Jimmy shoots the policeman instead. Later, Mia reflects upon what has happened: "If I had been able to act, I would have done as [Jimmy] had, simply in order to stay alive.... Jimmy was always a more humane, open, warmer person than I, and it cost him greatly to shoot the man" (p. 223). Nonetheless, it was Jimmy, the male, and not Mia, the female, who did the killing. This traditional sex role behavior appears again, very shortly thereafter.

To regain the signal they must have to summon the scout ship which retrieves them at the end of Trial, Mia and Jimmy break into an army complex. After they recover the device, Mia must knock out one of the officers so they can make their escape. She "took out [her] pistol and somewhat squeamishly hit him with it under the ear" (p. 230). Since her blow is ineffective, he does not stay unconscious long enough for them to get away. To Jimmy's question, "Couldn't you have hit the officer harder?" Mia replies, "I don't like to hit people" (p. 231). Jimmy doesn't like to kill people, but when he had to, he did. Mia's squeamishness is not only traditionally female; it is also calculated to do her in. In this situation, she has to blow up a good part of the army complex before she and Jimmy can finally escape. Looking at the destruction she has caused, Jimmy comments: "You know, that's an awful lot of trouble to make simply because you can't bring yourself to hit somebody" (p. 234).

In these two examples, Mia does not show the survival skill which should have resulted from her training. Instead, she lapses back into classic female sex role behavior. This is a weakness in the work, and there are others of the same ilk. For example, on Tintera Mia is often mistaken for a boy because she dresses and behaves like Tinteran males: she wears pants and she roams the countryside alone on horseback. Tinteran females wear feminine garb and stay at home or travel only with family groups. Even though Mia notices the sexist pattern of life on Tintera, she is not smart enough to realize that on a sexist world, it is to her advantage to be mistaken for a male. Her gender is extremely important to her. She thinks of herself as the "Compleat Young Girl" rather than the "Compleat Young Person." She is angered when she is called a boy. She even goes out of her way to leave a note saying, "I'm a *girl*, you Mudeater!" (p. 218), for the ruffian who had mistaken her for a boy and beaten her up. What the ruffian would have done to her had he known she was a girl, we can only conjecture. Also open to conjecture is why being known as a girl rather than as a boy is so important to Mia, who has been raised in a society that does not make sexist distinctions between females and males.

Another weakness in Panshin's almost non-sexist work shows up in Mia's discussion of her chosen profession. At first, Mia wants to be a synthesist; gradually, she realizes that her natural talent is better suited to ordinology. Her aptitude for one or the other of these demanding professions is never considered a result of her gender. Interestingly, Jimmy Dentremont originally wants to become an ordinologist, but Mia persuades him that his natural aptitude better prepares him for a synthesist's duties. This should be convincing evidence that their roles are interchangeable, that individual aptitude rather than sex should be the deciding factor. But synthesists must be creative; ordinologists must only be organized. Because creativity has so long been considered a male preserve, Panshin falls—perhaps unwittingly—back into a traditional pattern here. Mia compares the work of an ordinologist to that of a librarian:

> If you think of the limits of what we know as a great suite of rooms inhabited by vast numbers of incredibly busy, incredibly messy, nearsighted people, all of whom are eccentric recluses, then an ordinologist is somebody who comes in every so often to clean up. He picks up the books around the room and puts them where they belong. He straightens everything up. He throws away the junk that the recluses have kept and cherished, but for which they have no use. And then he leaves the room in condition for outsiders to visit while he's busy cleaning up next door. He bears about the same resemblance to the middle-aged woman who checks out books in the quad library as one of our agriculturists does to a primitive Mudeater farmer, but if you stretched a point, you might call him a librarian. (p. 29)

Or a housewife. In contrast, she describes the work of a synthesist this way:

> A synthesist ... is a person who comes in and admires the neatened room, and recognizes how nice a copy of a certain piece of furniture would look in the next room over and how *useful* it would be there, and points the fact out. Without the ordinologists, a synthesist wouldn't be able to begin work. (p. 29)

In these descriptions, the ordinologist's work is like that of a traditional wife; the synthesist's, like that of a husband. Also relevant is the fact that when Mia gets depressed and doubts her ability to enter her chosen profession, she thinks she "might well wind up as a dorm mother or something equally daring" (p. 22). All occupations on the Ship are clearly not of equal appeal, and "dorm mother," traditionally and linguistically a female occupation, is the least desirable Mia can think of. This looks like another lapse into ingrained, traditional sexist thought patterns.

There is another flaw in the novel, and this one is major. There are no adult female role models for Mia. The only adult women who are mentioned in the story are Mia's mother—and Mia doesn't like her; a neighbor who is always complaining to Mia's father about her behavior; an old woman who reports Mia and Jimmy to the authorities when they are having one of their adventures; Mrs. Mbele, who plays the role of dutiful wife and surrogate grandmother by supplying refreshments for Mia and Jimmy when they have their tutoring sessions with Mr. Mbele; and a woman who is exiled from the Ship because she has gotten pregnant for the fifth time—and against the Eugenist's advice. In an apparently non-sexist society, which requires all its girls to undergo the same rigorous training and Trial that it requires of its boys, adult women seem to disappear from the scenes: the teachers and tutors are male; the council members are male; the ship pilots are male; the survival class leaders are male. All those who take an active part in the society are male, and all the significant others for Mia are male: her father, the Chairman of the Ship's Council; her tutor and mentor, Mr. Mbele; and her friend, lover, and later husband, Jimmy Dentremont. Although these men all encourage Mia's freedom of action and choice, they prefer her when she dresses up and wears pink.

In the novel's "Epilogue," which is subtitled "Rite of Passage," Mia makes clear that her most significant change is a newly gained maturity:

Maturity is the ability to sort the portions of truth from the accepted lies and self-deceptions that you have grown up with. It is easy now to see the irrelevance of the religious wars of the past, to see that capitalism in itself is not evil, to see that honor is most often a silly thing to kill a man for, to see that national patriotism should have meant nothing in the twenty-first century, to see that a correctly-arranged tie has very little to do with true social worth. It is harder to assess as critically the insanities of your own time, especially if you have accepted them unquestioningly for as long as you can remember, for as long as you have been alive. If you never make the attempt, whatever else you are, you are not mature. (pp. 241-2)

If we, as readers of the novel, accept this definition and apply it to ourselves, to be mature we must try to assess critically the insanities of our time, insanities which include sex roles and sexist rites of passage. Panshin's novel can help us by showing an alternative society against which we can measure our own and by reminding us how difficult it is to see beyond one's time and societal conditioning.

Notes

[1] *Studies in American Fiction*, 3 (Spring, 1975), 27-37.
[2] Ginsberg outlines the significant differences between the traditional literary patterns of

female and male initiation stories in American fiction:

1) Girls are introduced to a world where their relationships with men are more important than their relationships with other women. Significant relationships for boys are those with other men.

2) Boys who achieve adulthood have a choice of roles they might fill in society; girls see their future roles as those defined by their relationships with men.

3) The initiation process for girls is almost always portrayed in terms of sexual experience; this is much less often the case for boys.

4) Many of the girls in female initiation stories are dressed in boys' clothing or bear boys' names at the beginning and drop these as the stories progress. Never are boys portrayed wearing girls' clothing or bearing girls' names.

5) Boys often have a male mentor to guide them, but girls seem never to have a female mentor. If they have a mentor at all, it is usually an older male.

6) The range of settings varies: boys are often initiated into a relationship with the natural world; girls are not.

Alexei Panshin, *Rite of Passage* (New York: Ace Books, 1968), p. 10. Subsequent quotations from the novel are from this edition and will be cited parenthetically in my text.

I can think of none that are not, nor does Ginsberg cite any.

II Paradise Lost

James D. Merritt

"She Pluck'd, She Eat"

THE OLDEST, MOST pervasive myth in western civilization is a peculiar hybrid of good and evil. Eve is the mother of us all and as such she is the object of reverent love, but she is also the source of all our misery, for it was Eve's sin which brought death and pain into the world. I have taken my title from *Paradise Lost*, Book IX, 781. For thousands of lines Milton had been leading up to this moment, but when it comes, the effect is brutal:

> So saying, her rash hand, in evil hour
> Forth reaching to the fruit, she pluck'd, she eat.

Eve's sin brings universal pain into the world:

> Earth felt the wound, and Nature from her seat
> Sighing through all her works gave signs of woe
> That all was lost.

Milton was obliged to believe the story of man's fall because he was an orthodox Christian; he lived in a world in which belief in the authenticity of the Biblical story was rarely questioned. *Paradise Lost* is more than three centuries old, but the story Milton tells is still with us in some modern works of science fiction, that branch of contemporary literature least bound by the old orthodoxies. Milton's poem is full of the devices employed by contemporary science fiction writers—journeys through space, terrifying monsters, and visits to unknown planets, but I want to discuss examples of Eve—the sinful Eve who plucked and ate the forbidden fruit—in three very different examples of twentieth century science fiction, C.S. Lewis's *Perelandra,* H.P. Lovecraft's *The Dunwich Horror,* and Carolyn Neeper's *A Place Beyond Man.*

C.S. Lewis was certainly one of the most literate men who ever turned his hand to science fiction. He was professor of Renaissance literature at Oxford and an internationally known scholar whose specialities were the works of Spenser and of Milton. He was also a self-declared Christian apologist, and he took his inspiration for the science fiction stories from orthodox Christian sources and saw

37

them through the eyes of a believer. In *Perelandra* he invented a brilliant plot. The story takes place on the planet of Perelandra which we come to learn is Venus. The narrator is a man named Ransom, a professor who, for reasons too complex to explain here, is sent to Perelandra for some unknown purpose. The planet is a watery, incredibly beautiful paradise with only two pieces of fixed land. It is inhabited by exquisite little creatures that look like dragons out of heraldry, by various almost invisible spirit creatures and exactly two human-like creatures of great physical beauty. They are the King and the Queen and they are obviously Adam and Eve and Perelandra is obviously the Garden of Eden. Ransom has landed *before* Eve has disobeyed God and is in the amazing position of being able to prevent the sin of this woman and its consequent horrors for the millions of people who will follow her.

Satan is personified by Weston, an English scientist, who tempts the Queen on the same level that Satan tempted Eve in *Genesis* or *Paradise Lost,* through her pride. Her feminine intellect is insufficient to protect her against the wiles of the devilish argument, and it takes the combined male strength of the King and of Ransom to prevent this second fall. She is, of course, beautiful, but Lewis has a little trouble in depicting his Eve and goes wandering off into vague sophistries; female sex is simply one of the things that have feminine gender. "...the eyes of (Eve) opened inward, as if they were the curtained gateway to a world of waves and murmurings and wandering airs, of life that rocked in winds and splashed on mossy stones and descended as the dew and arose sunward in thin-spun delicacy of mist" (pp. 200-1). Eve is inward looking and therefore subjective and therefore temptable; Adam, the King, is objective, outward looking, and, therefore, able to look at the long view.

Lewis's twist in *Perelandra* is, of course, that paradise is not lost, but saved. This Eve reached for the fruit, but she did not pluck and she did not eat.

My second example is from H.P. Lovecraft's great 1928 classic, *The Dunwich Horror.* This Eve is named Lavinia Whately and she is the devilish image of both Eve and the Virgin Mary. She is described by Lovecraft as a deformed, unattractive albino woman of thirty-five. During a night of unspeakable happenings, she mates with some horror from the gulfs of time and space and becomes the fallen creature through whom the comparative Eden of Earth will be transformed into a hell populated by the waiting monsters who wish to return to possess it. In the same way that Eve's sin in the Garden of Eden opened the door for death and pain to enter paradise, Lavinia Whately's fall would open the door for the destruction of all humanity and all that is beautiful on Earth. Like Eve she is not very bright. Like Eve she is given to looking into things which she has no business looking into; in effect she becomes too aware of the knowledge of good and evil, just as Eve did when she ate the fruit in Eden. A woman, without innocence, according to all the old myths, is a demon of destruction.

After her fall, Lavinia is more like a fiendish Virgin Mary than an Eve, for she bears a hideous humanoid creature who feeds on the blood of cattle until that is insufficient and he feeds upon his mother, and also—and this is the wonderful twist of Lovecraft's plot—his invisible twin brother who is the Lovecraftian equivalent of Milton's sin and death loosed upon the world by a woman.

Once again, it is a man, and once again it is a professor, who saves us from the horror. He, too, delves into forbidden knowledge, but he does it to save the world, whereas the woman had done it to destroy the world.

My final example comes from a novel published in the far more liberated year of 1975: *A Place Beyond Man,* by Cary (Carolyn) Neeper, and the heroine is Tandra Grey, a biologist. She is brilliant, generous, fast with a witty ripost, and we are obviously supposed to admire her. Yet, this reader found her a troubling modern image of the destructive Eve. We see her as free of father, of mother, of influences in general, but yearning for motherhood. The Earth of the near future in which she lives has become the antithesis of Eden. Though it contains beautiful spots where the crickets chirp and the pine trees rustle in the night air, it is terribly overpopulated, the air in most places is polluted, the natural resources have been dissipated, and greed is the ruling factor. This Earth is, in short, the product of Eve's rash act in the Garden of Eden. Tandra Grey is chosen by aliens who have been observing Earth from a moon base for one hundred years, to be the new mother of a new race. They want her "if she is fertile."

The aliens are *varoks* and *ellls.* The *varoks* are superrational creatures, altruistic and brilliant, who resemble perfectly formed humans. The *ellls* are creatures of sensuality who school together like fishes and are intensely emotional. They are green and have plumes and can only see in ultraviolet light. The males are also very handsome and have long, lean bodies. Tandra, the human, can find no human males to match her needs, but these two aliens both attract her. The aliens have created a sort of paradise at the moon base, and the entrance of Tandra marks the beginning of the end of happiness. She even introduces jealousy and disease, albeit unwittingly.

After various adventures which include contact with humans who have landed on the moon for further exploration, Tandra deserts humanity with all of its failings, leaves it to the corruption and decay which her ancient predecessor had introduced, and mates with the aliens. While she has introduced pain and suffering into the aliens' world, she will be the great Eve/mother from whom the next race will arrive. In the same way that we, Eve's descendants, are genetically programmed to carry her evil ever forward, so we must conclude that Tandra's heirs will carry their Eve's human corruption forever onward.

These three women, the Perelandra Queen, Lavinia Whately, and Tandra Grey, have all deliberately chosen to act a role which, without intervention, would lead their race to destruction or, at least, terrible suffering. In the original story Eve is led to her downfall by the temptation of Satan—who is, it is true, a male and thus we may say that she was not entirely to blame for her downfall, yet the Biblical story makes it clear that she was warned against eating the fruit, and Milton's retelling of the story in *Paradise Lost* reminds us constantly that Adam tried to protect Eve from her impending doom; he is loath to leave her alone even for a moment, fearing that she will succumb to whatever evil may come near her. I feel that Milton may be excused, for he lived in a world of rigid hierarchies, where even stones had their assigned place, but Lewis lived in a democratic age in which the rigidity of the old chain of being class structure was at least suspect. Lovecraft was the opposite of the self-proclaimed atheist and rationalist who felt absolutely no compulsion to stick with the old myths. Eve/Lavinia was an agent that introduced those horrors to our world, just as Eve was the agent who introduced death into *this* world. I know nothing of Ms. Neeper's religious or political viewpoint, but I find her Tandra Grey to be a variation of the old theme. Everyone can think of further illustrations, all of those old space operas where vicious Venusians and Amazonian horrors, great, terrible reproducers thunder around causing trouble.

But my point is this: The basic archetypal myth of the Western world is that of the woman who brings suffering death and pain into the world. Notice that I am distinguishing between the *femme fatale* who lures men to their destruction, and the Eve figure whose actual and deliberate *act* is responsible for all the world's troubles. I need only point out another obvious parallel: Pandora who opened a box out of curiosity and let loose the troubles of all mankind. Eve, out of pride, out of curiosity, and because of intellectual strength, did the same.

Science fiction has its roots in the gothic novels of the middle and late eighteenth century, and those novels are certainly full of evil women, but its possibilities are, literally, limitless. Of all the world's literature, nothing but science fiction is by its very nature so free of the necessity of sticking with the old myths. Ursula Le Guin, in *The Left Hand of Darkness*, made a sort of breakthrough when she placed her story on a planet where there is only one sex; that book says more about gender and sexuality than Lewis is able to do with his awkward definitions. But Le Guin stands alone in this. Science fiction women are too often Las Vegas showgirls—exaggerated, Amazonian beauties, skimpily dressed and insatiably hungry for their man's love—or they are Eves upon whom we can place all the blame. They are the mothers of us all who will make us suffer for the rest of our days.

Scott Sanders

Woman as Nature in Science Fiction

IF ALL THE science fiction ever written filled a boxcar, the stories that deal maturely and seriously with women might fill a bushel basket. I don't guarantee those statistics. But anyone who has read widely in the genre will probably concede that the proportion is roughly accurate. I honor those fictions in which women do appear as complex, intelligent, independent selves. In order to understand the genre, however, much as we value the bushel, we must talk about the boxcar. Until very recently SF was written primarily for a male audience, about heroes for whom women are toys, threats or enigmas. As late as 1966, in *The Moon Is a Harsh Mistress*, Robert Heinlein could present us with a narrator who observes, "Women are amazing creatures—sweet, soft, gentle, and far more savage than we are" (14).[1] And in a story published the following year, Theodore Sturgeon could describe a rocket-drive as "a device somewhat simpler than Woman and considerably more complicated than sex."[2] For the male audience implied by Sturgeon and embraced by Heinlein's sly *we*, women are "amazing creatures," alien and obscure.

In much of the genre, women and nature bear the same features: both are mysterious, irrational, instinctive; both are fertile and mindless; both inspire wonder and dread in the hero; both are objects of male conquest. Just as men in SF embody consciousness, the agency through which nature knows itself, so women embody fertility, the agency by which nature reproduces itself. Men belong to the realm of mind; women and nature, to no-mind. Women are the bearers of life; men are life's interpreters and masters.

This series of contrasts might be charted as follows:

science	mental	rational	conscious	deliberate	male
nature	physical	emotional	unconscious	instinctual	female

The features on the upper line are commonly associated, in SF as in our culture generally, with the activity of science and with the "masculine," those on the bottom with nature and the "feminine." Most SF is built upon an opposition between the upper and lower terms of one or more of these pairs. The confrontation between male and female, my concern in this essay, is cognate with the fundamental opposition between the scientific mind and the material universe. Insofar as scientific knowledge is regarded as purely mental, logical, rational, while intuition and instinct and the body are excluded from the process of knowing, the male appears as the epitome of the knower, the female as the epitome of that which is known. This analogy between woman and nature does not hold for all SF by any means; but I hope to show that it is sufficiently common to give us insight into both the sexual stereotypes and the epistemology characteristic of the genre.

*   *   *

For someone who wishes to argue that women and nature bear analogous features in SF, the first objection to be overcome is that, whatever their features, women play so little role in the genre at all. The view of women in the bulk of SF would seem to be implicit in their absence: they simply are not there, unless, like Penelope, they are symbols of home and humdrum to the questing Ulysses on his return, or, like Circe, they are distractions along the way.

The most obvious reason for the absence of women in SF is that women have for so long been discouraged from taking part in the scientific and technological enterprise itself. I believe there are also more subtle reasons, stemming from the fact that SF first gained popularity, in the 1930s and 1940s, as an entertainment for adolescent boys. Many of the genre's influential authors, including Heinlein, Sturgeon and Asimov, were schooled in the pulp stories of that era, first as readers and then as writers. The genre is not inescapably shackled by its origins; but it has been shaped by them—particularly, in its treatment of women, by the psychology of its early audience. Abraham Maslow argues that the adolescent boy feels threatened by "femininity"—with which he associates emotion, instinct, tenderness—and he clings to "masculinity"— which to the boy signifies thought, will, hardness. Such a boy, Maslow contends,

has to tear himself loose—in our society at any rate—from his love for his mother. It is a force pulling him backward, and he fights it and her. He tries to achieve both independence and freedom from dependence on woman. He wants to join the company of men, to be the autonomous companion of his father rather than his dutiful, subordinated son. He sees men as being tough, fearless, impervious to discomfort and pain, independent of emotional ties, dominant, quick to anger and frightening in their anger, earthshakers, doers, builders, masters of the real world.[3]

There you have a psychological matrix for those innumerable stories about all-male space crews setting out to master the cosmos. On most of those flights the only "she" involved is the rocket ship, an artificial womb bearing men, while men bear consciousness.

There you also have one source of the taboo against sex that marked the genre until the early 1960s. For sex would disrupt the monastic fraternity of scientists, engineers, and space explorers. (Why were no women admitted to the US astronaut corps during the first 20 years of its existence?) On a deeper level sex would subvert the rationalist, disembodied stance on which much of the genre is predicated. Science, as popularly imagined and as generally depicted in SF, depends upon the mind's estrangement from nature: a gulf between the observing consciousness and the natural phenomena being observed. The emotions, particularly sexual desire, dull the sharp edge of reason and overcome this estrangement. So in practical terms woman is a distraction to the male scientist. In psychological terms her presence and her appeal are reminders of the scientist's own biological being, his identity with the nature he is observing. By succumbing to woman, the male scientist merges, however briefly, with the material world.

In *A Canticle for Leibowitz* (1959) Walter M. Miller, Jr., reminds us that the association between celibacy and spiritual conquests extends back to the monastic traditions of the Middle Ages. His own bearers of knowledge, abandoning earth at the novel's end, are literally monks and nuns, whose prospects for childbearing on other planets are discreetly left unexamined. Some authors, such as Cordwainer Smith in "Scanners Live In Vain" (1948) and Samuel Delany in "Aye, and Gomorrah..." (1967), actually render their adventurers neuter, splitting body off from brain so their heroes might conquer space in celibate peace. The Martians imagined by H.G. Wells in *The War of the Worlds* (1898) likewise "were absolutely without sex, and therefore without any of the tumultuous emotions that arise from that difference among men" (2:2). But Wells adds a caution: "In the Martians we have ... a suppression of the animal side of the organism by the intelligence.... Without the body the brain would, of course, become a mere selfish intelligence, without any of the emotional substratum of the human being" (2:2).

The psychological movement Maslow describes is dual: away from those qualities our culture defines as "feminine," toward those defined as "masculine." Pursuit of father entails flight from mother. In the same manner, the absence of women and the taboo against sex in much SF, aside from reflecting our social preconceptions about the place of females, reflects also an active repudiation of "feminine" qualities.

*   *   *

When women do appear in SF they are frequently identified with the principle of fertility, and hence with the procreative powers of nature. On an overpopulated planet human fecundity is a menace. But on an earth scourged by war or plague, or in a distant planetary colony, women may be imagined and revered simply as breeders. When chemical warfare leads to the sterilization of nearly all women on earth in D.F. Jones's novel *Implosion* (1967), for example, those few women who remain fertile are herded into state-run Homes and are dedicated "to the sole task of producing children." Guards protect them from the vengeance of the sterile ones, since "Among that lot there'll be hundreds to whom the prospect of children is their sole reason for living, and they'll be like ravening tigers...." (4). The fictional Prime Minister of England offers his opinion that "A strongly maternal woman is close to nature—she knows too that Mother Nature produces nothing useless; yet a sterile woman with strong maternal instincts *is* useless, and knows it. She feels useless—that's why some of 'em are so bitchy" (4). Through indoctrination and their presumed "maternal instincts" the fertile women become contented breeding stock, each one typically bearing thirty children, while the rest form a "Woman's Union": "This highly militant organization, with no very clear aims, was attracting a lot of sterile women, serving as a focus for their growing frustrations" (12). By 1967, when those dismissive lines were published, the women's movement both in this country and in Britain had attacked this simple equation of fulfillment with fertility. *Implosion* keeps the equation feebly alive: to be a woman is to be a stand-in for Mother Nature, and to populate the earth.

When it comes to populating remote colonies, women must at last be admitted aboard the rocket ships, if not on the pioneering flights then on the routine flights that follow. The lunar colony imagined by Robert Heinlein in *The Moon Is a Harsh Mistress* includes "host-mothers," who bear children for a living. One such woman is a major character in the book, and between children she takes an active part in the moon's rebellion against earth. Lest his readers puzzle over this assertive woman, Heinlein arranges for his narrator to tell us that she "Really was a man in some ways—her years as a disciplined revolutionist I'm sure; she was all girl most ways" (4). The "all girl" part of her was earlier described as follows:

"Pleasant face, quite pretty, and mop of yellow curls topped off that long, blond, solid lovely structure" (2). The distinction between the world-conquering man and the breeding woman is even extended to the novel's computer, which is said to manifest both male and female personalities. In its male phase it is rational, omniscient, aggressive; it masterminds the revolution and eventually governs the liberated moon. In its female phase the computer is described as letting down its hair and chatting with the heroine—the one with the "blond, solid, lovely structure"—about gynecology, pregnancies and childbirth.

In *The Word for World is Forest* (1972) Ursula Le Guin satirizes this image of women as planetary breeders. An all-male crew, patterned on the Marines in Vietnam, is in the process of conquering the planet of Athshe, clear-cutting its forests and enslaving its native peoples. Once the conquest appears secure a rocket load of earth women arrives, for the dual purpose of entertaining the men and populating the colony. When the native Athsheans revolt they shrewdly murder the women first, explaining to the outraged men, "We killed them to sterilise you" (6). Stripped of their women, the men become futureless machines, mastering planets they cannot settle. Le Guin's rich allegorical references to the Vietnam war remind us that the attitudes toward women we are considering, even when the setting is a galaxy away, are rooted in our history. Those endless "virgin" planets in SF are virginal in the same sense North America was when white people first landed here: ripe for our designs. In most SF, as in the settlement of this continent and in the conduct of our wars, those designs have been almost exclusively male. Women have followed men into the newly "pacified" territories, as playmates and mothers.

Occasionally, women appear in full regalia as goddesses of fertility. No fewer than three such goddesses appear in Philip José Farmer's *Flesh* (1969), which is deliberately modeled on the Great Mother myth outlined by Robert Graves in *The White Goddess* (1948). Some nine hundred years in the future, after global catastrophe, large portions of the earth are governed by a matriarchy. Under the rule of women technology regresses and science all but disappears, industry gives way to farming, and the reign of reason gives way to instinct, superstition and the cult of fertility. An all-male starship crew, after a trip to far-flung "virgin" planets that consumed eight hundred years (but only a short span in the lives of the men, thanks to the ever-useful dilation of time near the speed of light), are dismayed upon their return to find this government by women, and the consequent regression to a near-animal state. The starship doctor informs us that these women believe "Nature ... to be a living goddess," and he laments their "worship of Nature and fertility" (2). After undergoing an operation at the hands of the women the starship captain fulfills an adolescent boy's dream by becoming an inexhaustible male god who is sought after by every virgin girl in the land. Under the sway of women and sex, however, he loses all rational control, becomes "one great pulse that throbbed in unison with the buried heart of earth itself"; he suffers a "transformation from an individual man into a force of nature. Mindless ecstasy, body obeying the will of a Principle. He was an agent who had no choice but to obey that which possessed him" (9). Now there is a cautionary tale for you. Loss of control, loss of reason, loss of identity—these are the predictable symptoms of submission to women and, through women, to nature.

As Farmer's title suggests, it is flesh itself, the simple fact of our biological existence, which the male scientists fight against. For eight hundred years these men have lived celibately aboard their artificial ship. They are not about to surrender their rational paradise to the slovenliness of nature. By developing a machine that revivifies the dead they have even peeled away this final integument of flesh. Killed by the chief fertility goddess, the starship captain is revived by this miraculous device. What flesh betrayed, science restores. The only ill effect suffered by the captain is losing the memory of his orgiastic stay among the matriarchs. In fact his memory is restored to the moment when he decided, before the novel's opening, to return to earth; so all the woman-dominated nightmare is wiped from his mind and he becomes once more the rational hero, in command of his starship. When the men decide to flee what one of them calls this "woman-ridden" land, intending to establish colonies elsewhere in which science and patriarchs will once again prevail, they abduct the women whom they will need to populate their new world. Appropriately enough, the women are carried aboard unconscious, and they pass the trip in Deepfreeze. Presumably they will be thawed when the new colony is ready for children.

Fertility goddesses also appear in Samuel Delany's *The Einstein Intersection* (1967) and J.G. Ballard's "The Ultimate City" (1976). The first of these, as Delany himself informs us in the diary entries recorded in the novel, is based on the myth of Orpheus and Eurydice. The Orpheus figure accordingly goes through death defying trials, right to the very gates of hell, in his pursuit of the Eurydice figure, who is identified with animals, the underworld, the unconscious. At the doorway of hell Delany's hero encounters a white goddess, "the one men search out from seeding to seeding," "the thing that allows them all to go on loving."[4] More cagey than his mythic original, this hero avoids the fate of Orpheus, which, as you will recall, was to be torn limb-from-limb by women angered at the vow of chastity he took upon the second (and final) death of Eurydice.

In the Ballard novella a woman with the deliberately Shakespearean name of Miranda plants flowers and vines amidst the ruins of a technological city. Meanwhile her father, whose name of Buckmaster is clearly meant to summon up the ghost of R. Buckminster Fuller, is dedicated to restoring the machine society. While he works at his monuments to technology, Miranda is "gazing up at her hanging garden, as if waiting patiently for the jungle to return. In some way she seemed almost at odds with her father, trying to undo his work and transform it for her own purposes."[5] Here is a true fertility goddess, who can say, "wherever I touch, a flower springs up": "Miranda moved tirelessly through the city, seeding the glass-filled streets with poppies and daisies, trailing vines over the fallen telephone wires."[6] To one of the men who join with Buckmaster in an attempt to restore scientific civilization, her plants appear to be carnivorous. His response to this threat is again reminiscent of Vietnam, for he sprays her "botanical gardens" with defoliants. But no amount of poison can extinguish the threat posed by Miranda, for she embodies that power in nature which proliferates new life and disrupts the settled orders of men.

This equation between woman and the procreative power of nature emerges transparently from Ray Bradbury's "Here There Be Tygers" (1953). The customary all-male crew, on an expedition in search of minerals, lands on a planet which sounds remarkably like the Garden of Eden, minus the snake. "If ever a planet was a woman, this one is," a crewman declares.[7] After one of their number is killed by the planet in return for his persistent efforts at mining the idyllic countryside, the crewmen simultaneously dream of enchanting "women who would make fine wives, and raise beautiful children."[8] They are chagrined to learn that their dream-women are only projections of the planet, meant to lure them into staying and to distract them from their technological mission. Forcing his men to rocket away from this world of sensual delights, the captain reflects upon the planet: "Yes, she was a woman all right.... She wanted to be loved, like every woman, for herself, not for her wealth. So now, after she had offered us everything, we turn our backs. She's the woman scorned. She let us go, yes, but we can never come back."[9] Other crews have failed to return from their missions of conquest, and we are led to believe that some of them have been seduced by the womanly charms of other pastoral planets.

*   *   *

As a goddess of fertility, whether a humble breeder of colonists or a deity of mythic, even planetary proportions, the woman in SF is a two-sided figure, both temptation and threat. She thus resembles the White Goddess described by Robert Graves, and partakes of the ambivalent character of nature itself, both giver of life and bringer of death. "The fear of woman and the mystery of her motherhood," according to Joseph Campbell,

have been for the male no less impressive imprinting forces than the fears and mysteries of the world of nature itself. And there may be found in the mythologies and ritual traditions of our entire species innumerable instances of the unrelenting efforts of the male to relate himself effectively—in the way, so to say, of antagonistic cooperation—to these two alien yet intimately constraining forces: woman and the world.[10]

The name Aldous Huxley gives to this two-sided nature goddess is the Great Mother, whom he describes as "the principle of life, of fecundity, of fertility, of kindness and nourishing compassion; but at the same time she is the principle of death and destruction."[11] When Ballard's Miranda sows carnivorous plants, when Bradbury's female planet nearly seduces his amorous crewmen, when Farmer's fertility goddess temporarily kills his starship captain, or when Delany's women threaten to dismantle his Orpheus, we are exposed to the darker, the deathly side of the Great Mother.

Women frequently endanger men in SF in more humble ways. Humblest of all is the damsel-in-distress. Invariably she faints at the very feet of the monster or alien, or else she lapses into hysterics just at the moment when the male hero must keep his wits most firmly about him. In one sense such a woman is secretly in league with the external menace, because her emotionalism, her giving in to the body, is precisely the kind of surrender the male hero must avoid. She renders him vulnerable, not simply as all male myth figures from Adam onward are rendered vulnerable by their consorts, but she also weakens him specifically as a scientist, as a rational creature, because she calls out in him compassion and fear and desire. She is a reminder of that irrational nature which has just thrust some monster or mystery before him.

At the point of crisis, when the woman's body is draped unconscious across the arms of the scheming man, the polarization of male and female roles in conventional SF can be seen most clearly. For an early example of this endlessly repeated tableau, recall H.G. Wells' harried traveller in *The Time Machine* (1895) rescuing his maiden, Weena, from drowning, and then carrying her senseless body through woods infested with bloodthirsty Morlocks. In defending her body he all but loses his own. "But the problems of the world had to be mastered," he reminds himself at one stage. "I had not . . . come into the future to carry on a miniature flirtation. . . . I had as much trouble as comfort from her devotion" (5). Weena is a winsome distraction from the Time Traveller's real business, which is the almost universal science fictional task of mastering the world. She is one in a long line of female distractions in the genre, always ready with a naive question, prepared to faint on a moment's notice.

Almost as common as the damsel in distress, and equally distracting from the business of mastering the world, is the stupid wife. You will find her in the works of many SF authors, particularly in stories from the 1940s and 1950s, forever nagging, forever meddling with the instruments, incapable of understanding any mathematics more complicated than a grocery bill. As Fritz Leiber notes in the "Afterword" to one of his own stories in which a nagging wife appears, "For the modern American male... the ultimate bogey may turn out to be the Mom figure: domineering-dependent Wife or Mother, exaggerating their claims on him beyond all reason and bound."[12] I choose two examples from Robert Heinlein. In "The Roads Must Roll" (1940), while the Chief Engineer is dealing with a threatened breakdown in the transport system on which his whole society depends, his wife keeps pestering him with phone calls about the guest list for dinner, and comparable domestic matters. The engineer's secretary—naturally a woman and therefore attuned to the wife's pettiness—is ordered to "calm her down" so that he can run the technological system in peace. Heinlein provides the world leader in *Stranger in a Strange Land* (1961) with another dithering wife. While the husband is quite literally managing the entire planet, the wife is interviewing astrologers in her bedchamber, or addressing women's groups on "Motherhood in the New World." Again we find the coupling of superstition, fertility and political irrelevance in the woman's character. Such wives are impediments in the root sense of that word: pieces of baggage their managerial husbands must lug through life.

We have already seen that women threaten the monastic discipline by which many SF quests are governed. Because the adventure of reason derives at least some of its energies from the sublimation of sexuality, a woman disrupts the all-male enterprise. In Tom Godwin's "The Cold Equations" (1954), for example, when a woman stows away aboard an all-male ship that is on its way to deliver medicine to an all-male exploration party, the captain reluctantly decides he must jettison her into space in order to avoid jeopardizing the entire mission. We are told that her weight is the problem; given the make-up of the crew, one suspects the real problem is her sex. She is naive and emotional, while the captain, true to the story's title, is coldly rational. In space, we are informed, there is no scope for sentiment: "The men of the frontier knew—but how was a girl from Earth to fully understand?"[13]

Like many other women in SF, this girl comes from earth in more than one sense: presumably she was born there; and she is also a reminder of those earthly, sensual pleasures the spacemen have left behind. There is a deep connection, I believe, between the menace of female seduction and the recurrent warning in SF against the dangers of living in harmony with the environment. We have already seen one illustration of this in the Bradbury story, where the female planet nearly wrecks the technological mission by satisfying the crew's every bodily and sensory need. Once again Wells provides us, in *The Time Machine*, with an early formulation of this pseudo-Darwinian view: "It is a law of nature we overlook, that intellectual versatility is the compensation for change, danger, and trouble. An animal perfectly in harmony with his environment is a perfect mechanism.... There is no intelligence where there is no change and no need of change" (10). These sentiments have been echoed innumerable times within the genre. To take one more example, a character in Frank Herbert's *Dune* (1965) explains the decadence of a race as follows:

We came from Caladan—a paradise world for our form of life. There existed no need on Caladan to build a physical paradise or a paradise of the mind—we could see the actuality all around us. And the price we paid was the price men have always paid for achieving a paradise in this life—we went soft, we lost our edge.[14]

Sensual fulfillment saps the reservoirs of aggression. Rational conquest of the cosmos is routinely linked in the genre to the struggle for existence—the true business of men—just as softness, yielding, harmonious dwelling within nature is linked to women.

Sometimes the menacing female appears directly in her guise as death mother. In Delany's *Einstein Intersection*, in addition to the woman who guards the gates of hell and steals men's souls, there is a computer named Phaedra, who refers to herself as "Mother" and imprisons the damned in a perpetual state of illusion. Like the furies who dismember Orpheus, the mythical Phaedra is another woman so angered by a man's vow of chastity that she connives at his death. In "A Toy for Juliette" (1967) Robert Bloch offers us a heroine who tortures and slays human "toys" brought to her from the past. Her career ends abruptly when she is inadvertently delivered Jack-the-Ripper, who butchers her.

Often women serve as instruments for some alien power that seeks to gain control over humanity. Thus women in John Wyndham's *The Midwich Cuckoos* (1957) serve as mothers for otherworldly offspring whose purpose is to supplant the human race. In both Murray Leinster's *The Brain-Stealers* (1954) and Jack Finney's *The Body Snatchers* (1955) (whose titles between them sum up about all there is for a man to lose), a male hero is nearly lured to destruction by a woman who has already succumbed to the aliens. To avoid being possessed the man must shun the woman. Some remote and hostile civilization seeks control over earth in Fred Hoyle and John Elliot's *A for Andromeda* (1962) by tricking scientists into building a computer and then into synthesizing a woman, Andromeda herself. Newly minted, she is said to look "like a princess in a fairy tale," (9) "like a young goddess" (10). Among the deities with whom she is compared is our old friend from the underworld, Eurydice. For the practical business of winning over generals, politicians and scientists, almost all of whom are male, Andromeda is furnished with the regulation curvaceous body and blond hair. During most of the story she is the mindless will less creature of the computer. Only by arousing her emotions through carefully planted kisses can the novel's hero woo her away from the machine, and thus succeed in its destruction.

The alien force at work in Stanley Weinbaum's "A Martian Odyssey" (1934) attempts to destroy a spaceman by mesmerizing him with images of his sweetheart: "The dream-beast uses its victim's longings and desires to trap its prey."[15] Given the gender of most SF protagonists, the dream-beasts scattered throughout the genre usually come up with female images. In Stanislaw Lem's *Solaris* (1961), for instance, the planetary being that gives the novel its title—the ocean of Solaris—presents itself to the party of investigating scientists by means of projections from the scientist's own unconscious. The only two projections we see are women, each haunting a male scientist with recollected guilt and desire. The original team leader is driven to suicide by his woman-phantom. His successor, who narrates the novel, falls in love with his own woman-phantom, abandons his scientific mission, succumbs to eros. By novel's end the entire study of the planet is forsaken. Arriving without memory or purpose these women are mindless, selfless extensions of the shape-giving ocean, which Lem clearly means for us to regard as nature. Lem could have chosen other manifestations of nature, other messengers from the unconscious; but he chose women. They are outgrowths of the very world the men are seeking to understand, but outgrowths so disturbing they divert all attention to themselves.

Lem's female phantoms come upon his scientists in sleep, like the medieval figure of the succubus. (Sleep, like sex, is menacing to the rational hero because it means a loss of consciousness, an abeyance of the will, a yielding to natural forces.) In a poem entitled "The Succubus" (1930), Robert Graves echoes Freud and Jung, and anticipates Lem, by tracing this devouring female home to the male's unconscious:

> Why with hot face,
> With paunched and uddered carcase,
> Sudden and greedily does she embrace,
>   Gulping away your soul, she lies so close,
> Fathering you with brats of her own race?
>   Yet is the fancy grosser than your lusts were gross?[16]

Male dread of the *femme fatale* has multiple sources, as Freud, Jung, de Beauvoir and other commentators on the sexual imagination have argued. SF is certainly not immune to any of those sources. But because within the genre women are commonly identified with nature, and because nature is both the object of the rational hero's conquest and the obstacle in his way, women often carry a special charge of menace in SF. Since the "feminine" is actively repressed, when it does surface it unsettles the masculine order.

*   *   *

The element missing from all these impersonations of the Great Mother is the one largely reserved in SF for men: logic, reason, the analytic workings of the mind. Even when not menacing, women in SF are often depicted as irrational creatures whose powers, however great, are distinct from those wielded by men. I have already noted the polarization between female instinct and male science in *Flesh*, between female sentiment and male logic in "The Cold Equations," between female superstition and male reason in *Stranger in a Strange Land*. In the latter novel Heinlein even projects these sexual stereotypes onto the Martians, whose developmental psychology he describes as follows: "Martian nymphs [the young] were female, all adults were male.... Adults were huge...; they were physically passive, mentally active. Nymphs were fat, furry spheres, full of bounce and mindless energy" (11). The passage from youth to maturity, from a state of "mindless energy" to one of mental activity, is identified with the leap from female to male. His earthly characters in the novel obey the same pattern, since all the reasoning figures are men—detectives, politicians, scientists— while all the women—secretaries, nurses, consorts—are indeed "full of bounce and mindless energy."

When Isaac Asimov invented an other-worldly psychology in *The Gods Themselves* (1972), he was considerably more thoughtful than Heinlein about sex roles, yet the stereotypes still show through. In Asimov's para-universe the aliens are divided, when immature, into a triad of personalities. The rational and parental thirds are referred to as "he," the emotional or intuitive third as "she." At maturity these three selves fuse into a single adult, called a "hard one" (remember those masculine qualities of toughness), who is referred to exclusively by the male pronoun. While the parental and emotional qualities are supposed to survive the transformation, in fact the adults appear to be wholly rational: "They had only the mind, only the inquiry into the Universe" (2b). When Asimov returns to the human sphere late in the novel, he offers us a female intuitionist working with a male scientist: the man is a master of logic and mathematics, able to implement the discoveries which the woman can intuit but can neither explain nor prove.

A female religious order in *Dune* achieves influence over an entire galaxy through shrewd use of superstition, mysticism and "higher powers." By careful breeding over generations they prepare the way for a messiah, whom they hope to harness to their will. But when at last the messiah comes he is a man, he quickly outstrips them in powers both occult and rational, and *he* bends *them* to his will. The female sorceress, dealing in spells and visions, is set off against the male Mentat, who is "the embodiment of logic." This polarity between irrational women and rational men is linked to the polarity between women as life-bearers and men as world-shapers, for at one point the messiah observes:

There is in each of us an ancient force that takes and an ancient force that gives. A man finds little difficulty facing that place within himself where the taking force dwells, but it's almost impossible for him to see into the giving force without changing into something other than man. For a woman, the situation is reversed.[17]

So the male force is the one that takes, the female the one that gives. At least in regard to sexual roles, Dune is not so unlike earth.

Sometimes the opposition between rational men and irrational women is carried to absurd lengths. For instance in *The Robot Brains* (1967), by Sydney Bounds, we learn of a far-future race divided between males who are the "Brains" of the title, mere walking craniums with spindly bodies, and nine foot tall females who are described, through the hero's eyes, as "all remarkably alike, superbly built and blonde-headed, as if cast from a mold. It made him think of a beauty contest carried to an insane conclusion. He suspected that they were devoid of any intelligence whatever" (10). His suspicion proves true. A visit to the female nursery suggests why these women have lost whatever vestiges of intelligence might once have lingered in their giant bodies: "The girls ... paraded between mirror-walls, constantly adjusting their scanty drapes and remaking their faces with cosmetics" (10). In this admittedly trashy novel we find the sex-role polarization of more sophisticated SF crudely presented; but it remains the same convention, the same identification of men with thought and women with thoughtless flesh.

*   *   *

In order to re-imagine the lives that women might live, in fiction and in the real world, we need also to re-think our relationship to nature. In most SF, as in technological societies generally, that relationship has been viewed as antagonistic, as a struggle for domination. Despite frequent appeals within the genre to wonder, to knowledge for its own sake, much of what *happens* in SF involves the expansion of human control over the material world. Knowledge is literally power: the more of the universe is understood scientifically, the more is subject to human purposes. Most heroes within the genre, to recall Maslow's phrase, are "earthshakers,... doers, builders, masters of the real world." Most heroines, because of their supposed affinity with nature, are acted upon rather than acting.

Toward the end of the last century Wells echoed a view popular in industrial society when the protagonist of his *Time Machine* dreamed of a day when "The whole world will be intelligent, educated, and co-operating; things will move faster and faster toward the subjugation of nature" (4). Some thirty years later, unable to believe so sanguinely in "progress," Alfred North Whitehead could still declare: "The primary function of Reason is the direction of the attack on the environment."[18] Because of our present ecological crisis it is unlikely that anyone as intelligent as Whitehead or Wells would now speak of "subjugating" nature or "attacking" the environment. Yet as recently as 1969 Buckminster Fuller, that great visionary of a technological future, wrote that "the essence of human evolution upon Spaceship Earth" is the "metaphysical mastering of the physical."[19] Although his diction is less aggressive, his meaning is the same: as rational creatures it is our business to gain control over nature. That is what it *means* to be a thinking animal. The very metaphor, "Spaceship Earth," implies that the planet is here *for us*, is wholly ours to use.

This ethic of domination rests on the deeper assumption that mind stands over against nature, observing and manipulating it from the outside. Fuller speaks, for example, of "the progressive mastery of matter by mind."[20] In personal terms, this division between consciousness and nature translates as a split between mind and body; in sexual terms, it often translates as a split between male and female. To speak of subjugating nature or attacking the environment is also by implication to speak of subduing the body, and also, in many cases, to speak of subduing women.

From the seventeenth until the early twentieth century, science was based on this Cartesian opposition between consciousness and the material world. Modern developments in physics and psychology have largely erased that dualism from the philosophy of science, yet it still lingers on in popular thinking and in much SF. I have already mentioned the "Scanners" of Cordwainer Smith and the "Spacers" of Samuel Delany, creatures who are literally divided between brain and body, the better to function amidst the sensory deprivation of outer space. Spaceflight itself, one of the central motifs of the genre, represents a divorce from all organic systems. The major thrust of technology, both in society and in SF, is the attempt not just to dominate nature but to cancel it out: to eliminate disease, weather, species antagonistic to our purposes; to overcome barriers of time and space; to postpone and if possible vanquish death. Think how many science fictional elements suggest a wrestling with the limits of material existence: telepathy, faster-than-light travel, instantaneous communication, perfect healing, omniscient intelligences, machineries of immortality.

In the fictions of Arthur Clarke we find memorable expressions of this yearning to escape our material limits. At the end of both *2001* and *Childhood's End*, for example, children are translated from flesh into spirit, are reborn as patterns of pure energy, without benefit of sex or mothers. At some distance behind that imagined rebirth lurks St. Paul, with his doctrine that the human spirit has somehow been trapped in a house of flesh, and awaits release. Once divide human existence between soul and body, between spirit and nature, and it is but an easy step to divide the sexes along the same lines, as St. Paul himself did: "I permit no woman to teach or to have authority over men; she is to keep silent. For Adam was formed first, then Eve; and Adam was not deceived, but the woman was deceived and became a transgressor. Yet woman will be saved through bearing children, if she continues in faith and love and holiness, with modesty" (1 Timothy 2:12-15). The woman's inferiority, her penance, is marked here as in Genesis by her fertility. Describing the same Biblical couple, Milton put the case even more directly:

> Not equal, as their sex not equal seemed;
> For contemplation he and valor formed,
> For softness she and sweet attractive grace;
> He for God only, she for God in him.[21]

The sexual polarization we have found in SF could not be more neatly stated: man is created for thought and heroic deeds, woman for love or sex.

The point of summoning up St. Paul and Milton is to remind us how deep in our culture runs this dual suspicion of nature and women. SF writers have certainly not invented the structure of thought I have been examining. The association of men with reason and women with unreason, of men with the conquering of nature and women with nature itself, is a commonplace of our intellectual inheritance. Indeed, as Alan Watts wrote in his own study of attitudes toward nature, "The catalogue of popular images, figures of speech, and customs which associate spirit with the divine, the good, and the male and nature with the material, evil, sexual, and female could go on indefinitely."[22]

In his study of world mythologies Joseph Campbell traces this sexual polarization to the displacement of matriarchal social orders by patriarchal ones. When the Earth Mother, with her intimate links to nature, is ousted by the Spirit Father, who stands outside the natural world, all that had been associated with the "feminine" is actively repressed:

the female principle is devaluated, together with its point of view, and, as always happens when a power of nature and the psyche is excluded from its place, it has turned into its negative, as a demoness, dangerous and fierce. And we are going to find, throughout the ... orthodox patriarchal systems of the West, that the power of this goddess-mother of the world, whom we have here seen defamed, abused, insulted, and overthrown by her sons, is to remain as an ever-present threat to their castle of reason, which is founded upon a soil that they consider to be dead but is actually alive, breathing and threatening to shift.[23]

Stripped of its Jungian overtones, Campbell's passage rests on the sound notion that to deny any portion of our psyche or any segment of our population is to throw ourselves out of balance both psychologically and politically. We do not need to accept his reading of Western culture in order to agree that any rigidly patriarchal order will be haunted by the ghosts of matriarchy, by those powers associated with the rule of women. Because so much SF excludes and belittles women, and repudiates those qualities culturally defined as "feminine," women, when they do appear in the genre, often are figures of menace, threatening the heroes' "castle of reason."

Occasionally an author stands this conventional view of sex-roles on its head. In my reading, almost every such reversal has been imagined by a woman writer. Thus Marion Bradley, in "The Wind People" (1959), presents a mother who is bound by her scientific training to deny the existence of the ethereal creatures who give the story its title, while her son intuits their presence directly. She remains cut off from the life of the planet by the barrier of reason; he merges into nature. In "Vaster Than Empires and More Slow" (1971) Le Guin assigns a woman to be the doggedly rational leader of a scientific expedition, and assigns a man to be the crew's "empath" or intuitionist. As in the Bradley story, the woman can never overcome her dread of the forested planet they have come to explore; but the man, yielding to the forest's emanations, once again merges with nature. Le Guin also reverses the customary sexual roles in *The Word for World is Forest* (1972). Among the Athshean people whom she describes there, women run the practical affairs while men seek wisdom through dreaming. Women are the hard-nosed, tough-minded ones, upon whom the men depend for sustenance and government.

Even these inversions of a paradigm still leave us with the paradigm, however: the choice we are offered remains either/or. Either one reasons, or one intuits; either one lives from the mind or one lives from the body; either one masters nature or one vanishes into it. What we need, in SF as in society at large, is an end to this polarization, a reunion of those human qualities falsely sundered under the labels of "masculine" and "feminine." Writers, especially the creators of speculative fiction, can imagine such a reunion within individuals and entire societies, even when the actual world in which we live provides few promising models. By taking thought, as Marx sardonically reminds us, we do not change the world. An effort of consciousness will not by itself alter the facts of our existence; but it might offer us designs for that revolution.

Notes

[1] Numbers in parentheses indicate that the passage quoted appears in the chapter number given of the text cited. Because a particular science fiction text often appears in more than one edition, and because these editions often differ significantly in pagination, I use this convention for referring to chapter divisions whenever possible. If a text is divided into books as well as chapters, it is annotated thus: 2:4, meaning book 2, chapter 4.

[2]Theodore Sturgeon, "If All Men Were Brothers, Would You Let One Marry Your Sister?" in *Dangerous Visions*, ed. Harlan Ellison (New York: Doubleday, 1967), p. 346. Even Sturgeon's title implies a male reader.

[3]Abraham H. Maslow, *The Psychology of Science* (New York: Harper and Row, 1966), p. 36.

[4]Samuel Delany, *The Einstein Intersection* (New York: Ace Books, 1976), pp. 140, 142.

[5]J.G. Ballard, *Low-Flying Aircraft and Other Stories* (London: J.C. Cape, 1976), p. 48.

[6]Ballard, pp. 70-71.

[7]Ray Bradbury, "Here There Be Tygers," in *Tomorrow, and Tomorrow, and Tomorrow*, ed. Bonnie Heintz, et al. (New York: Holt, Rinehart and Winston, 1974), p. 365. "Here There Be Tygers" was first published in *Amazing Stories, 1953*.

[8]Bradbury, p. 373.

[9]Bradbury, p. 374.

[10]Joseph Campbell, *The Masks of God, I: Primitive Mythology* (New York: Viking Press, 1959), pp. 59-60.

[11]Aldous Huxley, *The Human Situation*, ed. Piero Ferruci (New York: Harper and Row, 1977), p. 200.

[12]Fritz Lieber, "Gonna Roll Them Bones," in *Dangerous Visions*, p. 254.

[13]Tom Godwin, "The Cold Equations," in *The Science Fiction Hall of Fame*, ed. Robert Silverberg (New York: Doubleday, 1971), p. 559. This story was first published in *Astounding Fiction, 1954*.

[14]Frank Herbert, *Dune* (Philadelphia: Chilton, 1965), p. 204.

[15]Stanley Weinbaum,"A Martian Odyssey," in *The Science Fiction Hall of Fame,* p. 31. This story was first published in *Wonder Stories,* 1954.

[16]Robert Graves, *Collected Poems 1955* (New York: Doubleday, 1955), p. 84.

[17]Herbert, p. 356.

[18]Alfred N. Whitehead, *The Function of Reason* (Princeton: Princeton Univ. Press, 1929), p. 8.

[19]R. Buckminster Fuller, *Operating Manual for Spaceship Earth* (Carbondale: Southern Illinois Univ. Press, 1969). p. 36.

[20]Fuller, p. 94.

[21]*Paradise Lost,* Book 4, lines 296-99.

[22]Alan W. Watts, *Nature, Man and Woman* (New York: Pantheon, 1958), p. 143.

[23]Joseph Campbell, *The Masks of God III: Occidental Mythology* (New York: Viking Press, 1964), p. 86.

III Paradise Regained

Carol Pearson

Coming Home:
Four Feminist Utopias and
Patriarchal Experience*

FEMINIST UTOPIAN FICTION implicitly or explicitly criticizes the patriarchy while it emphasizes society's habit of restricting and alienating women. Each work discussed here assumes that the patriarchy is unnatural and fails to create environments conducive to the maximization of female—or male— potential. Upon discovering a sexually equalitarian society, the narrators have a sense of coming home to a nurturing, liberating environment.[1]

The creators of feminist utopias envision societies which are surprisingly similar. Mary Bradley Lane's *Mizora: A Prophesy*[2] and Charlotte Perkins Gilman's *Herland*[3] were originally serialized in newspapers and grew out of the nineteenth-century women's movement. The contemporary feminist movement influenced Dorothy Bryant and Mary Staton. Bryant's *The Kin of Ata Are Waiting for You*[4] is mystic in its primary focus, while Staton's *From the Legend of Biel*[5] is a highly symbolic novel about consciousness. This essay will discuss the surprisingly numerous areas of consensus among such seemingly divergent works, agreement which can be explained by the similar conditioning and experiences women share.

Feminist utopias tend to emphasize forces which most directly oppress women. One major concern is the low status and pay for "women's work." The narratives often emphasize the particular value of certain traditionally feminine occupations. The citizens of *Mizora's* classless society, for example, have particular respect for cooks, and school teaching is one of the most valued occupations in Herland. Everyone is employed and everyone's job is meaningful. This does not mean, however, that no one works at jobs the patriarchal society would judge to be "menial." For instance, in Ata, the cultivation of the soil enriches the people's dreams.

*This article is a revised version of "Women's Fantasies and Feminist Utopias" which first appeared in *Frontiers: A Journal of Women's Studies,* (Fall 1977), pp. 50-61. Many of the ideas in this essay will also appear in the final chapter of *The Female Hero in British and American Literature,* co-author, Katherine Pope (New York: Bowker, 1979).

These feminist utopias assume that individuals naturally work for love rather than for profit. Because of their experiences in the patriarchy, women may find it easier than men to imagine societies in which labor is free and people do not compete for scarce jobs which have status. Although housewives have never earned a salary, a sense of love, pride, or duty motivates them to serve their families. Women who have worked outside the home as secretaries, nurses and elementary school teachers have done their jobs efficiently and well—without the hope of becoming executives, doctors or principals. Ironically, it may be women's experiences in a sexist society which have enabled them to see truths about human motivations.

The novels challenge and correct biases about innate female "nature." They counter stereotypes by emphasizing women's strength, courage and intelligence. These female characters desire to take risks and they seek adventure. The authors celebrate the liberation which results from an absence of rape or other assault. Lane and Gilman assert the superiority of female gentleness and challenge the assumption that women are weak and need male protection. The male explorer who discovers Herland wonders how the women survived without protective men. He soon learns that "stalwart virgins had no men to fear and therefore no need of protection" (p. 128). The following statement from *Mizora* takes a prositive view of men's absence: "I noticed with greater surprise than anything had excited in me, the absence of men. . . . There was not a lock or bolt on any door" (p. 28).

Violence, coupled with a desire to master others, is antithetical to a feminist utopian vision. In all cases, feminist utopias allow citizens to control their own lives. These women are free from the rape of their minds as well as their bodies. No one is owned by anyone else. In *Herland*, two male explorers see the evil of their ways and embrace a nonviolent, noncompetitive, equalitarian ethic. Instead of labeling men as the enemy, Bryant and Staton point out the need for different patterns of socialization and education. All four authors portray women as the creators of a new consciousness and a new vision.

Women are, after all, the victims of sexism. Since they alone know where the shoe pinches, they are more motivated than men to seek the means for alleviating the discomfort. Perhaps even more importantly, their experience is just different enough from men's practical knowledge to enable them to challenge the dominant masculine public culture.

Feminist utopias do away with the division between the inhumane marketplace and the humane hearth. This is not accomplished by moving both men and women out into a brutal public world. Instead, the entire society is patterned after the principles which (ideally) govern the home. Herland, for example, is "like a pleasant family—an old, established, perfectly-run country place" (p. 238). The metaphor "coming home" is evident throughout these feminist utopias. The protagonists typically assume that they will be alienated in a public world which demands the denial of such vital parts of the self as emotion, vulnerability and spontaneity. The nurturing utopian societies allow for the full development of each individual within a supportive, secure environment. When an outsider reaches the alternative society, he stops repressing valuable human qualities and feels rejoined to the self. In *From the Legend of Biel*, for example, as Howard Scott entered a building "he felt that if he could stay here, in this room, he would come together with that in himself which was not realized.... The pieces of shattered mosaic which was himself could come naturally, easily together, matching edge to edge, and click into a whole" (p. 46).

In these novels, reclaiming the self is often associated with coming home to mother. However, in contrast to the stereotype of a smothering, dependent, maternal woman, the authors take pains to define that mother as a fully human, free person. The explorer who decides to marry one of the women of Herland describes his love in terms of "coming home" to a mother of this type:

I found that loving 'up' was a very good sensation after all. It gave me a queer feeling, a way down deep, as of the stirring of some ancient dim pre-historic consciousness, a feeling that they were right somehow—that this was the way to feel. It was like—coming home to mother. I don't mean the wide-flannels and doughnuts mother, the fussy person that waits on you and spoils you and doesn't really know you. I mean the feeling that a very little child would have, who had been lost—for ever so long. It was a sense of getting home; of being clear and rested, of safety and yet freedom, of love that was always there, warm like sunshine in May, not hot like a stove or a featherbed, a love that didn't irritate and didn't smother (p. 323).

The turn of the century utopias sentimentalize motherhood and assert women's moral superiority.[6] *Herland*'s narrator notes that women in that society "had no enemies; they themselves were all sisters and friends" (p. 129). They are all mothers whose "power of mother love, that maternal instinct we so highly lauded" is developed to the fullest and complemented by a "sister love" (p. 128). The success of Herland's society is attributed to mother love: "The children in this country are the one center and focus of all our thoughts. Every step of our advance is always considered in its effect on them—on the race. You see we are *mothers* she repeated, as if in that she had said it all" (p. 152).

These writers, however, do not naively assume that the bond

between mother and child is always positive. Even though mother/daughter love forms the pattern for all other relationships in *Herland, Mizora* and *From the Legend of Biel,* this bond differs from its patriarchal equivalent. There is no illegitimacy because all children have mothers; children are not seen as the property of their parents. The idea of having two parents is ludicrous in *Mizora.* When asked about her father or "other parent," a young girl laughs: "You have a queer way of jesting. I have but one mother, one adorable mother. How could I have two?" (p. 2).

In *From the Legend of Biel* we learn that the nuclear family must be destroyed because it is always composed of captor parents and a captured child: "The whole object of the family is to repeat itself, to create the future in the image of the past. Consequently it is a very effective brake on change because it keeps all children within the boundaries of cultural tradition. In the family learning is a process of psychological brutality at the end of which a child knows nothing but what is permissible to the tribe" (p. 219). Patriarchal parents entrap their children by expecting them to justify their own sacrifices. A mother who lives her own life does not need to live through her child.

From the Legend of Biel severs the link between parent and child, since, in this novel, women do not give birth to children in the customary natural fashion. This dissolution of the nuclear family leads to a redefinition of the parent/child relationship. The story of the love between Mikkran and Biel, her young charge, forms this culture's central myth: "The mentor/charge relationship is based on mutual sovereignty—not on imitation. The one truth in the Federation which has maintained equilibrium in the absence of prescribed morality, in the absence of unquestioned basic tenets, is this relationship which teaches that two persons of relaxed and curious mind who learn and share together, who confront the unknown, also create joy" (p. 22). Furthermore, no person assumes total responsibility for child care.

In Bryant's *The Kin of Ata,* chidbirth is seen as a communal responsibility. The narrator, a visitor from a patriarchal culture, watches as a young girl in the preliminary stages of labor is assisted by the three men who might have conceived the child. When she is nearing delivery, the entire community gathers to help. A citizen explains, "We try to take some of the pain on ourselves, to share it. We try to give some of our strength for the hard work. We try to make the girl feel happy that, once she has done this, she need no longer carry the burden of the child alone. Then she will labor in joy" (p. 149). However, although the mother/child relationship is celebrated, child rearing is the responsibility of professionals. Even the women of Herland who emphasize the overriding power of mother love, entrust young children to trained teachers.

Just as they redefine the mother/child bond, the authors envision families of equals, families which are not claustrophobic and nuclear. Rather, they are relatively large extended groups who freely choose to live together. The members of these groups are not divided into male and female roles. In *The Kin of Ata*, "kin" replaces words which signify gender differences. This novel's narrator has difficulty discerning sexual distinctions. Similarly, Herland's newcomers are somewhat shocked to realize that the women "don't seem to notice our being men.... They treat us well—just as they do one another. It's as if our being men was a minor incident" (p. 69).

Economic and racial prejudice are absent from these families. In fact, respect for the individual is an integral aspect of the feminist utopian vision. The opinions of individual citizens are respected in Herland, where decisions are made by a community family council. These societies essentially function without strong governments and repressive laws. A citizen of *Mizora* explains, "in a country like ours, where civilization has reached the state of enlightenment that needs no law, we are simply guided by custom" (p. 28). Such procedures coincide with Ursula K. Le Guin's conception of the "female principle": "To me the 'female principle' is, or at least historically has been, basically anarchic. It values order without constraint, rule by custom, not by force. It has been the male who enforces order, who constructs power-structures, who makes, enforces, and breaks laws."[7]

The societies in these novels use persuasion, rather than force, to establish order. And, in contrast to their traditional domestic duties, mothers enforce the public law. Their controlling hand is almost free of restraint. For instance, a policy of noninterference governs the mentors in *From the Legend of Biel*. Mikkran desires to protect Biel without interfering with the child's journey. The mentor learns that it is possible to offer guidance without disrupting a young person's natural growth. And, she realizes that she is most effective when acting as an equal rather than as a master. The mothers of Herland also respect their children's natural inclinations. These children learn when they play; the creation of children's games is seen as one of the society's supreme achievements. In this way, the adults provide direction without limiting the next generation's natural desire to explore and experiment. Contrary to our expectations, the children who have been allowed to do exactly as they wish learn to be wise and productive adults. Time after time, the discoverers of feminist utopias marvel that they "never heard a baby cry" (Bryant, p. 20).

The children of Ata are also encouraged to experiment freely. Such lenient methods of raising children result from a belief that the interests of the individual and the group are not in conflict. Yet, although these novels assume that people prefer to act in an ethical manner, they do not romanticize human behavior. The reason for the kin of Ata's decision to have a low birthrate exemplifies this point: children "are pure desire.... They must try everything, have everything—too many would destroy our way of life faster than any invasion from outside" (p. 152). People learn from both their negative and positive experiences.

Citizens of feminist utopias tolerate rather than deny unpleasant human behavior. For example, instead of being punished for violating Herland's customs, the narrator is cared for by sympathetic women. And, after the protagonist of *The Kin of Ata* accidentally kills a revered old man, his action results in a surprising consequence: the kin perform a rite of purification and ask forgiveness for their violent feelings. Such resolutions are based upon the assumption that crime is bad for the perpetrator as well as for the victim. However, tolerance of this sort is more than a manipulative method of making sin lose its appeal. Instead, as Le Guin explains, it is based upon a philosophical rejection of dualistic thinking:

> Our curse is alienation, the separation of Yang from Yin. Instead of a search for balance and integration, there is a struggle for dominance. Divisions are insisted upon, interdependence is denied. The dualism of value that destroys us, the dualism of superior/inferior, ruler/ruled, owner/owned, user/used, might give way to what seems to me, from here, a much healthier, sounder, more promising modality of integration and integrity (IGN, pp. 138-9).

A feminist utopia's most common plot structure emphasizes the relationship between the repression of parts of the self and the oppression of other people. *The Kin of Ata* is typical: although the narrator is an extremely successful man in a patriarchal society, he is an alienated, unhappy misogynist. When this man stops repressing the metaphorical woman within himself, he is free from his need to dominate and conquer people in the outside world. Staton's characters also develop an ethic based upon the full and free attainment of the self. They learn that "equilibrium is a natural state for persons, and ultimately inevitable, once the screen for systems has been removed" (p. 297). Systems, are "Basic Tenets, Constitutions, Morals, Law, Belief, Ethics—any construct which presumes to decide what is appropriate human behavior" (p. 297).

Coming home to the self, then, is based upon an organic, anarchic ethic of growth rather than a dualistic pattern of ownership, denial and repression. The mothers of Herland, who "had no theory of the essential opposition of good and evil; life to them was a growth; their pleasure was in growing and their duty also" (p. 240) exemplify this point. Similarly, in *From the Legend of Biel*, morality is based upon one question: "How do we manifest potential?" (p. 300). Process is more important than product. An attempt to extract "truth" from this process freezes or kills experiential reality. The kin of Ata avoid writing down their sacred myths for just this reason. They prefer an oral tradition, a tradition which allows their myths to be enriched by the dreams and interpretations of each storyteller.

Eliminating hierarchies changes the spatial metaphors which people use to understand their world. The kin of Ata arrange their circular village buildings in a spiral pattern. A vertical infinity sign is a sacred symbol in *From the Legend of Biel*. The enclosed space symbolizes the known; the space outside represents the unknown. The infinity sign signifies the capacity of the human brain to "embrace all concepts and all reality" (p. 174) when it forgets the patriarchal desire to "own mates, progeny, land, knowledge, or emotions" (p. 176).

Inhabitants of feminist utopias typically reject the assumptions behind terms like "abstract" and "objective." They best understand outer phenomena when they combine analysis with empathic and intuitive understanding. Again, women's experiences in the patriarchal society undoubtedly contribute to this emphasis. Women have not been encouraged to interpret experiences in a scientific fashion. Consequently, they have often developed intuitive skills, or "women's intuition," which are often denigrated.

Despite this stereotypical denigration, science in feminist utopias is not at a low level. Their science is not inferior; it is just different. Howard Scott, for example, enters the "cerebral cortex" of the Thoacdien dome where he becomes aware of "a large, benevolent heart which was glad he was there, and in beating, spoke to him" (p. 47). Such technology, which is designed to include natural processes, results from a consciousness which fuses thought and feeling.

Although this consciousness does not call for the worship of a "god," a vision of an earth mother goddess often personifies the philosophical vision underlying a feminist utopia. The patriarchy has associated woman with nature to justify and perpetuate the oppression of women. Yet, for these writers, such an association forms a basis for potential strength. As opposed to the judgmental patriarchal god who reigns above nature and humankind, the mother goddess represents life in all its fluidity and contradictions. The goddess personifies a vision which is consistent with female experience. In Herland "mother love ... was a Religion.... All they did related to this power" (p. 266). And, as a young girl dies in

Mizora, she regrets that she cannot "go to sleep in the arms of my mother. But the great mother of us all will soon receive me in her bosom" (p. 210). In feminist utopian fiction, then, religious feeling is associated with self-affirmation and a sense of unity with all life.

The metaphors for the birth of a feminist consciousness and society are patterned after women's actual procreative experiences. However, the new woman and the new society do not spring full-blown from a diety's head. As children emerge from a woman's body, the utopian future is an outgrowth of women's actual situation. The utopian novels I have discussed seek to transcend the limitations of female experience. They suggest new institutions and new visions which are derived from women's experience in the patriarchy. They acknowledge that, like babies, societies are inevitably engaged in a process of growth which is beyond the control of the mother who gave them life.

Notes

*This article is a revised version of "Women's Fantasies and Feminist Utopias" which first appeared in *Frontiers: A Journal of Women's Studies* (Fall 1977), pp. 50-61. Many of the ideas in this essay also appear in the final chapter of *The Female Hero in British and American Literature,* co-author, Katherine Pope (New York: Bowker, 1979).

[1]Works were assumed to be feminist utopias if they portrayed complete equality between the sexes. This article does not discuss novels such as Thomas Berger's *A Regiment of Women* which envisions a society where men are oppressed by women. And, it considers only the work of women authors.

[2]Mary Bradley Lane, *Mizora: A Prophesy* (Boston: Gregg Press, 1975). All further references will be cited in the text. *Mizora* was originally published in 1890.

[3]Charlotte Perkins Gilman, *Herland*, serialized in the *Forerunner,* 6 (1915). All further references will be cited in the text. *Herland* has been reprinted (New York: Pantheon, 1979).

[4]Dorothy Bryant, *The Kin of Ata Are Waiting for You* (New York: Random House, 1976). Originally published as *The Comforter* in 1971 by Moon Books. All further references will be cited in the text.

[5]Mary Staton, *From the Legend of Biel* (New York: Ace Books, 1976). All further references will be cited in the text.

[6]For a discussion of turn of the century female moral reform societies, see Carol Smith Rosenberg, "Beauty, the Beast and the Militant Woman: A Case Study in Sex Roles and Social Stress in Jacksonian America," *American Quarterly,* 22 (1971), 562-84.

[7]Ursula K. Le Guin, "Is Gender Necessary?" in *Aurora: Beyond Equality,* ed. Vonda N. McIntyre and Susan Janice Anderson (Greenwich, Conn.: Fawcett, 1976), p. 134. Further references will be cited in the text followed by IGN and page number.

Joanna Russ

Recent Feminist Utopias

IN THE LAST FEW YEARS science fiction in the United States has seen a mini-boom of feminist utopias, a phenomenon obviously contemporaneous with the women's movement itself. Of the books and short stories considered in this paper, the earliest—not actually American but possibly a catalyst for some of the others—was Monique Wittig's *Les Guérillières*,[1] brought out in English translation by Viking in 1971. The latest—Suzy McKee Charnas' *Motherlines*,[2]—was published by Berkley Putnam in 1979. Of the group of works I will be considering here, Ursula Le Guin's *The Dispossessed*[3] was published in 1974 and Joanna Russ's *The Female Man*[4] in 1975. The remaining seven works (two of which are by a single author) appeared in 1976. These are Samuel Delany's *Triton*,[5] Marion Zimmer Bradley's *The Shattered Chain*,[6] Marge Piercy's *Woman on the Edge of Time*,[7] Sally Gearhart's *The Wanderground: Stories of the Hill Women*,[8] Catherine Madsen's "Commodore Bork and the Compost,"[9] and two stories by Alice Sheldon, "Your Faces, O My Sisters! Your Faces Filled of Light!"[10] under the pseudonym of Raccoona Sheldon and "Houston, Houston, Do You Read?" under the pseudonym of James Triptee, Jr.[11]

Although "utopia" may be a misnomer for some of these works, many of which (like *Triton* or *The Dispossessed*) present not perfect societies but only ones better than our own, "feminist" is not. All these fictions present societies (and in one case, a guild organization) which is conceived by the author as better in explicitly feminist terms and for explicitly feminist reasons. In only one work, *The Dispossessed*, is feminism *per se* not the author's primary concern; it is secondary to Le Guin's communitarian anarchism. No doubt such a formulation does less than justice to Le Guin's work, but oversimplifications are necessary in dealing with so many works in so short a space. Even though *The Dispossessed* is feminist and utopian (rather than a feminist utopia as such) and though the society in *The Shattered Chain* is a group (the Guild of Free Amazons) within the larger society of the planet Darkover, these works form a remarkably coherent group in their presentation of feminist concerns and the feminist analyses which are central to these concerns.

71

Moreover they imagine their better—and feminist—societies in strikingly similar terms. Science fiction is a small field and it's likely that these writers have read one another (with the exception of Wittig, who could not have read the others' works although they have probably read *Les Guerillières*); nonetheless it is significant exactly what these writers choose to imitate. In Carol Pearson's recent "Women's Fantasies and Feminist Utopias,"[12] an essay covering six modern works (five of which I also examine in this paper) and two which "grow out of the nineteenth-century women's movement," Charlotte Perkins Gilman's *Herland* and Mary Bradley Lane's *Mizora*, Pearson finds "surprisingly numerous areas of consensus among such seemingly divergent works."[13] She does not, in fact, find it necessary to distinguish between the two older novels and their modern cousins. It seems to me reasonable to assume that, just as Gilman and Lane were responding to the women's movement of their time, so the works I discuss here are not only contemporaneous with the modern feminist movement but made possible by it.* Both sets of books become even more interesting in the light of the twentieth-century tradition of American science fiction. I have argued elsewhere that American science fiction (until the 1970s) has in general ignored both woman's estate and the problems of social structure with which feminism deals.[14] Even such honorable exceptions as Theodore Sturgeon and Damon Knight, to name only two, could only indicate their distress at a state of affairs in which women were perceived as inferior and men were encouraged in machismo without providing the political analysis which did not, at that time, exist, since earlier feminism had been buried and the new feminism of the late nineteen-sixties had yet to occur. For example, Sturgeon's *Venus Plus X*[15] presents no political analysis of sex class and its solution—literal unisex— places the blame for oppressive social conditions on the biologically innate temperament of the sexes, a solution the authors I am considering here would certainly reject, either because of the assignment of blame to biology or the assignment of blame to both sexes equally. Aside from such atypical works, most American science fiction can be divided into three categories according to its attitude toward sex roles: the status quo (which will be carried into the future without change), role reversals (seen as evil), and fiction in which women (usually few) are shown working as equals alongside men, but the crucial questions about the rest of the society

---

*Pearson covers some of the materials I focus on in this paper, notably the communal nature of the societies portrayed, the absence of crime, the relative lack of government, and the diffusion of the parental role to the whole society. She also treats the lack of dualistic thinking, the importance of mothering, and the philosophical/religious attitudes of the societies portrayed.

(e.g. personal relations and who's doing the work women usually do) are not answered. When science fiction between 1965 and 1975 has dealt with feminist insights, it has usually been by the expansion of that last category, with the usual evasions: parenting and human nurturing take place offstage, as do the effects of such work on the personalities of those who do it. The work women do in acting out sexual and power fantasies for the emotional R & R of men is either not present or it is taken for granted as a natural part of the human scene. Work that is both sex- and class-limited (for example, the drudgery of maintenance and production as well as the drudgery of housework) is usually ignored altogether. When such work occurs, it is part of the natural world and is not examined; it is something the superior hero must escape from or something that is to be done away with (vaguely) by machinery, or something that, although boring and dehumanizing, is nonetheless better than the boredom presumed to follow (in the mass of ordinary people, not in the hero) from its absence.

In view of this general previous neglect, the works treated in this paper are remarkable not only for their explicit feminism but for the similar forms the feminism takes. They not only ask the same questions and point to the same abuses; they provide similar answers and remedies.

For one thing, the societies portrayed in these tales are, with one exception, *communal* even *quasi-tribal.* Government does not exist or hardly exists, although there is sometimes a council dealing with work assignments (seen as the main problem of government). *Les Guérillières* is self-consciously "tribal" in its imagery. The Anarresti of *The Dispossessed* are anarchists; their communities recall in flavor the Israeli kibbutz. The core of social structure in *The Female Man* is families of thirty to thirty-five persons; children have free run of the planet past puberty and "the kidnap web is world-wide."[16] In "Your Faces, O My Sisters!" the society imagined by the mad, present-day protagonist practices common worship in the open, as do the characters in the Gearhart stories, who live in small groups in a setting so natural as to recall primatologists' descriptions of the nightly nests gorillas make in trees. In "Houston, Houston" government exists largely to shift people from job to job; families are groups of women cloned from the same stock who refer to each other as "sisters" and keep a family book.

The two Judys in the story (their names, Judy Dakar and Judy Paris, recall the feminist painter Judy Chicago) refer to "The Book of Judy." The society in "Commodore Bork and the Compost," a spoof of *Star Trek,* is a small, closed society in a spaceship, in which everyone is related, while in *Woman on the Edge of Time* the world consists of many such family-communities, in which everyone knows and is a relative of everyone else. *Motherlines* is literally tribal, with its horse-riding nomads who raid each other's camps for horses. Carol Pearson has suggested that women's visions of utopia use the family as a model for social structure, but the unowned, non-patriarchal family, headed by nobody.[17]. Certainly the groupings in most of these tales go beyond small-town neighborliness into genuine family cohesion, or at the least (in *The Dispossessed)* the co-operation and comradeship expressed by the Anarresti word "ammari." (Le Guin translates the word as "brothers.") Only in *Triton* is there an urban society in which one can meet real strangers, though even here we're told that Lux, the biggest city on Triton, numbers only ten thousand people.

Without exception the stories are ecology-minded. Such concern is common in science fiction nowadays. However, many of the stories go beyond the problems of living in the world without disturbing its ecological balance into presenting their characters as feeling a strong emotional connection to the natural world. The Gearhart stories are the most insistent about this, the characters on occasion talking to (and listening to) trees. A native of the Ark in "Commodore Bork" describes in lyrical terms the ship's compost room, in which "the eggshells, the cabbage leaves, the tampons softly moldering" make the visitor from the *Invictus* feel ill, and tells a defector from that ship (the only female officer on it) "If you get homesick for metal surfaces, I'll even take you up to the navigation rooms."[18] *Woman on the Edge of Time* is so suffused with the feeling of harmony with nature that one quotation would understate the importance of this in the novel, while in "Houston, Houston" the spaceship of the utopian society contains not only chickens but an enormous kudzu vine, and the women who run the ship talk excitedly about the possibility of getting a goat. The Anarresti spend much of their time out-of-doors (it would be interesting to do a line count of outdoor versus indoor scenes on Anarres) and the most lyrical parts of *The Dispossessed*, to my mind, take place outdoors, as do most of the Whileawayan scenes in *The Female Man*. Only in *Triton* is there no connection with the out-of-doors, since in this case the "out of doors" is the surface of a moon of Neptune, an environment lethal to life.

Triton is also an exception to another rule that prevails in this group of fictions; except for it, all the societies presented are *classless*. Le Guin's book is a long discussion of this fact; the other stories simply take it for granted. Even Bradley's Guild of Free Amazons, which exists on a feudal world in which class is omnipresent, an absolutely-assumed social constant, abolishes class distinctions within its own organization, i.e., it does not model its structure on the hierarchy of the world around it. Even

"Commodore Bork," while it pokes fun at the *Invictus's* chain of command and casually mentions its own job-shifting, does not argue the point. So pervasive are the results of this classlessness— e.g. the informality of tone, the shifting of jobs from person to person, the free choice of jobs whenever possible—that the authors' not discussing their worlds' forms of government seems neither ignorance nor sloppiness. Rather classlessess is an assumption so absolute that it need not be discussed. Similarly few of these societies (except perhaps *The Dispossessed*) examines gender strereotypes to see if they are true, or argues against them. We merely see that they are not true and do not apply. For example, on the Ark one of the natives asks the woman officer from the *Invictus* (in mild bafflement), "Do they make you do that to your hair?"[19]

Triton, the only utopian society here that is class-stratified, is also the only society engaged in international (or rather, interplanetary) war. However this war is very different from those usual in science fiction, for example, Joe Haldeman's *The Forever War* or Robert Heinlein's *Starship Troopers,* in which inter-species war resembles (respectively) the Korean war or the Pacific front in World War II, with more advanced technology. Delany's war, science-fictional ingenious, consists almost entirely of sabotage, the results of which are like natural disaster. In *Motherlines* there are occasional clashes between the border guards of the Riding Women and the Holdfasters (the gynocidal society of the Eastern seaboard) who accidentally stray into their territory. In *Woman on the Edge of Time* there is a war going on between the utopian society of the novel and a dehumanized, class-stratified, mechanical society which holds the moon and a few remote bases on earth—and yet this war may be only a possibility in another continuum. Even the possibility is kept on the margins of the book. In *Les Guerillieres* there is a war between the women and the men—presented, however, pretty much in metaphor (as is everything else in the book). The Anarresti of *The Dispossessed* constitute one, warless society, nor is there a war going on between them and their mother/sister planet, Urras. There are no wars in the other utopias, although in at least two cases ("Houston, Houston" and one society of the four in *The Female Man*) there were—or rather, may have been—wars in the past. Even these are not national, territorial wars, but in one case a sexual Cold War and in the other a general breakdown of society caused by biological, natural disaster.

In short, the violence that does occur in these stories (with the exception of *Triton*) is that of ideological skirmish, natural disaster, social collapse, and/or something that may have occurred in the past but is not happening in the present. (One might argue that women's usual experience of war is just that: social collapse and natural disaster. Certainly few women have experienced war as part of a military hierarchy and few expect to do so.) None are dramatically full-scale shooting wars and none are central to the plots of the stories. (The war in *Triton* is confined to its effect on helpless civilians; it occurs in two, fairly brief episodes.) In general violence occurs seldom and is taken seriously when it does occur, *Triton* in particular focusing on the anguish of helpless people harmed or killed by the sabotaging of Triton's artificial gravity. Violence in these tales has emotional consequences and is certainly not presented as adventure or sport.

Classless, without government, ecologically minded, with a strong feeling for the natural world, quasi-tribal in feeling and quasi-family in structure, the societies of these stories are *sexually permissive*—in terms I suspect many contemporary male readers* might find both unspectacular and a little baffling, but which would be quite familiar to the radical wing of the feminist movement, since the point of the permissiveness is not to break taboos but to separate sexuality from questions of ownership, reproduction and social structure. Monogamy for example, is not an issue since family structure is a matter of parenting or economics, not the availability pf partners. *Woman on the Edge of Time* is reproductively the most inventive of the group, with bisexuality (they don't perceive it as a category and so don't name it) as the norm, exogenetic birth, triads of parents of both sexes caring for children, and all three parents nursing infants. Exclusive homosexuality (also not named) is an unremarkable idiosyncracy. *The Shattered Cabin*, the most conservative in its sexual/reproductive arrangements (necessarily since its Guild is only an organization embedded in a larger, feudal society), nonetheless presents two separate, legal forms of marriage—one more than we have!—and the Free Amazons are casual about male and female homosexuality. In *The Dispossessed* monogamy (which has no legal status), casual promiscuity, homosexuality, and heterosexuality are all acceptable, and adolescent bisexuality is the norm. I find that Le Guin's biases for monogamy and heterosexuality show (there seems to be only one male homosexual on Anarres and no female ones and the monogamous people we see are clearly nicer—at least in adulthood—than the promiscuous) but the auctorial intention is clear. "Commodore Bork" is cheerful about homosexuality, heterosexuality, promiscuity and a reproductive technique that allows one woman to have a baby "with" another; everybody

---

*The matter is amply dealt with in the literature of the feminist movement. Briefly, these stories would be very much out of place in *Playboy* and its imitators, as well as in the underground press (e.g. underground comics).

parents. The response to all of this by the Captain of the *Invictus* is to try to seduce all the young women he meets, telling them (in effect): What's a nice girl like you doing in a place like this? *Triton*, always the exception, goes beyond the permissiveness of the other works into an area of argument I suspect the other authors might find both witty and unpleasantly mechanical, since Delany divorces sex from affection (as the other works do not) and both recognizes and, philosophically speaking, honors erotic specializations like sadism that the other authors ignore. That is, he considers no uncoerced form of sexuality privileged. *Triton*'s is the only society in the group which provides for sex-change surgery, although the novel's detestable protagonist is the only character in the book who takes the change as seriously as do contemporary transsexuals. The other characters seem to see it as a form of cosmetic surgery. On Triton, transsexing as gender-role change is impossible, since Triton's is a society in which it is impossible to be "masculine" or "feminine." As in Piercy's book, parenting is shared by all the members of a family and men suckle infants.

There remain six works in which the only sexuality portrayed is matter-of-factly Lesbian, and necessarily so, since the societies described contain only women. Since Lesbianism is a charge routinely made against feminists (the recent sexual-preference resolution at the women's conference in Houston was passed in part to combat the disuniting of women that arises from such a charge) and since many men appear to believe that the real goal of all feminists is to get rid of men, it is important to investigate the reasons why these authors exclude men from their utopias. In the two-sexed utopian societies, Lesbianism is one among many forms of freedom, but a world without men raises two questions: that of Lesbianism and (lurking behind it) the question of separatism. I believe the separatism is primary, and that the authors are not subtle in their reasons for creating separatist utopias: if men are kept out of these societies, it is because men are dangerous. They also hog the good things of this world.

In "Houston, Houston" the intruders into an all-female world (men from our time) are given a dis-inhibiting drug. The results are megalomania, attempted rape, horrifying contempt, and senseless, attempted murder. One of the women comments with obvious irony, "You have made history come alive for us." The men will be killed; "we simply have no facilities for people with your emotional problems."[20]

In "Your Faces, O My Sisters" (by the same author) a madwoman who believes she is living in a future, all-female utopia, and is therefore safe anywhere at any time, is raped and murdered by a male gang in a city at night.

In *Motherlines* the heroine, a native of the society of the Holdfast, where all women are chattel slaves owned in common by all men, escapes only because she has been trained as a runner. She carries a child, the product of rape. She meets the Riding Women, strong, free, nomad Amazons who travel adventurously over the Great Plains. Gathering an army of women from among the free fems (escaped slaves), she becomes a chief and leader of her people.

In *The Female Man* women of the all-female utopia are farmers, artists, members of the police force, scientists, and so on, and: "there's no being out too late in Whileaway, or up too early, or in the wrong part of town or unescorted.... There is no one who can keep you from going where you please... no one who will follow you and try to embarrass you by whispering obscenities in your ear.... While here, where we live!"[21]

In *Les Guérillières* bands of strong women roam freely everywhere, run machinery and control production.

Sally Gearhart's characters, with their hard-won training in paraphysical powers, travel freely over forests and plains. But they avoid the cities, for men still rule there.

The physical freedom to travel safely and without money is emphasized also in the two-sexed societies, though *The Dispossessed* shows such freedom being enjoyed by a male character. Most of *The Shattered Chain* is taken up with the travels and adventures of bands of Free Amazons, who are twice taunted and attacked by groups of men (for no good reason). Even Triton— urban, class-bound, money-economy that it is—is far freer physically than any American city; indeed Delany emphasizes that the "Unlicensed Sector" of Lux, the part of the city without laws, is safer than the rest. (This sort of unpoliced part of town is usually used in science fiction as a pretext for showing various kinds of violence.) It's hardly necessary to stress here that physical mobility without cultural restraints, without harassment or the threat of it, is denied women in the United States today (not to mention elsewhere) and that access to most professions and public activities is similarly restricted.

Careful inspection of the manless societies usually reveals the intention (or wish) to allow men in... if only they can be trusted to behave. *Les Guérillières*, the most lyrical of the group, has the women allowing men back into their society, but only after the women have won. *Motherlines* (the sequel to a previously published novel, *Walk to the End of the World*, which depicts the Holdfast society) has a sequel in which the escaped slaves return to the Holdfast as an army, though the Holdfast may have destroyed itself in the interval.[22] In *The Female Man* Whileaway is one of a number of possible societies, none of them in our future.

Whether tentative or conclusively pessimistic, the invented, all-female worlds with their consequent Lesbianism have another function: that of expressing the joys of female bonding, which—like freedom and access to the public world—are in short supply for women in the real world. Sexually this amounts to the insistence that women are erotic integers and not fractions waiting for completion. Female sexuality is seen as native and initiatory, not (as in our traditionally sexist view) reactive, passive, or potential. (Earlier sexist views, which see women as insatiable, do not really contradict the later view. Both address themselves, in reality, to problems of male sexuality, i.e. the problems of controlling women, and both perceive female sexuality as existing in relation to male fears or needs.)

Along with physical mobility and the freedom to choose one's participation in the world goes a theme I shall call the rescue of the female child. This theme occurs in only three works under discussion here, but it also turns up in two recent, non-utopian, science fiction novels, both of them concerned with feminist themes and both written by women.

In *The Shattered Chain* occurs the clearest example of this event: Free Amazons rescue a twelve-year-old girl, Jaelle, and her mother from the gynocidal Dry Towns in which pubertal girls' wrists are chained together and the chain fastened to their waists so that never again will they be able to extend both arms fully. Jaelle (her name echoes Jael in *The Female Man*) later becomes a Free Amazon.

In *Walk to the End of the World* the fem Alldera is pregnant when she flees slavery. Her daughter, born after her own rescue by the Riding Women, is adopted by them and eventually goes through an adolescent rite of passage, as Alldera puts it: "I really did it. I was no mother, I didn't how how to become one—I was just a Holdfast dam. But I got her away from the men and I found her a whole family of mothers, and saw her into a free life as a young woman."[23]

Woman on the Edge of Time also shows a serious rite of passage undergone by a female child at puberty. Connie Ramos, the heroic and abused woman of our own time, able to visit this future utopia witnesses the beginnings of the rite (survival in the woods alone). At first disgusted by the future society, Connie finally wishes that her own daughter—taken away from her three years before by the state—could somehow be adopted by the people of the novel's utopia.

The two subsequent novels are Joanna Russ's *The Two of Them*,[24] written before my acquaintance with these other examples, and Vonda McIntyre's *Dreamsnake*.[25] In *Two* a twelve-year-old girl living in a quasi-Islamic, misogynist society, who wants to be a poet, is taken off-planet at her own request by a man and woman from an interstellar espionage organization. In *Dreamsnake* the heroine rescues a pubertal girl from a brutal male guardian who beats and rapes her. The author of *Dreamsnake*, told of this paper, objected that the little girl's oppression did not come from the realities of the non-sexist society depicted in the novel. However, she then added that the character's oppression might very well come out of the conditions of the author's society.

Puberty is an awakening into sexual adulthood for both sexes. According to Simone de Beauvoir in *The Second Sex*, it is also the time when the prison bars of "femininity," enforced by law and custom, shut the girl in for good.[26] Even today entry into woman's estate is often not a broadening-out (as it is for boys) but a diminution of life. Feminist utopias offer an alternative model of female puberty, one which allow the girl to move into a full and free adulthood. All the novels described above not only rescue the girl from abuses which are patriarchal in character; they provide something for her to go to, usually an exciting and worthwhile activity in the public world: healer (*Dreamsnake*), Free Amazon (*The Shattered Chain*), Riding Woman and horse-raider (*Motherlines*), or poet (*The Two of Them*). We are used to envisioning puberty for girls as a sexual awakening, usually into reactive sexuality (Sleeping Beauty, *q.v.*). This is one aspect of puberty missing in the above examples; the children therein are sexual beings, certainly, but the last thing (say the tales) that matters for the adolescent girl is that she be awakened by a kiss; what is crucial is that she be free.

A discussion of these recent feminist utopias would be incomplete without some reference to their anti-feminist opposite numbers: the role reversal (or battle of the sexes) science fiction novel which assumes as its given the sexist assumptions the feminist utopias challenge and attack. I have discussed this subject elsewhere.[27] Briefly, the battle of the sexes stories present all-female or female-dominated worlds (of which there are none among the feminist utopias) which are returned to the normalcy of male dominance by male visitors from our own society or male renegades from the world of the story. These men overthrow a gynocracy that is both awesomely repressive and completely inefficient. The method of overthrow is some form of phallic display: flashing, a kiss, rape. The books are badly written, apolitical, and present women as only potentially sexual; they also present rape as either impossible or desired by the woman. These stories are not only strikingly violent; they are violent without feeling, and in contrast to the all-female, feminist utopias, never propose an all-male world as a solution to their problem. Their authors are not, it seems, willing to do without women. However the books are surprisingly non-erotic, sex being a matter of power in them and not pleasure.

It seems clear that the two kinds of novels are not speaking to the same conflict. That is, the battle of the sexes stories envision what is essentially (despite science fiction trappings) a one-to-one confrontation between one man and one woman, in which the man's sexual power guarantees his victory, while the feminist utopias, if they present a conflict at all, see it as a public, impersonal struggle. One might expect public war to be more violent than personal conflict; thus the relative gentleness of the feminist books is all the more surprising.

However, it may well be that the feminist books, because their violence is often directed *by women against men* are perceived as very violent by some readers. For example, *The Female Man* contains only four violent incidents: a woman at a party practices judo on a man who is behaving violently toward her and (by accident) hurts him; a woman kills a man during a Cold War between the sexes after provocation, lasting (she says) twenty years; a woman shots another woman as part of her duty as a police officer; a woman, in anger and terror, shuts a door on a man's thumb (this last incident is briefly mentioned and not shown). A male reviewer in *Mother Jones*[28] quoted at length from the second and fourth incidents (the only quotations from the novel he used), entirely disregarding the other two. Ignoring the novel's utopian society, which is one of four, he called the book "a scream of anger" and "a bitter fantasy of reversed sexual oppression," although the only fantasy of reversed sexual oppression in the novel appears to be the reviewer's. There is one scene of reversed sex roles in the book and that involves not a woman and a man but a woman and a machine.

What are we to make of these books? I believe that utopias are not embodiments of universal human values, but are reactive; that is, they supply in fiction what their authors believe society (in the case of these books) and/or women, lack in the here-and-now. The positive values stressed in the stories can reveal to us what, in the authors' eyes, is wrong with our own society. Thus if the stories are family/communal in feeling, we may pretty safely guess that the authors see our society as isolating people from one another, especially (to judge from the number of all-female utopias in the group) women from women.

If the utopias stress a feeling of harmony and connection with the natural world, the authors may be telling us that in reality they feel a lack of such connection. Or perhaps the dislike of urban environments realistically reflects women's experience of such places—women do not own city streets, not even in fantasy. Nor do they have much say in the kind of business that makes, sustains and goes on in cities. (For example, according to the popular culture fantasies about cities expressed on TV cop shows, cities are places where women and powerless men are threatened with bodily harm by powerful men and saved (if at all) by other powerful men. Since truly powerful men, one would think, don't need fantasies about being powerful, such fantasies must be addressed to ordinary, powerless men. They are certainly not addressed to women.)

The stories' classlessness obviously comments on the insecurity, competitiveness, and poverty of a class society.

Their relative peacefulness and lack of national war goes hand in hand with the acceptance of *some* violence—specifically that necessary for self-defense and the expression of anger, both of which are rare luxuries for women today.

The utopias' sexual permissiveness and joyfulness is a poignant comment on the conditions of sexuality for women: unfriendly, coercive, simply absent, or at best reactive rather than initiating.

The physical mobility emphasized in these books is a direct comment on the physical and psychological threats that bar women from physical mobility in the real world.

The emphasis on freedom in work and the public world reflects the restrictions that bar women from vast areas of work and experience.

The rescue of the female child speaks to an adolescence that is still the rule rather than the exception for women, one made painful by the closing in of sexist restrictions, sexual objectification, or even outright persecution.[29]

Some of the above is common to thoughtful people of both sexes, like the dislike of war and the insistence that violence has consequences, but most are specific to women's concerns. Noticeably absent are many wishes common in contemporary fiction and contemporary science fiction: material success, scientific triumph, immortality, being admired for one's exceptional qualities, success in competition, inherited status, and so on. In general competitiveness and *the desire to be better than* are absent. Also absent is a figure who often appears in women's novels: the Understanding Man, a love affair with whom will solve everything.* There is only one Understanding Man in the group and he is a spectacular failure, put into the story to illustrate the ineffectuality of undoubted good will and intelligence in dealing with great differences in power between groups. As the women's movement slogan goes, there is no personal solution.[30] *The Shattered Chain* presents a nice young fellow for the Free Amazon,

---

*For example, the unconventional, non-masculine lover, Duncan, in Margaret Atwood's *The Edible Woman* (New York: Popular Library, 1969).

Jaelle, to fall in love with; he too is a spectacular failure, not (I suspect) because the author intended him to be one, but because having set the book's terms up so uncompromisingly in the first two-thirds of the novel, Bradley cannot make him a real character and still have her love affair even remotely workable.

Comparison between *Triton* and the other books is instructive; it seems to me that for better or worse the one male author in the group is writing from an implicit level of freedom that allows him to turn his attention, subtly but persistently, away from many of the questions which occupy the other writers. For example, *Triton* argues that no form of voluntary sexuality is privileged, while the other books deal with rape and the simple availability of sex that is neither coerced, exploitative or unavailable. *Triton* enjoys its sophisticated urban landscape while the other stories are preoccupied with escape from an urban landscape which they do not own, do not enjoy, and in which they are not safe or happy. *Triton* makes a point of the financial discrimination suffered by children, while the other authors are busy saving their children from solitary imprisonment, madness, rape and beatings, or being chained for life.

In short, most of these utopias are concerned with the grossest and simplest forms of injustice. I do not believe that this fact detracts from their value any more than it detracts from the value of, say, *The Fear and Misery of the Third Reich*. And in these recent feminist utopias we certainly have part of the growing body of women's culture, at least available in some quantity (however small) to readers who need and can use it. I need not recommend *The Dispossessed* to anyone—it's already famous in the science-fiction community—nor does Samuel Delany lack for readers. But it might not be amiss to mention that *Woman on the Edge of Time* is a splendid book in the tradition of nineteenth-century utopias, with all the wealth of realistic detail that tradition implies, and that women's studies classes might also tap the raw power of "Your Faces, O My Sisters," to mention only two of the works discussed here. Here is Alice Sheldon's mad young woman, unable to stand our world and so by sheer imagination trying to inhabit another, the woman who will be killed because she thinks she's free:

Couriers see so much. Some day she'll come back here and have a good swim in the lake, loaf and ramble around the old city. So much to see, no danger except from falling walls, she's expert at watching for that. Some sisters say there are dog-packs here, she doesn't believe it. And even if there are, they wouldn't be dangerous. Animals aren't dangers if you know what to do. No dangers left at all in the whole, free, wide world![31]

And here is Piercy's Consuelo Ramos, trapped for life in a big state mental hospital (a much worse place than a prison), later to be the subject of an experiment in brain control through surgery which is not in the least science-fictional but very much of the present.[32] Connie's longing for and assent to utopia states eloquently the suffering that lies under the utopian impulse and the sufferer's simultaneous facing of and defiance of pain:

> Suddenly she assented with all her soul.... For the first time her heart assented.... Yes, you can have my child, you can keep my child.... She will be strong there, well fed, well housed, well taught, she will grow up much better and stronger and smarter than I. I assent, I give you my battered body as recompense and my rotten heart. Take her, keep her!.... She will never be broken as I was. She will be strange, but she will be glad and strong and she will not be afraid. She will have enough. She will have pride. She will love her own brown skin and be loved for her strength and her good work. She will walk in strength like a man and never sell her body and she will nurse her babies like a woman and live in love like a garden, like that children's house of many colors. People of the rainbow with its end fixed in earth, I give her to you![33]

Notes

[1]Monique Wittig, Les Guérillìeres (Paris: Editions de Minuit, 1969), English trans. David Le Vay (New York: Viking Press, 1971).

[2]Suzy McKee Charnas, *Motherlines* (New York: Berkley Putnam, 1978).

[3]Ursula Le Guin, *The Dispossessed* (New York: Harper & Row, 1974).

[4]Joanna Russ, *The Female Man* (New York: Bantam, 1975).

[5]Samuel Delany, *Triton* (New York: Bantam, 1976).

[6]Marion Zimmer Bradley, *The Shattered Chain* (New York: Daw Books, 1976).

[7]Marge Piercy, *Woman on the Edge of Time* (New York: Doubleday, 1976).

[8]Sally Gearhart, *The Wanderground: Stories of the Hill Women* (Watertown, Mass.: Persephone Press, 1979).

[9]Catherine Madsen, "Commodore Bork and the Compost," *The Witch and the Chameleon*, No. 5/6 (1976).

[10]Raccoona Sheldon, "Your Faces, O My Sisters! Your Faces Filled of Light!" in *Aurora: Beyond Equality*, ed. Vonda N. McIntyre and Susan Janice Anderson (New York: Fawcett, 1976).

[11]James Tiptree, Jr., "Houston, Houston, Do You Read?" in *Aurora: Beyond Equality.*

[12]Carol Pearson, "Women's Fantasies and Feminist Utopias," *Frontiers*, 2, No. 3 (1977).

[13]Pearson, p. 50.

[14]Joanna Russ, "The Image of Women in Science Fiction," in *Images of Women In Fiction: Feminist Perspectives*, ed. Susan Koppelman Cornillon (Bowling Green, Ohio: Bowling Green University Popular Press, 1972).

[15]Theodore Sturgeon, *Venus Plus X* (Boston: G.K. Hall, 1976).

[16]Russ, *The Female Man*, pp. 81-82.

[17]Pearson, p. 52.

[18]Madsen, p. 16.

[19]Madsen, p. 16.

[20]Tiptree, p. 97.

[21]Russ, *The Female Man*, pp. 81-82.

[22]Volume III is in progress. The author refuses to divulge what the free fems find at the Holdfast or what happens there.

[23]Charnas, p. 234.

[24]Joanna Russ, *The Two of Them* (New York: Berkley Putnam, 1978).

[25]Vonda McIntyre, *Dreamsnake* (New York: Houghton Mifflin, 1978).

[26]Simone de Beauvoir, *The Second Sex* (New York: Bantam, 1961), pp. 306-47.

[27]Joanna Russ, "Amor Vincit Feminam: The Battle of the Sexes in Science Fiction," *Science-*

Fiction Studies, 7 (1980).

[28]Michael Goodwin, "On Reading: A Giant Step for Science Fiction," *Mother Jones* I (1976), 62..

[29]"Persecution" may strike some readers as too strong a word. But surely father-daughter incest (which, to judge from the publicity recently given the problem, is usually unwanted by the daughter and enforced by the father through threats of emotional blackmail) deserves to be called persecution, as do wife-battering and rape.

[30]See Suzy McKee Charnas, *Walk to the End of the World* (New York: Ballantine, 1974).

[31]Sheldon, p. 17.

[32]See Peter Roger Breggin, "The Second Wave," in *Madness Network News Reader* (San Francisco: Glide Publications, 1974). Amygdalotomy, the operation with which Connie is threatened, is part of the contemporary repertoire of psychosurgery. So are the other operations described in Piercy's book.

[33]Piercy, p. 141.

Robert Scholes

A Footnote to Russ's "Recent Feminist Utopias"

I WAS ASKED TO respond to Joanna Russ's essay on feminist utopias. Actually, I don't have much of a response. It would take a brand of idiocy more extreme than mine to find fault or take issue with the cool, balanced thoughtfulness of that essay. In short, I think she is right on the mark—but who am I to say so.

If I could add a footnote to Russ's essay, it would be to mention Philip Wylie's neglected novel *The Disappearance*. First published in 1951 and recently reissued by Warner Books, Wylie's novel consists of alternating sections in which earth is deprived of all women and all men. The results in both cases are dystopian, partly because of the suddenness of the disappearance, which leaves a lot of jobs undone, cars driverless, and so on. The book also suffers from some purely literary problems, as Wylie indulges himself with some long, quasi-philosophic mutterings—and he was no philosopher. But for our present purposes one important idea emerges: though both worlds are horrible enough for everyone to desire a return to a world with two sexes, the women's world is not anywhere near as horrible as the men's. I think Wylie reached this conclusion in spite of himself, by honest extrapolation; and I think any honest extrapolater would arrive at the same result. The women suffer from defects in education, mainly—not enough doctors and engineers in their world. The men suffer from defects of personality—too many angry, selfish, violent people in theirs.

If we can accept this as likely, for a moment, we can raise a fascinating question. Russ points out that the all-female utopia is common, the all-male utopia virtually nonexistent; and she rightly suggests that this is because in our present world women feel exploited and men do not—not by women, anyway. Thus, for a woman to imagine a world without men is to assume a kind of liberation—much the way Americans felt about kings in the eighteenth century. It is plain to me that if we had a niceness Olympics, the women's records would far exceed the men's. Women are better people than men—by and large, with considerable overlap, to be sure, and so on. But they are kinder, less violent, and

86

quicker to learn the lessons of ecology—as a group. For these and other reasons, a utopia of women seems much more plausible than a utopia of men. But is it biology or conditioning that presently gives women their superiority? In an all-female utopia would women remain what they are? Or would release of their oppression by men change them in ways unforeseeable?

Personally, I have a sinking feeling that men are what they are all too biologically: the males of a species selected for survival in a primitive universe now destroying their social fabric to buy more largely lethal weapons. Maybe an all-female world is the only hope for the future of the human race. It's worth considering.

Lyman Tower Sargent

An Ambiguous Legacy:
The Role and Position of Women in the
English Eutopia*

"Can man be free if woman be a slave?"
Shelley, *Revolt of Islam*

THE UTOPIAN NOVEL has provided a means for many authors to present their conceptions of an ideal society, and while there have been hundreds of such novels written, they have rarely been explored in any systematic manner. The definitional and bibliographic problems have been severe and many of the works are rare and difficult to locate. Still, it is unfortunate that this vast resource has been ignored, if for no other reason because the ideal often illuminated the reality.

In what follows I shall look at one set of questions, the role and position of women in the English eutopia.[1] I shall focus on the nineteenth century because that period includes most of the utopias that are concerned with the question. In doing so I shall use only the positive utopia or eutopia.

Early English Utopianism
The English eutopia began, of course, with More in 1516, and while there were relatively few eutopias published before 1800, they are important. These early eutopias are on the whole, conservative and present authoritarian, hierarchical societies[2] or are concerned with constitutional or legal reform. Women are largely ignored. In the few exceptions, women are placed in a distinctly inferior position.

More's *Utopia* provides a good example of the inferior position in which women are placed. In *Utopia*, although women work outside of the home, there is little or no notion of equality. "Wives wait on their husbands, children on their parents, and generally the younger on their elders." And again, "On the Final-Feasts, before they go to the temple, wives fall down at the feet of their husbands.

*Originally published in *Extrapolation*, 16 (May, 1975). Reprinted by permission of the author and editor.

children at the feet of their parents. They confess that they have erred, either by committing some fault or by performing some duty carelessly, and beg pardon for their offense." Finally, although in More's famous premarital ritual each potential partner is shown nude to the other, *all* the reasons given for the practice relate to the possible deformity of the woman.[3] The other eutopias of this period provide similar pictures. Bacon's *New Atlantis* (1627) provides a distinctly inferior place for women, and in Eliot's *The Christian Community* (1659) women and children are not even counted in establishing the number of people in each governmental unit. Lupton (1580) also presents a typical picture when he says, "There are no wives on the earth more obedient to their husbands than ours be."[4] On the other hand, Edward House (1671) at least notes that matrimony establishes "the tyranny of men...."[5]

Most of these eutopias are based on sets of superior-inferior relationships. For example, Samuel Gott says of the working classes, "The education of all these goes no further than reading, writing, arithmetic with geometry, and other such studies as are a help to the mechanical arts, for the higher culture is considered out of place in this station of life, and even prejudicial, from its tending to make the working classes dissatisfied with their humble duties...."[6] With appropriate changes in the focus of the learning, this statement could be applied to women's education in most English eutopias. Thus, in the early eutopias it could be argued that the position of women was merely a reflection of other status relationships rather than being singled out for special treatment. For example in Francis Gentlemen's *A Trip to the Moon* (1764), he says, "...know that our method of salutation between the different sexes is, the man holds his hand over the female's, without touching, and says, *may virtue and constancy ever flourish:* to which she replies, her right hand pointing to her left breast, with love and obedience...."[7]

The Nineteenth Century Eutopia

All eutopian literature should probably be divided into those published before and those published after Edward Bellamy's *Looking Backward* (1888) since most of the post-Bellamy works are stimulated by the reception of *Looking Backward*, and there was a tremendous upsurge in the writing of eutopias as a result.[8] Bellamy simply ignored the subject of women except for a rather inane romance.[9]

1811-1887—The pre-Bellamy Nineteenth-Century eutopias are generally characterized by a concern with economics and education. Education becomes the main avenue to eutopia. There is also a strong anti-urban, pro-rural theme.

Most significantly for present purposes, women's position is still ignored. While it is always questionable to make an argument based on the lack of a theme, in this case it seems justified. Without overemphasizing the point, it is fairly clear that authors of most eutopias up to 1887 believe that woman's position would be exactly the same in an ideal society as it is in contemporary society. In other words, women are already living in eutopia, and in that eutopia they serve men. This seems to imply an important point about the character of men and women. First, if women are already living in eutopia, it is clearly not a eutopia appropriate for men. Women are seen as suited for dull, placid inferior roles. It is almost as if two species are being described. Of course, a simpler explanation is possible—that women weren't considered important enough to take into account.

There are exceptions, and among these exceptions some argue for what they see as a significantly improved position for women. Probably the most sustained argument is found in James Lawrence's *The Empire of the Nairs; or, the Rights of Women* (1811). I shall let Lawrence speak for himself:

What awaits our glory abroad, if we are slaves at home? What public liberty, if one half of mankind be slaves to the other? But the children of nature are not the tyrants of beauty. She neither chains nor wears chains—she neither lessens the freedom of others, nor risks her own—she is an attraction; but no tie; allowed to choose and to change, to sue and to reject, she meets a refusal without affronting—she rejects without affronting; she gives to many; and has enough for all; her favours are unconfined; like the sun, she may shine on all mankind. The duration of the amour depends on the temper of a pair; caprice separates those whom inclination united; without blushing, they cease to love, and without complaints, to please. Sure at every hour to find a sympathizing heart, the forsaken lover broods not over his loss, nor bears rancor against him who was preferred. Though all men were rivals, they would all be friends. Nor look the other nymphs with aversion on him, whom a suiter favors, or proposes to favor in his turn. Hence, maternity alone is certain and fixed; the name 'father' is unknown.[10]

Lawrence says that "This work was designed to show the possibility of a nation's reaching the highest civilization without marriage" [Vol. 1, p. ii].

A man's only responsibility is to the state; women must raise and educate the children. "...mother is the most respectable title that a woman can bear" [Vol. 1, p. 8]. Each man, or better, noble, is provided with two horses, a groom and an annuity. He is expected not to encumber himself further so that he can be free to fight [Vol. 1, p. 96]. Slightly in opposition to this point is the fact that monogamy is common [Vol. 1, pp. 48-49].

But again, Lawrence believes his system provides equality. "...every mother receives a set sum out of the public treasury, according to the number of her children. We consider the maternal duties the chief duties of her sex; and the woman, who augments its population and the man, who fights its battles, have an equal claim on the gratitude of their country" [Vol. 1, p. 97]. Or again, "...every male belongs to the state, which may claim his services and exertions. Every man is a public character; he is a member of a great republic; but every female, like the queen bee, the mother of the hive, is the sovereign of a little monarchy" [Vol. 1, p. 78].

Now it is possible to see what Lawrence is doing. He has defined two mutually exclusive roles for which he believes the sexes are best fitted. Equality is found in fulfilling the appropriate role, one that cannot be filled by the other sex. He does not, though, seem to see this as a superior-inferior relationship. In the establishment of society women led the male warriors, but when the eutopia is fully functioning that is unthinkable.

Still, there is sexual freedom (couples who dance the final dance together usually spend the night together); [Vol. 1, p. 39] women appear to be fully educated, ("it seems that ye Europeans endeavor by all possible means to render your women simpletons"); [Vol. 1, p. 88] and both sexes, but women in particular, have been freed from the limitations of contemporary fashion.

Both men and women enjoyed the perfect use of their limbs. No restraint proceeded either from the materials of fashion or their habits; the same spirit of liberty, which had inspired all their laws and manners, seemed to have presided at the toilets of the Nairs—no unnatural ligature repressed agility of the men; no whalebone imprisoned the shape of the women, no hoops impeded their motions, no high heel gave them a tottering step—they moved as nature had designed them...[Vol. 1, p. 36].

There is no other sustained attempt to present an eutopia stressing any form of equality between the sexes before 1888. There are a number that simply assume some degree of equality without developing the point. For example *New Britain* (1820) by Mr. Ellis (pseud.?) stresses separate but equal education. The point here is obvious: certain skills are appropriate for each sex. On the other hand, if the father dies, the mother is given the household's vote rather than the oldest male child.

Henry Wright in *Mental Travels in Imagined Lands* (1878) also assumes equality and even provides for sex education in his very moral, uplifting eutopia—e.g., only good literature is available and the major recreation is work. In *Erchomenon; or the Republic of Materialism* (1879) [by H.C.M. Watson] men and women dress alike, there is free love, and children are cared for by women other than their mothers in order to avoid too exclusive attachments.

Others that make some provision for an improved place for women are John Minter Morgan, *Revolt of the Bees* (1826), [Edward

Barnard Bassett,] *The Model Town* (1869), by Beta (pseud.), *Etymonia* (1875), and *Politics and Life in Mars* (1883). Therefore, there are a number of writers who believe that the contemporary position of women can be criticized, but it should be emphasized that almost without exception, women's position can be brought into the eutopian realm through the general improvement of society and man's place in it. Reforms specifically directed toward women are at best a secondary concern. And it should be noted that the reforms of women's roles are very limited; women are already closer to eutopia than men.

The writers who present an inegalitarian society bluntly say that women are inferior. In one society women are said to be fitted only for "the ornamental part of government." The same author says, "the faculties of women are not capable of following out the highest intellectual processes, since she has a less degree of pure Reason than the man."[11] Another put it as strongly:

The tendency of her [woman's] education is to qualify her for the position which nature intended her to hold as the companion and helpmate of men. However, she is instructed, though not to so great a degree, in many branches of art and science, cultivated by the stronger sex, the design being to enable her to appreciate the efforts of man and to encourage and comfort him in his progress, but not to take his place. With us women are happy and content, and words of complaint rarely fall from their lips.[12]

This work has, in addition, a complicated, rather confusing marriage system, which is the only other time women are mentioned. The system is carefully organized and controlled by men. Each district in the country has two councils, one of ladies and one of elders, who regulate the marriage system. They are checked by a male overseer. At the time of coming of age one girl and 85 men spend 31 evenings together, properly chaperoned of course. The girl then makes her choice. The next day the couple spends three chaperoned hours together during which time either one is free to reject the marriage. If the girl fails to make a choice or is rejected, there is a smaller version of the same ritual a year later. A third year is possible but has never been needed. The focus of women's life is this ritual followed by obedient service.

Other works presenting pictures of the best future for women achieved through less equality focus on a variety of points. Some, such as [Ellis James Davis's] *Pyrna* (1875) and Robert Dudgeon's *Colymbia* (1873), present women as having had equality and rejected it. Dudgeon says that women reveled in complete idleness. Davis says that women could be elected to office"... but by their own free will never presented themselves as candidates."[13] Another work, the anonymous *In the Future* (1875), has women in two castes, outdwellers, who are free, and indwellers, who are veiled and isolated. Men prefer the latter.

Without overemphasizing the point, these works again present men and women as having almost totally separate sets of social roles. Wise women choose to remain true to their appropriate roles and even if offered such male roles as political leadership are sensible enough to reject them.

1888-1914—The Post-Bellamy eutopias have no clear pattern. The eutopia is used as a vehicle for comment on all topics including, of course, the position of women. The major changes are that during this period very few writers ignore the question and the pictures presented are much more egalitarian. There is, of course, still significant inegalitarian material, from the confident assertion that women are inferior, such as in [Charles Wicksteed Armstrong] *The Yorl of the Northmen*, by Charles Strong'th'arm (pseud.) (1892); Leonard A. Magnus, *A Japanese Utopia* (1905); and C. Regnas, *The Land of Nison* (1906) to the argument that the aim of society is to develop asexual beings, such as in [John Macmillan Brown,] *Limanora; The Island of Progress* (1903). Although the latter argument presents a form of equality, this equality can only be achieved by ridding both man and woman of sexual characteristics.

But most of the eutopias of 1888-1914 are explicitly reformists where women are concerned. One play, Cicely Hamilton and Christopher St. John, *How the Vote Was Won* (1910), suggests a general refusal to work by woman as a means of gaining reform. Still, many of the reformers take away with one hand what they give with the other. For example, one stresses that women have the vote, but women choose not to be eligible for national office.[14] Others assert equality but restrict women, or married women, from work or politics because they are too busy in the home, as in Frederick Hayes, *The Phalanx League* (1893), G. McIver, *Neuroomia* (1894), Z.S. Hendow, *The Future Power* (1897), and Albert Ernest Taber, *Work For All* (1914). One of these, though, provides women with sufficient personal income so that they need not be financially dependent on their husbands. [Hendow, p. 11]. One comments "...the women had reduced the membership of political conventions to a few dozen, every man being carefully selected for his sensitiveness to parasols and feminine influence and outcry."[15] Surprisingly, the result is entirely positive.

There are many other reforms that tend toward equality, mostly centering on the vote, equal pay for equal labor, financial independence and marriage and divorce reform, as in Mme. F. Blaze de Bury, *The Storm of London* (1904), *Star of Morning* (1906), and Robert Blatchford, *The Sorcery Shop* (1909). There is one eutopia, Mrs. George Corbett, *New Amazonia* (1889), where celibate women rule. Most works where women rule are of the sex-role reversal type, where it is presented as a clear perversion of nature, as in Sir Walter Besant, *The Revolt of Man* (1882), Thomas Pinkerton, *No Rates and Taxes* (1902), Allan Reeth, *Legions of the Dawn* (1908) and James Wilson, *When the Women Reign* (1909).

In general these works are based on the assumption that the author has identified specific areas in which the roles women play in society need to be changed. Some suggest that formal or legal equality is essential even though the wise woman will choose not to assert herself. On the other hand, others focus on such significant questions as the woman's financial dependence on her male relatives. Clearly a society that achieves the financial independence of women would have produced the potential for far-reaching changes in women's position. But the most interesting point is that the authors generally don't perceive that potential. For them, a financially independent woman will be able to free herself from abusive male relations, but she will not attempt to compete with men. The same point is made regarding marriage and divorce reforms, usually from an almost exclusively male perception even when the books are written by women.

One of the dullest eutopias ever written includes a striking courtship system that is designed to take all the trauma out of the engagement situation for both men and women. At the end of the last year in school, girls send their pictures and whatever statement about themselves they wish to the boys' school or schools where they are posted for inspection. Then the boys send back a proposal to a specific girl along with a photograph. The proposals, including statements of why the particular girls were chosen, are read to the girls in an open meeting. The girls publicly accept or reject the proposal immediately; the couple then meet for the first time.[16] The point in this case is fairly obvious. courtship and marriage get in the way of the important questions of career and future education. Thus if you get such questions settled within a two week period, neither society nor the individuals involved are seriously disturbed. But equally important is the fact that a wide range of career choices are open to men and women. This eutopia, however dull as a novel, at least seems to mean what it says about equality.

One other eutopia of this period requires at least passing mention even though only one copy is known to exist, and it is in a private collection. *A Woman of Tomorrow* by [Alice] Coralie Glyn (1896) was published in two editions by the Women's Printing Society of London and describes an egalitarian society only ten years in the future. It also manages to suggest with some sensitivity the problems that will be faced by the older women who had lived in the inegalitarian society that was being supplanted.

The final eutopias of the post—Bellamy reaction are in fact transitional works to the post World War I eutopia. One is H.G. Wells' *A Modern Utopia* (1905); another, *The Great State* (1912),while not written by Wells, is a product of Wells and his friends.

Wells demonstrates some sensitivity and some ambivalence on the subject, saying... "women may be free in theory and not in practice, and as long as they suffer from their economic inferiority, from the inability to produce as much value as a man for the same amount of work—and there can be no doubt of their inferiority—so long will their legal and technical equality be a mockery."[17] His solution is to see motherhood as a service to the state:

But—do not let the proposition in its first crudity alarm you—suppose the Modern Utopia equalises things between the sexes in the only possible way, in insisting that motherhood is a service to the State and a legitimate claim to a living; and that, since the State is to exercise the right of forbidding or sanctioning motherhood, a woman who is, or is becoming, a mother, is as much entitled to wages above the minimum wage, to support, to freedom, and to respect and dignity as a policeman, a solicitor-general, a king, a bishop in the State Church, a Government professor, or anyone else the State sustains [pp. 187-88].

Since marriage is, in Wells' view, primarily for the purpose of producing superior children, adultery by the woman is an offense against the state; "a reciprocal restraint on the part of the husband is clearly of no importance whatsoever..." to the state. Divorce is possible in the latter circumstance, but in the former she is "divorced as a public offender" [pp. 194-95].

Wells is trying to present a society that overcomes what he sees to be women's obvious disabilities. She is weaker and has children. The latter characteristic, if properly controlled by eugenic legislation, is advantageous but bothersome. It is the only basis he can find for providing women with economic equality. But it should be noticed that until she actually gives birth for the first time the wage is secured "from her husband" thus raising questions about her degree of economic independence. Wells rarely mentioned the position of women in his many other eutopias.

The essay on "Women in the Great State," by Cicely Hamilton, presents a different picture. "...woman in the Great State is recognized as an individual with capacities apart from domesticity, love-making, and child-bearing, with an existence independent of husband, lover or son...."[18] She continues, "What it [the State] has not the right to demand of her [the female citizen]—either directly or indirectly, by bribe or by indirect pressure—is that she, in return for its protection, shall consider herself under any obligation to produce its future citizens" [p 223]. This is, of course, a specific rejection of Wells' position.

She then specifies in more detail the relationship between women and the Great State.

1) Having recognized parasitism as an evil, the Great State will discourage that form of feminine parasitism which gains a livelihood through the exercise of sexual attraction. That is to say, it will render it unnecessary for any woman to earn her livelihood by means of her powers of sexual attraction.
2) Having recognized women as citizens and individuals—with a primary instead of secondary existence, a place in the world as well as in the house—the Great State will permit and encourage them to employ their energies and abilities in every direction in which they desire to employ such energies and abilities. That is to say, it will throw open to them every department of work at which they desire and can prove their fitness to occupy themselves thereby insuring, so far as it is humanly possible to insure, that marriage shall not be made by women, and children brought into the world by them, merely because there is nothing else for women to do but make marriages and bear children. The Great State, in short, will hold it better that a woman whose tastes do not lie in the direction of maternity should be a good spinster instead of an indifferent mother [pp. 233-34].

Here, finally, is a positive image of the role and position of women that presents men and women as capable of equally functioning in society. Unfortunately, it does not seem to have impressed other writers of eutopias.

Twentieth Century Developments

In the twentieth century two changes took place in the utopian tradition. First a growing disillusionment led writers to the dystopia rather than the eutopia. Second, most utopias came to be written as part of science fiction.[19] Still, the standard eutopia was written regularly and continued to present highly mixed pictures of the status of women. Quite a number have women in the home and with no political rights, such as in H[erbert] M. Vaughan, *Meleager* (1916); "Unitas," (pseud.) *The Dream City*; C.E. Jacomb, *And a New Earth* (1926); and C[harles] Wicksteed Armstrong, *Paradise Found or Where the Sex Problem has been Solved* (1936). One of these says that the role of woman is childbearing and to keep man from "his wandering and adventurous instincts."[20]

Until recently most of the positive pictures were narrowly political and all in the same way, the establishment of a dual political system based on the sexes. In other words, women elect women and men elect men to separate political bodies, usually divided as to function into traditional sex roles, such as in Kenneth Ingram, *England at the Flood Tide* (1924); A Daughter of Eve (pseud.) *A Woman's Utopia* [by Mrs. Ellen Warner (Olney) Kirk] (1931); and William Boyle Hill, *A New Earth and a New Heaven* (1936). There are, of course, a few works, such as *A Peaceful Revolution* (1916) by Gentle Joseph (pseud.) that suggests a fairly wide ranging equality, but most are surprisingly quiet about the role of women.

Among women writers of science fiction in the United States recently, there have been a number of individual works, most notably Joanna Russ' *The Female Man* (1975), and collections, most notably *Aurora: Beyond Equality* (1976), compiled by Vonda N. McIntyre and Susan Anderson and *Women of Wonder* (1974) and *More Women of Wonder* (1976), compiled by Pamela Sargent, that strongly present the case for an entire re-thinking of the position of women in society. England has not yet produced a similar movement. Therefore, the twentieth century adds little to the picture developed throughout the history of the English utopia, except that the complete rejection of women's rights is almost nonexistent.

The eutopia has been generally unimaginative regarding women's position in society. It can be divided into four categories— one insisting that she be clearly subservient to man, one saying that women are already in eutopia, and one suggesting that fairly minor reforms are all that is necessary. And finally, many eutopias view men and women as different species with specific, sex-defined social roles that will determine their position in any eutopia. For these works equality is found in women filling their sex role and not aspiring to change it.

In this survey I have been concerned primarily with describing the eutopia or, to put it another way, presenting evidence regarding the characteristics of a set of eutopian novels. I have made relatively few interpretations since the evidence speaks for itself on the whole. Still it seems appropriate to comment a bit further on the possible meaning of the evidence.

Obviously, the central message simply reinforces what we have learned from other sources about the role and position of women, but it is particularly important that the same points are made in pictures of supposedly *ideal* societies. Writers of eutopias are generally concerned to identify serious problems in their contemporary society and then present a vision of a society in which those problems are overcome. The fact that for most authors the position of women did not seem to be a serious problem must lead us to significantly strengthen our perception of the ways in which women have been treated. The fact that the position of women is generally ignored, or even is thought of as ideal, demonstrates the extent to which the assumption of the inferiority of women has become a truism. The fact that a significant number of authors believe that women are already treated too well only adds to the picture.

The other attitude that I have suggested as a possible interpretation of these eutopias is particularly striking. If it is generally believed, or accepted without thought, that men and women are so different that their roles do not overlap in any significant degree, it becomes possible to define inequality as equality. If men and women are to be judged by different standards, then it is possible to simply ignore women in an ideal society, since most such works focus on activities defined as male roles. In such works women play supportive roles to the main focus, the active political male.

But in conclusion it is helpful to be reminded of Cicely Hamilton and her plea for seeing women, and men, as whole human beings with a variety of appropriate roles rather than one sexually defined role.

Notes

*Originally published in *Extrapolation*. Reprinted by permission of the author and editor.

¹For a discussion and defense of the terminology used, see my "Utopia: The Problem of Definition," *Extrapolation*, 16 (May, 1975), pp. 137-48.

²I draw out some of the implications of this type of eutopia in my article "A Note on the Other Side of Human Nature in the Utopian Novel," *Political Theory*, 3 (February, 1975), pp. 88-97.

³Thomas More, *Utopia*, ed. Edward Surtz, S.J. (New Haven: Yale University Press, 1964), pp. 77, 143, 110-11. For a different interpretation of More's patriarchalism see Elisabeth Mann Borgese, *Ascent of Woman* (New York: George Braziller, 1963), p. 127.

⁴[Thomas Lupton] Suiqila. *Too good, to be true: Omen. Though so at a vewe, Yet all that I tolde you, Is true, I upholde you: Now Cease to aske why For I cannot lye. Herein is shewed by waye of Dialogue, the wonderfull manners of the people of Mauqsun, with other talke not frivolous* (London: Henrie Bynneman, 1580), p. 37.

⁵[Edward House,] *The Six Day Adventure; or, The New Utopia* (London: Tho. Dring, 1671), p. 27.

⁶[Samuel Gott,] *Nova Solyma the Ideal City; or Jerusalem Regained* (1648), ed. Rev. Walter Begley, 2 vols. (London: John Murray, 1902), 1, p. 238.

⁷[Francis Gentlemen,] *A Trip to the Moon. Containing an Account of the Island of Noibla. Its Inhabitants, Religious and Political Customs, etc.* by Sir Humphrey Lunatic, Bart. (pseud.) 2 vols. (York: S. Crowder, 1764-1765), 1, pp. 127-28.

⁸On this point see Sylvia E. Bowman, et al. *Edward Bellamy Abroad; An American Prophet's Influence* (New York: Twayne, (1962).

⁹See Sylvia Bowman, "Bellamy's Missing Chapter," *New England Quarterly*, 21 (March, 1956), pp. 47-65.

¹⁰James Lawrence, *The Empire of the Nairs; or, The Rights of Women. An Utopian Romance.* 4 vols. in 2 (London: T. Hookham, Jun. and E.T. Hookham, 1811), 1, pp. 32-33. Further references will be found in the text.

¹¹William Delisle Hay, *Three Hundred Years Hence; or, A Voice from Posterity* (London: Newman, 1881), p. 351.

¹²[Benjmin Lumley] *Another World; or, Fragments from the Star City of Montalluyah*, by Hermes (pseud.) 3rd ed. (London: Samuel Tinsley, 1873), p. 94.

¹³[Ellis James Davis,] *Pyrna: A Commune; or, Under the Ice* (London: Bickers and Son, 1878), p. 64.

¹⁴William Stanley, *The Case of The. Fox; Being his Prophecies Under Hypnotism of the Period Ending A.D. 1950. A Political Utopia* (London: Truslove and Hanson, 1903), pp. 41-42.

¹⁵George Parsons Lathrop, "In the Deep of Time," *English Illustrated Magazine* (March, 1897), in George Locke, (ed.) *Worlds Apart* (London: Cornmarket Reprints, 1972), pp. 59-60.

¹⁶John Petzler, *Life in Utopia; Being a Faithful and Accurate Description of the Institutions that Regulate Labour, Art, Science, Agriculture, Education, Habitation, Matrimony, Law, Government, and Religion in the Delightful Region of Human Imagination* (London: Authors'

Co-operative Publishing Co., 1890), pp. 110-25.

[17]H.G. Wells, *A Modern Utopia* (Lincoln, NE: Univ. of Nebraska Press, 1967), p. 187. Further references will be found in the text.

[18]Cicely Hamilton, "Women in the Great State," in *The Great State: Essays in Construction* (London: Harper Bros., 1912), p. 222. Further references will be in the text.

[19]Attitudes toward women in science fiction have been studied by Joanna Russ, "The Image of Women in Science Fiction," in *Images of Women in Fiction: Feminist Perspectives*, ed. Susan Koppelman Cornillon (Bowling Green: Bowling Green University Popular Press, 1972), pp. 79-94; Beverly Friend, "Virgin Territory: Women and Sex in Science Fiction," *Extrapolation*, 14 (December, 1972), pp. 49-58; and Pamela Sargent, "Women in Science Fiction," *Futures* (October, 1975), pp. 433-41.

[20]C.E. Jacomb, *And a New Earth* (London: George Routledge, 1926), p. 123.

IV Women Writers

Suzy McKee Charnas

A Woman Appeared

IN THE WINTER OF 1972-3 I set about completely rewriting my first book, a science fiction novel. Written in what one editor had called a "private code," it was unreadable by anyone but its author. I had invented an elaborate future religion complete with mystifying terminology and underlying assumptions that I had never explained since they would have taken up the whole book. Sadly I dismantled all this. What was left was a thin, familiar tale set in a post-holocaust future about a young hero adventuring with two male companions in search of his father.

Then a woman appeared.

There were already women in the story, or rather in the background. Almost at once work gangs of "fems" had entered the scene under the supervision of male overseers. These fems, debased and enslaved, were the other face of the book's macho survival culture. My male protagonists, fleeing their enemies, ran for concealment to the town where the fems were raised and trained.

When they emerged to continue their travels, they had picked up another fugitive, a fem who stood out from the others. This fem, Alldera, was filling the place taken in so many stories, SF and mainstream, by "the girl"—she who stands for (and invariably lies down for) that half of humanity that is otherwise absent from the foreground. I know that's what Alldera was doing in the story because I remember saying to myself, there has got to be a woman in here someplace or things are going to look awfully lopsided. Readers, friends as well as strangers, will think you are very odd.

Now I had on my hands three major men and one grudgingly admitted woman. That seemed like a realistic representation of human diversity to me. I was writing an adventure story, and I knew from all my reading that adventure means male. Women are included only as prizes or so that they can be tamed and taught their proper place.

Unfortunately my reading did not give any clues about the part Alldera would play in my adventure tale: I knew why she was there, but not what she was supposed to do. There were literary models for my men, who had begun as easily recognizable stock figures—the cynical old warrior, the son seeking confrontation with his father, and the cheery young rogue. But none of the females in the war stories, Westerns, or tales of exploration and danger that I knew, helped me with Alldera. I had never read about a woman like her in these sorts of books. The men would never fight over her; she wasn't important enough. Similarly, given her low status she could never become the haughty lady broken to harness by her ordeal.

So I had to make Alldera up, and I composed her using aspects of a friend from my school days and aspects of myself. By page 140 this lowly fem had developed a tough character, a secret quest of her own, and a point of view so strong that a portion of the story had to be told through her eyes. At first, while bowing uneasily to this demand, I regarded the actual writing of her section as a grinding chore to be finished as quicky as possible so that I could get back to the real meat of the book. Instead, writing Alldera's part led to a series of revelations that gave the story a whole new balance of events, character and meaning. This reshaped the novel entirely, as is apparent in the finished book—*Walk to the End of the World* (Ballantine, 1974).

Looking back, I now recognize the obvious. During that same winter of 1972-3, I was doing what so many other women were doing and are still doing: reading books like Shulamith Firestone's *The Dialectic of Sex* (Bantam, 1971) and *Sisterhood is Powerful* edited by Robin Morgan (Vintage, 1970) and participating in consciousness-raising sessions with other women. As my awareness matured—and my anger at finding myself trapped in the powerless class of women—Alldera pushed her way more and more to the heart of the story I was writing, changing everything around her as my own perspective on her fictional world changed.

Walk could not remain a superficial tale of a young man in search of his father's power. It became a story of a society in which power is the crucial question, and the struggle between generations of males is the central form that question takes, while mothers and daughters figure only as labor, brood mares and objects of aggression. The book ended up being about sexism carried to a logical extreme, and it suggests, I hope, the inherent destructiveness of any society in which one portion of the population enslaves and dehumanizes another.

Inevitably and almost effortlessly, the last pages of *Walk* grew to be Alldera's. At that point the story had become her story. Whatever was to happen next, and clearly something was set to happen, would be up to her.

She was ready, which is to say that I was ready, or so I thought. A second book, a sequel to *Walk*, hove onto my mental horizon with Alldera at the helm. Her setting was to be a plains tribe of free, nomadic women, Amazons of the future. I was interested in the potentialities of an Amazon-like society unconstrained by our distorted and fragmentary notions of real, historic Amazons. This time, at least, I had some idea of what the book was about before I began.

I did not know until I had begun writing that in this sequel there would be no male characters at all. The decision to exclude men was not dispassionate and political. I tried to write them in; I wanted to do more of what came fairly easily.

No matter what I wrote, men would not fit. Every scene they entered went dead. I am hardheaded about my work; I tend to beat my brains out trying to force what I want onto the page. When I finally give up and do what a story demands, I remember too late that this is how it always is: if what I am trying to do will not go, the reason is that it's wrong.

Now I was terrified to discover that leaving men out altogether was going to be "right" for the new book.

To begin with, who would publish a science fiction book only about women? The field has long been considered a bastion of male readership, and most men seem willing to read about women only as victims (that is, compliant or conquerable objects) or monsters (insatiable or castrating subjects). I meant to write a book about women who were neither victims nor monsters. And if I succeeded, would more than a handful of women—science fictions readers or otherwise—ever read it? Female readers of popular fiction seemed hooked on badly written, numbingly predictable, sweet-savage Gothicry, a form of masochistic fantasy. Editors who might do books about women pander to that taste.

There were then (this was 1975) feminist publishing houses catering to a more enlightened and demanding female taste in reading; but so far as I was aware they did not handle science fiction. I was afraid that even if one of them were to accept my book, they wouldn't be able to market it effectively through their apparently limited distribution systems (that is, to get it onto the SF shelves as well as the "women's" shelves in the bookstores).

Then there was the problem of creating a whole bookfull of female characters. There were classical models of a variety of fictional women—Austen's Elizabeth Bennett, George Eliot's Dinah Morris or Dorothea Brooke, Woolf's Lily Briscoe, many others—but they were always shaped by and functioning in fairly sophisticated, male-dominated societies. My express purpose was to explore what women might be like without that domination, living the robust lives of horse-herding tribespeople.

Moroever, accepting at heart my culture's definition of women as a very limited type of people doing very limited things, I did not see how to invent a sufficient variety of these pastoral female people to hold even my own interest while writing the book. I was sure that I would end up inventing male characters, pulling out their chest-hair and attaching breasts—a betrayal, not a solution.

The book, *Motherlines*, took two and a half years to complete, and if you want to know what it felt like to do it, read George Sheehan on running a marathon. I have never run a marathon, but I recognize in Sheehan's description the experience of writing this book: warming up, working well, getting tired, growing desperate, hitting "the wall" where there is nothing left, dragging out previously unsuspected reserves, surviving to the finish, and then a long recovery period because, as they say, a marathon really "tears you down." And afterward being proud to have done it, and then wanting, and fearing, to try again. They also say that nobody runs one marathon; it's addictive.

Despite my original resolve, *Motherlines* did turn out to be partly about victimization: escaped fems, victims of the culture of *Walk*, try to heal themselves and succeed or do not succeed in a manless world. It also turned out to be about separatism as a solution to sexism—the heart of the book is the all-woman culture of the "Riding Women." Some readers will call the Riding Women monsters, since many people find monstrous the idea of women living good, full lives without men. I do not, though separatism is not my blueprint for Paradise and not the only answer to sexism that I hope to explore in fiction.

I became so involved in the Riding Women that the part of the novel introducing them had to be rewritten countless times to make the plotline clear. My impulse was just to follow the Riding Women forever, recording what it was like travelling and camping with them, living their life—as if I were one of those nineteenth century wanderers who vanished into the wild spaces of the world for years and came back to write books with titles like *My Life Among the Mongols* or *A Winter in Crow Camps*. The shape, rhythm and daily grit of that imaginary life fascinated me, and bringing that fascination under the discipline of telling a story was one of the hardest things I have ever tried to do.

Another reason that it took so long to finish writing *Motherlines* is that each of the women in it first came, I think, not from literature but from life. They were not impressions from some other book changed for use in my own. Each began as a scrap of the appearance or behavior of a real woman in the real world, however blurred and fragmentary the original observation. When I grew bored or exhausted, these characters tended to start talking and behaving like male stereotypes and had to be brought back to life again.

Then with the spectrum of human behavior in my story no longer split into male roles (everthing active, intelligent, brave and muscular) and female roles (everything passive, intuitive, shrinking and soft), my emerging women had natural access to the entire range of human behavior. They acted new roles appropriate to social relationships among a society of equals, which allowed them to behave simply as human beings—tenderly, aggressively, nurturingly, intellectually, intuitively, whatever suited a given individual in a given situation. The characters held my interest as a writer during the long period of their development because within the limits of their personalities they were capable of any action, feeling and attitude.

From the beginning I felt that the book was potentially so full and so sprawling that maintaining control of it would require more angles of vision than my own. Partly to slow down the whole process so that my own ideas could mature, partly to test the efficacy of what I was doing, and partly to clarify questions—and answers—that were still unclear to me, I submitted the working manuscript to a number of friends (including two men) for their reactions and criticism. Their contributions of thought, time, and encouragement proved invaluable. The working method that had produced my first, unreadable book—pounding around in secret, obsessive circles inside my own brain—had loosened up with *Walk*; the participation of others at even earlier stages of the new book opened the process out into something still more flexible.

This is not to say that *Motherlines* was written by a collective. But it demanded an approach that I think reflects some of the thinking about work and how to do it that has come out of the women's movement.

The editor who had accepted *Walk* had offered a contract on the sequel, sight unseen, and I had declined. Upon reading *Motherlines*, this editor informed me that the book was unpublishable and would have to be rethought and entirely rewritten. This time the judgment was wrong, although other editors turned the book down too. One said to me, "You know, if this book was all about *men* it would be a terrific story."

After a year or so, during which I engaged an agent to help find a publisher for *Motherlines*, the book was accepted by David Hartwell at Berkley/Putnam to be published in the summer of 1979. What sort of readership it will find remains to be seen.

As a result of writing *Walk* and *Motherlines* I think I have changed my way of looking at real women in the real world. When I meet a woman for the first time now, I am less likely than formerly to see only the feminine role that our culture allows her and more likely to glimpse her individuality and potentiality.

Another result is a change in the way I make judgments about women writers—myself included—and their work. We do not, I think, just shrug off the conditioning of patriarchal society at will. Most of us have our demons to exorcise—dusty, internalized patterns of masculinist thinking and creating. Beyond the demons lies the green prospect of writing fiction about women as they really are and women as they might become.

Susan Kress

In and Out of Time:
The Form of Marge Piercy's Novels

When I'm behind the writing desk, I'm the same full person I am when I'm any place else. I mean, everything is in play. In writing it always seems to me like even more is in play than maybe at any other time. I always feel that everything is lined up.... I don't leave my politics in the other room.... I'm not going to be called to account in the kind of weekly sense.... However, there's a deeper sense in which you can feel yourself in history, you can feel a sense of responsibility to the people of whom you are a part, you can have a sense that you draw energy from the lives of many people that have been submerged, that that energy flows through you, that you're responsible to those people living and dead and to come. And I do have that sense. And I have it fully as a writer.... I write as an individual, but I also write as a focus for that energy. And I do feel myself accountable to a constituency in a sense. Not accountable in a small sense. Not accountable to the petty prejudices and the day-to-day ups and downs. But accountable in a gross sense—for my life, for my work.

Marge Piercy[1]

MARGE PIERCY HAS BEEN writing novels for almost a decade now. Like Doris Lessing, she is intensely responsive to the political currents of her time, and, like Doris Lessing, her primary concern as a left wing radical is with the "individual conscience in its relation with the collective."[2] Clearly, a writer who is extremely close to contemporary events, and particularly the explosive events of the sixties, is faced with a number of difficult aesthetic choices. How does such a writer achieve distance from her own (acknowledged) strong emotions?[3] Conversely, how does such a writer ensure that rage is controlled but not eradicated? How does such a writer avoid the pitfalls of reporting—or even propaganda? How, in short, does such a writer handle the complexities of fictional form? Close examination of Piercy's five published novels—*Going Down Fast* (1969), *Dance the Eagle to Sleep* (1970), *Small Changes* (1972), *Woman on the Edge of Time* (1976), and *The High Cost of Living* (1978)—reveals that each work represents a different solution to the committed novelist's search for appropriate form. It is the task of this paper to examine the separate formal strategies Piercy adopts, to chart her progress from one novel to another, to reveal the significant patterns that emerge, and, in particular, to understand the logic behind her use of the science fiction genre.

Going Down Fast is a novel which, in reflecting the political and personal convulsions of the sixties, takes its shape from imagery of fragmentation and disintegration. The book's first page sounds the keynote: "The crane bit into a shiny yellow room, turned and with a tidy jerk spat the chewed wall in a dumptruck."[4] A large urban renewal project is under way in Chicago, a project designed to wipe out most of the cheap good housing near the University and to sweep back into the ghetto those who have dared to struggle out to the edges of middle classhood. The local tenants try to organize themselves against the plan to "redevelop," but the massed forces of State, University, planners and developers prove invincible. This area is indeed going down fast, and the implication is that crumbling there, too, in that debris, are some vital but fragile human structures; for in that fringe between University and slum proper—a place of small homes, small shopkeepers, small beginnings toward racial integration—a kind of village neighborhood has bloomed in the heart of the city.

Such breakdown is reflected in the lives of the characters, too. The book offers numerous examples of those who are deliberately or accidentally broken by the system. Rowley, the principal male protagonist, is engaged for the major part of the book in a quest for Black Jack, a singer of considerable power, who has dropped out of sight. Finally, he is discovered in a stinking hotel room, dying and defeated, vomiting his own blood. There are fleeting references to an old woman living in a tenement who refuses to be evicted by city officials, and must be finally removed in a straitjacket. There is a reference to (the real) Louis Sullivan, an architect with a new dream of city who dies in a flophouse worn down by a "Roman dream of empire he couldn't fight" (p. 190). Even Rowley's cat, Yente, in an act of gratuitous cruelty is burned alive. Such examples of irrational violence, of wasted human potential, pervade the book: Vera, a young black teacher, is burned to death when her school catches fire; Leon, after an act of protest in which he dumps disposal on renewal (heaps garbage in the shiny new shopping plaza) is committed to an institution, a place, observes one character, "simpler than the society and with the lines of control just as taut but more visible" (p. 346).

Most of the characters do work outside the established institutions of the social system. Rowley runs a radio music show, Leon is an independent film-maker, and Anna is an unemployed teacher, then (in desperation) a secretary to the Institute of Social Surveying, and finally, a member of a tenant organization. They are all resistant to the tugs of a capitalist system, although, as Rowley puts it for himself in a moment of insight, they have avoided, for the most part, direct opposition:

He had lived in the cracks where people could now and then get together, disaffiliated
but easy among themselves, and when a crack closed he found a new one. Thus he
had lived in his society without confronting it, and now he did not know where to
begin (p. 235).

None of these characters presents any convincing alternatives, any
whole coherent vision for change. Shelden Lederman, on the other
hand, Leon's father and one of the property tycoons involved in the
redevelopment scheme, does have a vision of his ideal city. All
garish glitter, his "city of light" is a gilded paradise of consumer
products. He will sweep away the poor, the ethnic, the misfit in
honor of an homogeneous "city of the clean, the fit, the socialized,
the acceptable, the good" (p. 270). Against such a nightmare, Black
Jack can only propose his own dream of total demolition: "To see
this supposed to be great city a hole in the ground" (p. 277).
Similarly, at the end of the novel, Rowley's vision of darkness, pain,
and despair is set up in direct contrast to the metallic brilliance of
Lederman's city:

Through the dark drifted the ashlight bodies of burned Vera and Black Jack and
Leon bound and Yente . . . and the thousands in the city burning with a stench more
suffocating than the soft coal favored by its landlords, burning in poverty, in
powerlessness, in blindness, in thousands of deadend graverooms where the smoke of
their angry flesh and charred nerves rose in their nostrils and choked them (p. 348).

These characters are cut off from one another, cut off from their
roots, cut off from a vision that will counteract the plastic paradise
of Sheldon Lederman and carry them into a war against a system
they despise. Trapped in history, they are unable to change it. Nor
do we get a view of events from outside those characters; no
authoritative, omniscient narrator tells this story. Instead, a
restricted narrator filters it through the consciousness of a number
of characters, sometimes in sequential, sometimes in parallel time.
The formal narrative strategy suggests that out of such times, out of
such characters, come only partial visions, fragments and
approximations.

But Piercy does propose a modest personal, if not political,
affirmation at the end of the book. The novel begins in late summer
with the breakup of Anna's and Rowley's relationship. Throughout
the frozen winter, characters huddle in unheated rooms, smothered
in layers of old clothing, seeking each other for warmth. Cold indeed
is this city of rubble where the characters try to make connections
with each other and with ideas, but rarely succeed. With February,
however, come the first thaw and the renewal of the tie between
Anna and Rowley. That they are together again is, we must assume,
positive, but neither of them is willing to make great claims for a
love relationship that failed once and must now struggle along in a

society expert in methods of demolition. Nor indeed can they, or the reader, forget the other abortive friendships in the novel (Anna and Leon, Leon and Caroline, Caroline and Rowley, Rowley and Vera) or the disquieting fact that this renewal is achieved in midst of the collapse of their friends' lives—most particularly Leon's who is left to crumble in an institution.

Dance the Eagle to Sleep offers the next stage in revolution, and proposes a very different kind of artistic form. If the characters in *Going Down Fast* have gone down to the bottom, have stripped themselves of illusion, and have analyzed their situation, then those in *Dance the Eagle to Sleep* suggest some ways of acting on that analysis, some ways of rebuilding. The form of *Going Down Fast* is appropriate for showing the perspectives of different characters engaging in reflection and self reflection. In general, the method of the novel is "realistic": the characters' context is carefully specified; there are no outrageous turns of plot or reversals of character. The novel has no chapter headings—only the name of the character whose views are expressed in that chapter—and, significantly, the date. These characters, then, are operating in a particular place (the city of Chicago) at a particular time; indeed, they are trapped in those very particularities, trapped, above all, in the present, the day-to-day, calendar time. In *Dance the Eagle to Sleep,* Piercy seems to have come to the conclusion that if she wants to express a coherent alternative to a capitalist system, she will need to locate the energy for that vision in a different group of characters, and channel that energy through a different formal structure.

In *Going Down Fast*, Rowley, contemplating his sister and her young husband, understands that from youth might come the necessary impetus for change:

The kids were more and less isolated than he was. They had a total mistrust of the whole shebang that startled him. Where his generation had taken honors and bitched at the system, they dropped out.... They had a sense of identity and community he had only in his music.... Thrown down in random flat cities they found each other, in Fort Wayne and Davenport, in Tangiers and Guatemala City. They invested much hope in small countries whose geography was blank to him. They made him turn and examine his youth as a piece of history. They could say "the revolution" without giggling, without quotes, without a sense of absurdity (pp. 326-7).

Such a group, then, becomes the focus in *Dance the Eagle to Sleep*. The characters are all teenagers, all escaping the horrors of the "Nineteenth Year of Service," a government plan to enforce State service (from army duty to "preschool socialization programs in the ghettoes")[5] on all nineteen year olds not engaged in the study of medicine, engineering, and the sciences. Various representative runaways (including Shawn the rock singer, Billy the brilliant young scientist, Corey the ex-dope-dealing Indian, and Joanna, daughter of an army officer) set up an alternate society based on tribal principles.

It will be obvious by now that Piercy has departed from the "realistic" novel. In a recent issue of the journal, *Frontiers,* devoted to the topic of "Fantasy and Futures," Piercy claims:

The reason for using a somewhat science fiction format in *Dance the Eagle to Sleep* was to gain some distance from my own very passionate involvement in SDS, and to be able to write about those experiences without aiding and abetting the government.[6]

Elsewhere, she has commented on her notion of the difference between the novel and the tale: the novel deals essentially with character development; the tale is closer to myth, to fairy tale, to ritual, its power deriving not so much from character as from the conflict of large forces.[7] Such a form not only allows artistic detachment, but also, by its very nature, confers universality and timelessness.

The rules and rituals developed by the tribes are in large part drawn from the youth culture of the sixties. The rebellion that expressed itself in unconventional dress, long hair, drugs, dancing, the peace movement, dropping out of school (and, by extension, the system), as well as some aspects of Indian tribal culture, is, in *Dance the Eagle to Sleep,* granted a mythic dimension and provides the energy for a separate youth-controlled and youth-populated society. Corey, the Indian, one of the group leaders, is the visionary. To him appears, appropriately enough, the buffalo, exhorting him, "Your generation is the last. You must lead the tribes to water. You must save your generation" (p. 32). The struggle between youth and system is thus expressed metaphorically in the conflict between the Buffalo of Corey's vision and the Eagle of Empire. But, as Billy the scientist points out, their "utopia" cannot possibly prevail. A remnant of nineteenth century American romanticism, it is a "throwback," another "Brook Farm—utopian cranks off in the woods...." (p. 93), and as such it will neither defeat "Empire" nor be tolerated by it. Hence the wholesale destruction of the Indians at the end of the tale—echoes of the vision established in *Going Down Fast.*

The tale is a fascinating formal experiment (and opens the way for *Woman on the Edge of Time*), but does, nevertheless, in important ways, lack conviction. Somehow, the characters do not seem large enough to bear their mythic burden. They are often forced to mouth clichés ("While there are people, we haven't lost. We were right and wrong, but the system is all wrong," p. 231), and the imaginative vision itself wears thin toward the end, as Joanna is co-opted back into the system, Corey is killed by a bulldozer that is clearing the ground for a state park and Ginny gives birth to her baby. The symbolism is heavy-handed; dogma weighs down the imaginative structure; and the book comes to a kind of visionary dead end. There is no way for such a band to defeat Empire.

In *Small Changes,* Piercy returns to the novel proper, and writes a book that is more ambitious and more powerful in a number of ways. Finally, Piercy has found a subject that releases her own artistic energy: the lives of women in society. In her previous works, Piercy has certainly been concerned with the roles of women. In *Going down Fast,* Anna drifts from Rowley to Leon and back to Rowley; she is essentially passive—willing to cook, clean, and nurture—a woman without real direction or sense of self; and Piercy grants Rowley most of the important insights. Joanna, in *Dance the Eagle to Sleep*, is a much more self-conscious character. She knows that she does not want to be "sombody else's wife or somebody else's mother. Or somebody else's servant or somebody else's secretary. Or somebody else's sex kitten or somebody else's keeper" (p.51), but, at the same time she is pulled into the tribe through her intense attraction to Corey. She also perceives that, even in the seemingly "advanced" culture of the tribes, "whatever the rhetoric ... women mostly ended up running the kitchen" (p. 145). Ginny is a much more revolutionary figure. She progresses from a state of passive self-hatred to one of strength and self-assurance. She is the one who disdains the men of the tribe for being "in love with apocalypse ... more in love with myths than with any woman" (p. 225); she is connected to the earth, to human tasks and aspirations. In *Small Changes*, however, Piercy concentrates predominantly on the lives of women, and charts the changes of the sixties and seventies through the experiences of two women—Miriam and Beth—whose lives converge and diverge.

If Piercy returns to the novel, however, she does so to overturn some of its formal assumptions. This book, unlike those traditional novels about women which *end* with marriage, begins with a wedding. Beth, about to be married, is already rebelling against convention, as, primped and curled and gowned, she is wrapped "like a package"[8] for her husband; and the novel continues its reversal of tradition by documenting her movement away from the convention of marriage. She runs from her husband, sets up house (room) in Boston, joins one then another commune, takes a male lover, a female lover, joins a theatre collective, and finally, pursued by the authorities for the kidnapping of Wanda's children, she and her lover, Wanda Rosario, hide out in Cleveland. Beth's ready exodus from her marriage and her disburdening of the conventional trappings of woman's role in contemporary society seem, perhaps, a shade too easy. For one so young, she seems to have analyzed too fast and acted on that analysis too promptly. Certainly, in terms of the structure of the novel, Piercy means her to offer a contrast with Miriam whose powerful intelligence and vital energy, while promising much, do not save her from following the traditional route of fictional heroines: marriage and children. If Beth is responsible for the novel's theory, for providing a polemical analysis of the plight of women and forcing us to confront the contradictions and inequalities of women's lives, then Miriam is responsible for dramatizing the conflicts of women in transition between old habits and new consciousness.

The book documents a number of changes in women's lives. Beth's odyssey is the grandest, but Dorine, too, moves from the position of house servant in one of the communes to become a woman of strength and self-esteem who becomes immersed in her work as a biologist. She is also primarily responsible for creating an equal relationship with Phil (one of Miriam's former lovers), a very significant accomplishment since he is then able to present the possibility that some men are capable of transcending the old sex roles. Even if people have changed and can change somewhat, however, society does not change much at all. Moreover, most of the small victories are won at enormous personal cost. At the end of *Small Changes,* Miriam is at a turning point. She has realized a number of things about her situation, and perhaps one expects the sequel, Piercy's next book, to portray a Miriam-like character breaking out of her painful dependence on her husband and building an independent future.

The sequel to *Small Changes,* however, is a very different kind of book. It is indeed about the future, but *Woman on the Edge of Time* is a science fiction tale. As we noted, Piercy had tried a "somewhat science fiction format" in *Dance the Eagle to Sleep,* and now she returns to it again for what is her most significant tale. Indeed, it will be worth pausing for a moment, before considering this most important tale, in order to review Piercy's movement toward such a formal strategy. In *Going Down Fast,* Piercy presented a somber vision of disintegration and breakdown—with characters unable to do much more than acknowledge and analyze their plight. Where does a politically committed and responsible novelist go from there? Well, she tries, in *Dance the Eagle to Sleep,* to have her characters, all young people and as yet not fully corrupted by society, form a tribal community based on ideal principles. But it does not, cannot, work because such an ideal society must operate in real time, in a real capitalist context. Nor, artistically, is the particular combination of realism and romance satisfying. Piercy is seemingly still looking for a way to combine political theory with the realistic novel—the novel of ideas and the novel of character. Additionally, the characters in *Dance the Eagle to Sleep* are required to be representative, which tends to undercut the reader's interest in them as particular individuals; and, as participants in a tale, they do not have the kind of imaginative power that will compensate for the overwhelming odds against them—the intractable fact of Empire.

In *Small Changes,* Piercy sharpens and intensifies her focus. She concentrates on the situation of women, and she incorporates her theory in the person of Beth, who is, however dry, still much more compelling and attractive than the characters in *Dance the Eagle to Sleep. Small Changes* offers a powerful critique of society, a critique informed by a passionate yet regulated rage. But Piercy is once again faced with the inflexibility of society itself, and the responsibility for presenting a coherent vision for change. Hence, *Woman on the Edge of Time,* a novel which undertakes an experiment in form that allows Piercy to combine novel and tale— the novel of character and the novel of ideas—with considerable success. This novel represents the culmination of much of the political thinking that has run through the other novels. Here we find caught up, extended, and explored, germs of ideas in the other works, and here, too, we find a coherent, complete, and consistent utopian vision of the future. Finally, Piercy seems to have discovered an integrated form that allows her to solve a number of difficult artistic and political problems.

In *Small Changes*, toward the end, Beth, in argument about the different fates of those powerless men and women at the bottom of the social heap, points out:

"Men get thrown in jail, women get pushed into mental hospitals. There you don't even learn survival skills and how to be a better criminal. You get drugged into forgetting why you were angry and what you knew" (p. 506).

Beth's words recall that haunting image from *Going Down Fast* of the woman being bodily removed from her building in a strait-jacket. This is the unlikely kind of woman that Marge Piercy takes for her protagonist in *Woman on the Edge of Time.* Connie Camacho Ramos is a Chicana, a thirty-seven year old woman from the lower reaches of society, and as such has four counts against her: age, poverty, race, and sex. Unlike the relatively privileged Beth and Miriam from *Small Changes*, this woman has little. Her breakfast of coffee and a scrap of stale bread must be extended with glasses of hot water to stay the pangs of hunger; a highlight of her day is to find in the street a pen that works. When she gets caught in a fight between her niece, Dolly, and Dolly's pimp, she finds herself checked into a psychiatric institution. Disadvantaged before, now she is completely powerless, with no control whatsoever over her own life. What she does have, however, according to the visitor from the future, Luciente, is the gift of receptivity. She is a "catcher," who can "receive" into her present world, Luciente, inhabitant of a future time (2137) and place (Mattapoisett). Through Connie, Luciente is visiting "The Age of Greed and Waste" as part of a time project being carried out in the future.

This is the device that allows Piercy the opportunity to compare the present with the future, as Connie herself visits Mattapoisett and discovers the conditions of life there.[9] But it also allows Piercy to question some assumptions about the nature of that future as well as assumptions implicit in the science fiction genre.[10] When Connie first visits Mattapoisett, she finds a future quite unlike her expectations: " 'No skyscrapers, no spaceports, no traffic jam in the sky' "[11] Mattapoisett is a village world, its roots in the primitive societies of the past; it is an implicit and explicit rejection of present technology (particularly the kind that aims to control and manipulate human beings),[12] and it is further a rejection of those novels about the future that tend to emphasize technological progress at the expense of human values. Connie is also amazed to discover that Luciente is a woman. Judging from her self-assurance, her manner of walking, talking, and taking space, Connie had been convinced she was a man. (Recall Beth from *Small Changes*, " 'We can get outside of roles, finally! We can!' " p. 521). The world of the future is a world for men *and* women, a world far removed from present patriarchy, a world where most of the inequalities of the present have been rectified, and most of the repressive institutions and practices have been reformed or abolished.

Marriage is gone, of course. No marriage has been seen to work in Piercy's novels; marriage (" 'the patriarchal way, where you lose your name and become property,' " *Small Changes*, p. 333) is seen as inevitably inimical to human relationships. But much more revolutionary than the abolition of marriage is the "birthing" of children, and this aspect of the future gives Connie, and perhaps the reader, the most trouble. In Mattapoisett, children are birthed in incubators, and genes are mixed to ensure a racially varied population. The children are reared by three parents, "comothers" of either sex, and parents of either sex are able to breast feed them. Such a concept brings to fruition many of the ideas in earlier works. We have not forgotten that *Dance the Eagle to Sleep* ends with the birth of a child who will have three "mothers" of both sexes (Ginny, Shawn, Marcus) of whom only Ginny is the biological mother. Nor indeed have we forgotten all the wars between "real" parents and children that rage through earlier novels. The communes in *Small Changes* try to deflect the tensions of one-to-one mothering by allowing communal responsibility for children; but just as Miriam rejects the method of the commune, so Connie is disgusted by the way of Mattapoisett. Much emphasis is given in *Woman on the Edge of Time* to the matter of educating and caring for children for a number of reasons: first, we saw in *Dance the Eagle to Sleep* and in *Going Down Fast* that faith in change, in the possibility of a good future, could only come from the young; second, Connie herself, suffering pangs of remorse because she once harmed her own child who was then taken from her by the authorities, is obsessed with the experience of mothering; and finally, as Luciente explains to Connie, the new methods of breeding and rearing, however shocking they may seen at first, are essential to women's freedom:

Finally there was that one thing we had to give up too, the only power we ever had, in return for no more power for anyone. The original production: the power to give birth. Cause as long as we were biologically enchained, we'd never be equal. And males never would be humanized to be loving and tender. So we all became mothers. Every child has three. To break the nuclear bonding (p. 105).

Suddenly, we recall a scene in *Small Changes* where Beth denounces Aldous Huxley whose *Brave New World* treats the subject of test tube babies: " 'He made it be associated with horrible people and a disgusting society where sex was a commodity. And it's remained a nightmare ever since' " (p. 385). Piercy, through Mattapoisett, gives the feminist response to Aldous Huxley, and makes the future work for women.

But it is not just family relationships, not just the rituals of birth, initiation, and death that Piercy has worked out in this tale. She proposes a thorough-going analysis of the present by demonstrating the solution to present problems in the future. Almost every detail of life is subjected to intelligent scrutiny as Connie discovers how Mattapoisett deals with government, work, energy conservation, automation, architecture, cities, living space, sex, food, dress, waste disposal, and festivals. Age, class, race, and sex discrimination are relics of our present. Piercy has even solved the problem of sexist pronouns with the witty, universal "per."

Piercy has picked an extraordinary protagonist for this tale. Not young. Not beautiful. Not white. Not rich. Not married or about-to-be. Not involved in any relationship with a man. Not brilliant. Not engaged in significant work. She is not even free, but trapped in an institution which monitors her every move. If Piercy does away with all the conventional plot tensions of realistic fiction, how does she maintain interest? At a basic level, she depends on the reader's desire to want to know this world of the future. The ways of Mattapoisett are revealed slowly, a little at a time, over the course of Connie's many visits. But extended exposition is not often guaranteed to compel the novel reader's rapt attention. Hence, plot tension is introduced on two different levels. Brought to the hospital by her neice's pimp, and signed there by her brother Lewis, Connie becomes the victim of a sadistic experiment to alter her brain by means of an implanted electrical device. Nothing could reveal more dramatically the difference between the benign future time and the horrors of the now; "they," in the attempt to get control over Connie's brain, have, as she puts it, "violated her frontiers" (p. 337). She realizes that she is at war, but more important, perhaps, she is made to realize by Luciente, that she is engaged in an even larger war, that the existence of such an ideal future depends on her—and others like her. Only if they fight against the system—and defeat it—will the new order prevail. Indeed, after the dialytrode has been implanted, Connie, while trying to reach Luciente, finds herself in a monstrous, alternate future time confronted by a woman who is a grotesque travesty of "femininity," cosmetically processed for sexual efficiency. And just as we can see Luciente as a possible descendant of Connie, so we can see this alien plastic woman as a possible descendant of Connie's niece, Dolly, who is drugged, smoothed, sleeked and starved—for sexual service. In order to ensure the ascendency of *her* descendants, then, Connie goes to war; tries her best to escape the institution; and when that fails, poisons the doctors' coffee with a substance fortuitously and appropriately stolen from her brother's plant nursery.

Toward the end of *Small Changes*, Phil explains the meaning of "Doing Time":

"You're a thing in their power. They can beat you, strip you, starve you, take away your letters and your pictures and piss on them and tear them up in front of you. Tell you waht to read, deny you paper and pencil, bust you for staring. They can take your health away real slow or break your back in two minutes. 'Desperate' just has no meaning till you're inside. Then nothing ever is the same again. Not touching a woman, not taking a crap or looking at the sky or buying a paperback or smiling in the mirror.... Doing *Time*" (p. 519).

This passage seems to suggest some of the meanings "Time" has in *Woman on the Edge of Time*, the richness of the concept Piercy has developed in this tale of past, present, and future time. In Connie's experience, exterior time, present time, is State time, system time, and even—male time. She has had her present time taken away from her, and by extension her very life—since life *is* time. She is controlled by institution time, by state time, depending on their time for food, sleep, recreation, medication. And she is at the disposal of their time for experiments and manipulation. Real or present time is her adversary, too, in that she only has so much of it left before the hospital officials, thwarted once in their attempts to implant the dialytrode, implant it again—and for good.

But Connie has her own time in her head, and that is her ally in that it allows her to modulate between past, present, and future. As she perceives it, "these men" wanted to chase "the crouching female animal through the brain with a scalpel" (p. 282), for this individual time, this interior, female time, allows her connections with her past, however painful that is, and her ability to connect with her history differentiates her not only from the characters in *Going Down Fast* (most particularly Rowley who is seeking Black Jack to regain touch with an adopted past), but also with Luciente herself who must, like the other future beings, rely, at least partially, on a "kenner" (a portable computer device) for her memory.

Of course, the primary achievement of Connie's inner time sense involves her ability to cross over into the future. Whether this future is a time outside of Connie's head is questionable. Nobody else in the tale ever corroborates the existence of Luciente; and we know that Mattapoissett is only one of a number of possible futures. Yet Mattapoisett is described in such minute detail. Would a woman like Connie have the means to imagine such a world, and detail so coherently so many practices that, at least initially, shock and dismay her? Piercy's skill is in keeping the matter ambiguous. The reader, too, feels torn between, on the one hand, wanting the future to be "real" and therefore possible, wanting Connie's war in the present to have real consequences in the future, and, on the other hand, wanting Connie, a poor, institutionalized Chicana woman, to be more than a passive "catcher," wanting her to transcend her present with such a vision of the future. If she has no control over her life, she does have control through her vision, for she has vision more powerfully and more clearly than anyone in *Going Down Fast*, *Dance the Eagle to Sleep*, and *Small Changes*. Unlike the characters in *Going Down Fast*, who cannot imagine a future, who are paralyzed in present, calendar time, Connie is able to touch a future which is truly a vision of light. For she is able, through her female time, to transcend present male time, and to reach a future time that will be a time for women.

Piercy's adoption of the science fiction form has provided her with the perfect solution to the problem of combining the novel of character and the novel of ideas. In *Woman on the Edge of Time*, Piercy is able to enlist our sympathy for the real, suffering woman, Connie, while she allows Luciente to carry the burden of theory, and assume quite naturally the role of teacher and guide to this new world. She is able to modulate between Connie's anger and Luciente's disengagement. And the notion of a future time utopia enables Piercy to present a compelling and coherent vision of an alternate society of the sort that was impossible in *Dance the Eagle to Sleep*. Additionally, by showing a future that Connie perceives to be radically different from her expectations, Piercy challenges both our normal assumptions about the kind of future we anticipate, as well as the assumptions often found in science fiction novels. Finally, through her brilliant exploration of the concept of time, she is able to draw some illuminating distinctions between the conditions of present patriarchy and future feminism.

There are, of course, some real questions to be raised about this utopian vision. Can any utopia be more than a play world where the complexities of life are simplified out of existence?[13] Is it possible that the reader (so uneducated in the ways of peace and happiness) would find Mattapoisett a nice place to visit but a dull place to live? Is the science fiction form itself, and particularly the time travel motif, an easy way out of present social and political problems? Whether or not she was guided by some such considerations as these, Piercy returns to the "realistic" novel for her latest work. Connie's Mattapoisett is light years away from the world of *The High Cost of Living*, a novel whose bleak vision is reminiscent of *Going Down Fast*. We have come full circle, back to a place where characters make futile attempts to connect with one another, back to the chaotic, painful, absurd present. The main character of *The High Cost of Living* is a lesbian graduate student who forms a friendship with a young girl, Honor, and, reluctantly, with a male homosexual, Bernie. Both Leslie and Bernie fall in love with Honor who seems to deserve neither of them, but instead opts for an affair with Leslie's graduate advisor. Nothing develops from this: a brief connection between Bernie and Leslie is abruptly broken; no real connection between Honor and Leslie ever develops. At the end, Leslie, in spite of his treatment of Honor, still returns to George, her advisor, realizing with some self-disgust that "she needed money and respect and prestige and a toehold in the middle class."[14] Piercy has moved back to the novel of character, but given those characters little to be and less to fight for.

Yet these, perhaps, are the conditions of our times, and it is unfair to Piercy to blame her for reproducing them too faithfully. It is just that *The High Cost of Living* reminds us all too forcefully of how far away we are from Mattapoisett, of what it means to live in the imperfect present. No wonder feminists like Marge Piercy and Joanna Russ opt for science fiction forms; only in some carefully imagined future or on some other planet does it seem possible to create "positive" images of women. As Ellen Morgan says, "the social reality in which the realistic novel is grounded is still sufficiently patriarchal to make a realistic novel about a truly liberated woman very nearly a contradiction in terms."[15] Consequently, those fiction writers who are committed to social and political change must revise old forms or invent new ones. Thus far, Marge Piercy has alternated between the novel and the tale, and found a shape perfectly adapted to her vision in *Woman on the Edge of Time*. Has she exhausted the possibilities of science fiction? It will be well worth watching to see where she goes from here.

Notes

[1]From a recorded panel discussion, "The Ordeal of the Woman Writer," with Toni Morrison and Erica Jong, intro. Heywood Hale Broun, Norton, 40061, 1974. (My punctuation.)

[2]Doris Lessing, "The Small Personal Voice," in *A Small Personal Voice: Essays: Reviews, Interviews,* ed. and intro. Paul Schlueter (New York: Vintage Books, 1975), p. 14.

[3]In "The Ordeal of the Woman Writer," Piercy claims, "Not to be in touch with your anger is to be very alienated from yourself. Alienated from your body, alienated from your own history, and alienated from your own emotions. And how can you write, then, except with what you learn from other books. Then you get very derivative literature. Very very literary literature. (My punctuation.)

[4]*Going Down Fast* (New York: Trident Press, 1969), p. 11. Subsequent references will be cited parenthetically in the text.

[5]*Dance the Eagle to Sleep* (New York: Doubleday, 1970), p. 5. Subsequent references will be cited parenthetically in the text.

[6]Letter, August 12, 1977, *Frontiers* 2, No. 3 (1977), 64.

[7]"The Ordeal of the Writer."

[8]*Small Changes* (Connecticut: Fawcett Crest Books, 1972), p. 14. Subsequent references will be cited parenthetically in the text.

[9]Robert Scholes, in an excellent article, "The Roots of Science Fiction," in *Science Fiction: A Collection of Critical Essays,* ed. Mark Rose, Twentieth Century Views (New Jersey: Prentice-Hall, 1976), p. 47, asserts: "Fabulation, then, is fiction that offers us a world clearly and radically discontinuous from the one we know, yet returns to confront that known world in some cognitive way."

[10]Pamela Sargent, in "Women in Science Fiction," her introduction to *Women of Wonder* (New York: Vintage Books, 1975), p. xiii, has this to say: "In the past, women, both as writers and as characters in sf novels and stories, were part of science fiction only sporadically. During the past twenty years, more women have entered the field. Some of them won acceptance initially by imitating the male writers, showing that they could do as well or better. Others explored the same material as male authors, but from a different perspective. There are signs that both female and male writers are beginning to work with new material and are questioning the assumptions which have dominated the field."

[11]*Woman on the Edge of Time* (Connecticut: Fawcett Crest Books, 1976), p. 68. Subsequent references will be cited parenthetically in the text.

[12]Carol Pearson in "Women's Fantasies and Feminist Utopias," *Frontiers,* 2, No. 3 (1977), 58, points out: "Feminist utopias are not only ecologically conscious, they assume a partnership between the natural and social world. A society which uses technology to work with the natural world rather than to "conquer it" produces a society which seems more pastoral and Edenic than a futuristic utopia."

[13]See the fascinating essay by Michael Holquist, "How to Play Utopia: Some Brief Notes on the Distinctiveness of Utopian Fiction," in *Science Fiction: A Collection of Critical Essays,"* pp. 132-146.

[14]*The High Cost of Living* (New York: Harper & Row, 1978), p. 266.

[15]"The Feminist Novel of Androgynous Fantasy," *Frontiers,* 2, No. 3 (1977), 40.

V Re-Creations

Norman N. Holland

You, U.K. Le Guin

WHEN I READ a novel as absorbing as *The Left Hand of Darkness,* I don't usually think about its author. Why, then, do I keep thinking out to you across the continent in Portland, OR? I think, in all honesty, it is because you are a woman. For someone whose airport reading these many years has been van Vogt, Sturgeon, Asimov, Dick, Blish and company, a woman writing science fiction is still a novelty. (Despite Joanna Russ or Suzy McKee Charnas.) And I wonder what kind of woman you are.

An old Bantam catalogue gives me the only picture I have: your portrait as part of an ad for *Orsinian Tales.* ("Orsino! I have heard my father name him.") Your cheekbone resting on one arm. Your strong wrist with pencil dutifully level on the paper for the photographer. An architectural position. A frank open face, close-cropped hair, broad cheekbones, planes between eyes and nose and upper lip, strong, dark direct eyes. A Western face. The desk is cluttered (as mine is) with books and papers. *Usage and Abusage.* (I don't know that one.) A box, "Current mail." Wedding ring, b. 1929. A lady of a certain age, like my wife. A stable, centered person.

*   *   *

Why all the cold? A whole planet of winter—Gethen, meaning "winter." Do you mean to imply sexlessness? That would be a bit crude. The Investigator from the Ekumen's first landing party thought it was the reason Gethenians did not make war: "The weather of Winter is so relentless, so near the limit of tolerability even to them with all their cold-adaptations, that perhaps they use up their fighting spirit fighting the cold. . . . in the end, the dominant factor in Gethenian life is not sex or any other human thing: it is their environment, their cold world. Here man has a crueler enemy even than himself."

Yet it is such a dominant image in the novel. From the first page to the last I am greeted by furred robes, fires, special eating habits, even a utensil for cracking the ice that has formed on your drink between sips—why did you put it there, Ukelele Lady? More accurately, how does it function in the thematic economy of the novel as a whole? Still more accurately, how do I integrate it into the rest of the novel?

Structure. Always think of the structure of a novel, they told me in graduate school. Here the novel alternates between two kinds of writing. First there is the straightforward telling of the story of Estraven and Genly and the Ekumenical embassy. Alternating with it are "transverse stories," folktales, creation myths, religious texts, a report from the first Investigator sent by the Ekumen, and so on. Then, the telling of the story is further divided. (A double doubled.) That is, we mostly hear the events of the novel in the first-person of Genly Ai, but starting with Chapter 11 we begin to hear a voice alternating with his: Estraven's. The alternation back and forth becomes strongest on the ice, when they are establishing their deep relation of friendship and trust. At times, I found it difficult for the first few paragraphs of the chapter to tell which of them was speaking.

The structure then (at least as I read it) mimics the double-doubled theme of the plot of the novel. First, there is the opposition between the Gethenians and the embassy, represented by Genly Ai and his ally Estraven. Then there is the relation between Estraven and Ai. The transverse stories, by giving us Gethenian culture, give me one opposition. The two first person speakers of the events of the novel give me the other.

*   *   *

But that's not what I'm really thinking about, U.K. Le Guin. Ukelele Lady (Dr. Jazz and the Ukelele Ladies being a Buffalo group). Le Guin. Guinevere. From Welsh *gwyn*, white: *hwyvar*, phantom. *Gwyn* is one of those words spun off from the incredible Indo-European root, *weid-* or *u(e)di-*: wit (you could write a history of English culture from the changes in that word's meaning), wisdom; vision; *eidos*, form, and all its spin-offs, idea, eidolon, idol; history; Rig-Veda—and on and on, oh white phantom. Here, in this book, the white phantom is a place on the journey across the glacier, the Unshadow:

> We stepped out of the tent onto nothing.... Estraven stood beside me, but neither he nor I cast any shadow. There was dull light all around, everywhere. When we walked on the crisp snow no shadow showed the footprint. We left no track. Sledge, tent, myself: nothing else at all. No sun, no sky, no horizon, no world. A whitish-gray void, in which we appeared to hang.

"No shadows. An even, white, soundless sphere: we moved along inside a huge frosted-glass ball. There was nothing inside the ball, and nothing was outside it." The place inside the Blizzard, where the body is wholly white, where the suicides live, shadowless and shamed.

By contrast, the elaborate Karhidish code of status (that substitutes for our macho contests) is *shifgrethor*: " 'It comes from an old word for *shadow*'." Except for the Unshadow, the other color on the glacier is the black of crag or distant mountain. Black as the dark alleyways of the escape from Ehrenrang; dark as in the night truck to the Orgota labor camp; black as "the void and terror and darkness" between the stars, so fearful to the Karhide King; black as Genly Ai himself (one of your little unexpected moves, U.K., that reveals the prejudgments in my tacit assumptions).

Around the white snow are the volcanoes: "Over Drumner in the dark now a great table of dull fire burns." "From time to time all things, clouds, icy rain, ice, air, would turn a dull red, then fade slowly back to gray." "The world's edge ... was a steep rubbly slope of white and red in a pallid noon light." White and red—the Renaissance's colors for a beautiful woman, but not here, not in this genderless world.

Red is the color of the palace: the King is "a short figure in the reddish gloom." "The face that turned towards me, reddened and cratered by firelight and shadow, was as flat and cruel as the moon, Winter's dull rufous moon." Estraven is given the Corner Red Dwelling as a mark of favor; it is taken away from him as a sign of his disgrace.

Palace red is treachery and murder. In the opening ceremony, the laying of a cornerstone, the King spreads red cement for the joint—a mortar of ground bones mixed with blood. In the transverse story about the question, On what day shall I die?, being asked of the Foretellers, the murder weapon is a red stone table. The Weaver who leads another group of Foretellers wears a scarlet cloak. I am startled to hear early in the novel that the hemmen, the commonest tree on the planet Winter, has "thick pale-scarlet needles," and I will be more deeply pained when Estraven dies after a day among "their reddish boughs bent low around us by loads of snow."

Red: the color of violence, murder, treachery, mystery, death.

White, black and red. The crossing of the ice has these three colors, a saga "from the sulphurous fire and dark of the pass between Drumner and Dremegole to the screaming gusts from mountain-gaps that swept the Bay of Gethen; with comic interludes ... and mystical ones, when he spoke of the sounds and silences of the Ice, of the shadowless weather, of the night's darkness."

White, black, and red—Robert Graves would tell us what they are: the colors of the Mother-Goddess. The three colors of the moon who defines the goddess' menses: the white or pale yellow of the full, high moon; the red of the moon close to the horizon; the black of the absent moon. But that is in Graves' man-and-woman world. Here, we have one gender and monthly kemmer. Nevertheless, the book speaks of "the dull-red halfmoon," and when Estraven—Harth (hearth?) is the more intimate name he lets Genly Ai use—goes into kemmer, "his face in the reddish light was as soft, as vulnerable, as remote as the face of a woman who looks at you out of her thoughts and does not speak."

Your own version, U.K., of the tradition, here on this genderless planet? Should I allegorize? White for the snow and ice that define the natural world of Gethen. Black as the darkness of night and as the shadow, emblem of a person's stature in the social world, visible, known to all. " 'We need the shadows, in order to walk'," says Estraven. Genly in reply draws the sign of Yin and Yang: "Light, dark. Fear, courage. Cold, warmth. Female, male. It is yourself, Therem. Both and one. A shadow on snow."

But then there is the red—*das ewige Weibliche*. Red, both of loveliness and of treachery—red for a palace murder to keep what one has. Faust's holding on to the moment. The eternal feminine: "To ignore the abstraction, to hold fast to the thing. There was in this attitude something feminine, a refusal of the abstract, the ideal, a submissiveness to the given, which rather displeased me"—so said Genly Ai. Holding on as the King holds on to his power and resists the reaching out to the Ekumen. Woman who holds her inner self complete within herself, not like man, at least as a Gethenian sees him. "There is a frailty about him. He is all unprotected, exposed, vulnerable, even to his sexual organ which he must carry always outside himself," muses Estraven about Genly.

From my point of view, though, the Gethenian must be always ambiguous, unpredictable, duplicitous—even more so than human women are said to be. Yet, despite my preconceptions, Estraven is not. Despite his completeness in himself, he reaches out for the Ekumen, for its "Increase of knowledge. The augmentation of the complexity and intensity of the field of intelligent life. The enrichment of harmony and the greater glory of God. Curiosity. Adventure. Delight." As the wise Faxe says, "The only thing that makes life possible is permanent, intolerable uncertainty: not knowing what comes next." The future is red.

*   *   *

Ursula K. Le Guin. An exotic name with its capitals, decisive *K.*, and the gap in the middle. "Gat-tothed was she?" "Ursula"—little she-bear. Orsinian. From the Greek, *arktos*, bear, yielding our *Arctic*. Or from the Celtic *arto-*, bear, yielding *Arthur*. But mostly I think of your father, maker of anthropological method, Alfred L.

Kroeber, and even more of your mother, Theodora, because of her book *Ishi in Two Worlds*, for so many of your books are between or "in" two worlds. Shevek, traveling between the mother and child planets of Urras and Anarres in *The Dispossessed*. The multiple universes of George Orr's dreams in *The Lathe of Heaven*. The underground night sky in "The Stars Below." Here, the twin countries of Karhide and Orgoreyn. Is Ehrenrang "Honor-rank?"

The anthropologist's mission: to explore the space between self and—what? The other's world. The space between father and other, mother and child, man and woman.

I think of a curious case, the last in a pop psychiatry book, Robert Lindner's *The Fifty-Minute Hour*. A physicist developed the delusion that he could teleport himself to another planet in a future time and bring back detailed records, maps, documents, and information of all kinds from that alien culture. The physicist had spent his earliest years on a Polynesian island where his father was Commissioner. His mother became apathetic under the tedious colonial routine and turned her child over to a Hawaiian nurse to whom the boy became utterly devoted. She in turn raised him in the warm, unclothed, sexually free style of her culture. The boy, in fact, spoke her language rather than English. On the small island where he was growing up, Kirk was the only white boy, in some respects treated as superior to the natives he went to school with, in others feeling a wall between him and them. The wall became a chasm when his beloved native nurse died. Other events in childhood contributed to his sense of alien worlds, but it was as an adult, when he began reading a series of science fiction novels in which the hero's name was the same as his own, that he began to spend a part of his life in that imaginary world. When the series of novels ran out, he took the decisive step of substituting his own discoveries through teleportation for those of the author. In effect, he re-created the alien culture of his lost childhood.

What about you, U.K. Le Guin? Is this some kind of a paradigm for the child who grew up "in two worlds" as an anthropologist's child might? I believe that a person acquires the drive we call artistic creativity in early childhood, when some artistic medium or activity becomes a central and habitual way of fulfilling the needs of inner and outer reality—becomes a central element in one's primary identity, the sameness that will run all through your life, that some people will think of as your style—you. For Hilda Doolittle, it was "making" through signs of a hieratic, mythological kind. For Scott Fitzgerald, it was having an experience and telling about it. For Robert Frost, it was managing big forces by small symbols.

For you, I think it is the act of naming—although I really have no good way of saying what I want to say. Putting things into words, perhaps. Putting things into words enables you to be two inconsistent things at once. "The novelist," you write, "says in words what cannot be said in words." "I am an artist ... and therefore a liar. Distrust everything I say. I am telling the truth." "The truth is a matter of the imagination." So that you are both. You are in two worlds at once, of both, but between both: a center that is not a center.

*   *   *

Gethen—Winter—is a planet of centers. "Humanity on the Great Continent of Gethen lives in a strip of land between two white walls. A further decrease of 8% in solar radiation, they calculate, would bring the walls creeping together; there would be no men, no land; only ice." At the center there is safety and life and warmth—yet ever so precariously so. "The centre cannot hold"—or can it? Can there be a center?

In the Orgota creation myth, men came out of a crevasse in the ice. The ice-shapes became the creators by saying, "I bleed," "I weep," "I sweat"—fluids from the melting of the ice. Life is fluid from a crevasse. How can I help seeing feminine symbolism? That is my problem throughout this book: in trying to conceive (yes, a pun) of these two-sexed people, I think of them as women—the Other. Yet you keep them poised between men and women—both, really. Centered rather than relegated to one pole or the other.

Gethenians structure time itself about such a center; they "always live in the Year One." That is,

In Karhide/Orgoreyn years are not numbered consecutively from a base year forward to the present; the base year is the current year. Every New Year's Day ... the year just past becomes the year "one-ago," and every past date is increased by one. The future is similarly counted, next year being the year "one-to-come," until it in turn becomes the Year One.

That way one does not ride on an arrow of time as we do, flying from past into future. Rather one stands at the center, looking from within at a receding past, looking equally from within toward an approaching future.

No wonder then that the King is afraid of time-jumps: "There's nothing in between the stars but void and terror and darkness, and you come out of that all alone trying to frighten me." That's *his* version of your theme of simultaneous sameness and separateness. "The people of Winter, who always live in the Year One, feel that progress is less important than presence." "If there are eighty thousand worlds full of monsters out there among the stars, what of it? We want nothing from them."

At the Center is life, presence—kindness. In the terrible, freezing night drive to the labor camp (so like the boxcars to the extermination camps),

... little by little we drew together and merged into one entity occupying one space, warm in the middle, cold at the periphery.

There was kindness. I and certain others ... were recognized as being least resistant to the cold, and each night we were at the center of the group, the entity of twenty-five, where it was warmest. We did not struggle for the warm place, we simply were in it each night.

"Meshe is the Center of Time." So begins an excerpt from a Gethenian religious book, one of your more beautifully vatic pieces of writing in this novel, Ukelele Lady. Meshe was a person who in one moment of his life, exactly thirty years after his birth and thirty years before his death, saw all things clearly. "And all the ages up until the Seeing were as long as the ages will be after the Seeing, which befell in the Center of Time. And in the Center there is no time past and no time to come. In all time past it is. In all time to come it is. It has not been nor yet will it be. It is. It is all. Nothing is unseen." This is a culture that finds its ultimate reality at the center, here thought of as that evanescent yet unchanging place of presence where one's changing self and the ever-different other meet, where the future tunnels into the past, where male and female are ambiguously poised. "As all the stars may be reflected in a round raindrop falling in the night: so too do all the stars reflect the raindrop. There is neither darkness nor death, for all things are, in the light of the Moment, and their end and their beginnings are one."

Is this a meaning for Estraven and Genly's winter journey across the glacier? "The good weather, you know, tends to stay over the great glaciers, where the ice reflects the heat of the sun; the storms are pushed out to the periphery. Therefore the legends about the Place inside the Blizzard." Not a mountain purification in the ordinary way of our writing, but a way for the two statesmen to situate themselves in the focal reality of Gethenian thought. "We are inside, the two of us, in shelter, at rest, at the center of all things. Outside, as always, lies the great darkness, the cold, death's solitude." Genly tells us he believes that is what "the real center of my own life is, that time which is past and lost and yet is permanent, the enduring moment, the heart of warmth." Is that the meaning of the cold in the novel? The cold of Otherness? (Even the Otherness who gives us birth?)

You, then, U.K., are our ambassador, like Genly Ai, at one neither with us nor with them—between, in your own center which is not theirs and not ours, but which you will make both.

For is it not the style of your stories to take a cold abstraction and turn it into a warm, centering relation of two people? You read the stories of others as "thought-experiments." "Let's say (says Mary Shelley) that a young doctor creates a human being in his laboratory; let's say (says Philip K. Dick) that the Allies lost the second world war; let's say this or that is such and so, and see what happens....thought and intuition can move freely within bounds set only by the terms of the experiment, which may be very large indeed." Perhaps, then, the act that energizes your own writing, that turns you on, is the transformation of abstraction into a relationship of thought and intuition. Some alienated two becoming one.

Let's say, instead of the world changing dreams, that dreams can change the world. Then we get *The Lathe of Heaven*, peeling off old histories and replacing them with new ones, until "To go is to return."

I think of my favorite among your stories, "April in Paris" (for I have loved that city, too). The modern American pedant; the medieval alchemist; Kislk, the beautiful archaeologist from Altair, 8000 A.D. (thank heaven they are still loving Paris); and Bota the Gaulish slave—two men, two women, and a little Parisian dog all come together in a fiery pentagram in a cold garret under the two great towers of Notre Dame. The pedant's abstract hypothesis about François Villon becomes friendship and love in a new and old space of past and future.

I think of your incredibly inventive "Direction of the Road." The great oak, who understands Relativity or, better, Relatedness, knows it is the trees' rushing along at sixty or seventy miles an hour that keeps the cars moving on the highway. It is the trees who have to strike and crush the cars who misplace themselves. It is the trees, therefore, who become construed as death, although they are life incarnate.

I think, Mme. Ambassador, you make it possible for me to turn an abstraction like relativity or time travel or double gender into relatedness: the sadness of a falsely accused tree; the joy of a middle-aged professor finding himself in Paris with truth and love; the love between Genly and Estraven, a bond born out of sexuality both accepted and declined. "It was from the difference between us, not from the affinities and likenesses, but from the difference, that that love came: and it was itself the bridge, the only bridge, across what divided us."

Is that your center—the creative joy at turning an Ekumen far off in space into a bridge between one-sexed and two-sexed people? Just the finding of a doubled doubling, a bond between one-sexed people and people who themselves have male and female doubled in their own centers? Is your enabling me to transform the abstractions I love to a human two-in-one I also love, is that the reason I enjoy your science fiction so much and your "mainstream" stories less?

I am saying, I think, that you are truly an ambassador because your theme of doubleness samed is precisely not mine, just as Genly and Estraven differ. Estraven recalls how "Ai brooded, and after sometime he said [to Estraven], 'You're isolated, and undivided. Perhaps you are obsessed with wholeness as we are with dualism'." I, certainly. I who directed a Center (for the Psychological Study of the Arts) am nevertheless obsessed with being on the outsides of things. " 'Duality is an essential, isn't it?,' " replies Estraven. " 'So long as there is *myself* and *the other*. I and Thou, he [Ai] said. 'Yes, it does, after all, go even wider than sex...'." Yes, I feel I have to assert the essential, separate me-ness of me against the merger, the one-ness, the unisex of this novel. And it is not a friendly act.

That most basic of dualisms requires, in the wise words of Marion Milner, "the primitive hating that results from the inescapable discrepancy between subjective and objective, between the unlimited possibilities of one's dreams and what the real world actually offers us...our whole traditional educational procedure tends to perpetuate this hate, by concentrating so much on only one half of our relation to the world, the part of it to do with intellectual knowing, the part in which subject and object have perforce to be kept separate" (*On Not Being Able to Paint*, p. 68).

...in the arts, although a bit of the outside world is altered, distorted from its 'natural' shape, to fit the inner experience, it is still a bit of the outside world, it is still paint or stone or spoken or written words or movements of bodies or sounds of instruments. It is still a bit of the outside world, but the difference is that work has been done, there has been a labour to make it nearer one's inner conception, not in the way of the practical work of the world, but in an 'as if' way. Thus it seemed that the experience of outer and inner coinciding, which we blindly undergo when we fall in love, is consciously brought about in the arts, through the conscious acceptance of the as-if-ness of the experience and the conscious manipulation of a malleable material. So surely it comes about that in the experience which we call the aesthetic one the cause of the primary hate is temporarily transcended. But not only is it temporarily transcended, surely also it is permanently lessened.... Since the object is thereafter endowed with a bit of the 'me,' one can no longer see it in quite the same way as before; and since the 'me,' the inner experience, has become enriched with a bit more of external reality, there is now a closer relation between wishes and what can really exist and so less cause for hate, less despair of ever finding anything that satisfies (*On Not Being Able to Paint*, pp. 131-32).

So Genly Ai is your ambassador, U.K., shaping a hateful, alien winter to himself so that you can show truth is a matter of the imagination. As Milner puts it (but she could be speaking for a generation of English psychoanalysts): "The substance of experience is what we bring to what we see, without our own contribution we see nothing." Thus, when I read your book, I can only do so to the extent that I bring something of myself to the Other who is you. You, the imaginer, the Weaver, provide me a way: "Space travel is one of these metaphors; so is an alternative society, an alternative biology; the future is another. The future, in fiction, is a metaphor. A metaphor for what?" And for whom?, I'd add. For me, it is a metaphor for that space where I, with my need to be separate, on the outside, male, can be for the long present of your book, one with an Other inside alien ice and pages, double-gendered. Then I, too, become an ambassador—from the kingdom of Me to your United Kingdom, U.K.

*   *   *

All the critics talk about gender in this novel, but, as you say, U.K., or rather, as you have your Estraven say, the ultimate Duality is "*myself* and *the other*." Genly agrees: " 'I and Thou,' he said. 'Yes, it does, after all, go even wider than sex....' " (I Freudianly wince. Symbolism like that we don't need.)

You speak of duality; I can put the theme in terms of completeness and incompleteness. It goes back to our earliest selves, unspeaking infants, who need the Other just to survive. Estraven remembers how he asked the ambassador's name "and heard for answer a cry of pain from a human throat across the night." Ai. But perhaps Ai also sounds the infant's cry for that Other, for it seems this whole novel reaches out for another—as Genly Ai's embassy is a reaching out from the Ekumen to cold, isolated Gethen. "...a Gethenian, being singularly complete..." Genry Ai, however, brings a sense of incompleteness. He needs something, an Other. His missing space ship, for example. A woman. "Gently, I..." " 'Genry Ai'—my name is Genly, but Karhiders can't say *l*." "Gen'ly I,...'? A name that is the beginnings of sentences. Incomplete.

Gethen, we learn, was nature's experiment in double gender. Hence, as Genly Ai says, " 'Your race is appallingly alone in its world. No other mammalian species. No other ambisexual species. No animal intelligent enough even to domesticate as pets." In that sense, Gethenians are incomplete. In the opposite sense, they are the only humans who are totally complete: both male and female. Yet, with their genitals inside, how would they look to an earthling like me? Incomplete, I think. The look of their genitals, however, is a subject on which you are discreetly silent. Or incomplete.

Genly knows mindspeech or telepathy, but it is particularly difficult for Estraven to learn. "Perhaps a Gethenian being singularly complete, feels telepathic speech as a violation of completeness, a breach of integrity hard for him to tolerate." Telepathy allows only perfect candor, perfect openness to the other between Genly and Estraven, yet at the end, in the moment of his dying, Estraven calls out in mindspeech to Arek, his lost, dead brother, as earlier, the first time he had heard Genly in his head in that perfect candor, he had cried, " 'Arek! is that you?' " He had had a child with this brother Arek; therefore he had had to exile himself from home to obey the incest taboo that permitted brothers to vow fidelity until the birth of one child but required them to part thereafter. Estraven, then, complete, double-gendered, yet longing for that other. He hears Genly in that other's voice. It is the missing other that he is waiting for even when he does not know he is waiting for someone.

It is Estraven's and Arek's son who pronounces the last sentences of the novel: " 'Will you tell us how he died?—Will you tell us about the other worlds out among the stars—the other kinds of men, the other lives?' " So the novel itself is incomplete. Genly Ai had begun it by saying, "I'll make my report as if I told a story, for I was taught as a child on my homeworld that Truth is a matter of the imagination." At the end, he promises to tell Estraven's father what he can of his friend's last days, in other words, the last third of the novel. " 'I should like to hear that tale, my Lord Envoy,' says old Esvans," but the boy breaks in and asks for another story, different from the one we have just read. This novel ends with the beginning of another, untold novel.

In a larger sense, though, all novels are incomplete that way, because they need a hearer to complete them. Your novel exists as a novel only as I—or someone else—make it into a novel. It is like a child, dependent for its very existence on an other; and, oddly, its final character will result from, will *be* the complex interaction of tale and hearer. Relationship again.

The Left Hand of Darkness talks about another kind of completing: patriotism. Is it the love of one's homeland or the fear of the other? In either case, I understand it as a relationship whose prototype is that earliest experience of otherness and incompleteness, here fulfilled through a nation's land, culture and language. The Ekumen is another way of completing—or trying to complete—the incomplete: its aims are "Material profit. Increase of knowledge. The augmentation of the complexity and intensity of the field of intelligent life. The enrichment of harmony . . ." and so on.

In short I can trace a theme of completing the incomplete through every phase of this novel. Genly Ai as ambassador aims to complete the Ekumen and to enable the Ekumen to complete Gethen. The doubled Gethenian gender is both complete and incomplete: "Room is made for sex, plenty of room; but a room, as it were, apart." Rather than being completely different, they have divided sexuality temporarily, isolating it into one sixth of the month, while we allow it all the time. "A strange lowgrade sort of desire it must be," muses Estraven, "to be spread out over every day of the year and never to know the choice of sex." Not one race complete, the other incomplete, but two races differently incomplete.

Deepest to me of all the completings is the relation of trust that has to be established between Genly Ai and Estraven. " 'It is strange'," says Estraven. " 'I am the only man in all Gethen that has trusted you entirely, and I am the only man in Gethen that you have refused to trust'." It is only after Estraven has rescued him from the labor camp and as they go out onto the ice that Genly knows he can trust the former prime minister.

Is that finally the meaning of the cold of Gethen? The symbol for our absolute need of an other, be it fire, tent, food (the Gethenians eat constantly), clothing, but above all perhaps a companion. Cold is wanting. "Here man has a crueler enemy even than himself." His own need.

As Estraven says to himself, "Up here on the Ice each of us is singular isolate, I as cut off from those like me, from my society and its rules, as he from his. There is no world full of other Gethenians here to explain and support my existence. We are equals at last, equal, alien, alone." Estraven has gone into kemmer and needs Ai sexually—but they do not take that route.

For it semed to me, and I think to him [Genly says to himself], that it was from that sexual tension between us, admitted now and understood, but not assuaged, that the great and sudden assurance of friendship between us rose: a friendship so much needed by us both in our exile and already so well proved in the days and nights of our bitter journey, that it might as well be called now as later, love. But it was from the difference between us, not from the affinities and likenesses, but from the difference, that that love came: and it was itself the bridge, the only bridge, across what divided us. For us to meet sexually would be for us to meet once more as aliens. We had touched, in the only way we could touch. We left it at that. I do not know if we were right.

Oh, U.K.! "We *left* it at that." Ye gods, were you conscious of your choice of idiom? I suppose so, for you put "right" in the next sentence, and you quote the key poem often enough:

Light is the left hand of darkness
and darkness the right hand of light.
Two are one, life and death, lying
together like lovers in kemmer,
like hands joined together,
like the end and the way.

Yet Estraven and Genly Ai are precisely *not* lying together like lovers in kemmer, but then the lines are also quoted by Arek in his letter to his brother before his death, and they *were* lovers in kemmer. Lovers and non-lovers, single and double-gendered—once more you double doubleness: you give us an incompleteness; you make it complete but paradoxically you give it a new incompleteness at the same time. Love comes out of difference, bridges difference, and leaves difference.

That is my feeling throughout the novel—a constant reaching out for completion. You give it to me, yet you simultaneously give me a need for completion again. I think that is why—to answer my opening question—I keep thinking about you. I don't usually think about authors, but reading this novel, my right, as it turns the paper pages, seeks an answer in your left, and I write this continent letter across a littered continent. I reach out to *you*, U.K. Le Guin, to join my hand to yours to re-create *The Left Hand of Darkness*.

Marleen S. Barr

Charles Bronson, Samurai, and Other Feminine Images: A Transactive Response to *The Left Hand of Darkness*

The criticism of literature originates in our personal experiences of individual works, and all criticism is a transformation of those experiences. This seems obvious, yet, implicitly or explicitly, it is the most frequently denied or avoided aspect of the professional study of literature. Indeed, the current crop of critical self-examinations of literary study yields a rich display of professional avoidance techniques.—Murray M. Schwartz[1]

A reader responds to a literary work by assimilating it to his own psychological processes, that is, to his search for successful solutions within his identity theme to multiple demands both inner and outer, on his ego.—Norman N. Holland[2]

Clearly face-saving was more important than honesty.——Genly Ai[3]

Brass Tacks I: Private "Feminine"* Personal Cost

> I'll [Genly] make my report as if I told a story, for I was taught...on my homeworld that Truth is a matter of the imagination. The soundest fact may fail or prevail in the style of its telling: like that singular organic jewel of our seas, which grows brighter as one woman wears it and, worn by another, dulls and goes to dust. Facts are no more solid, coherent, round, and real than pears are. But both are sensitive (LHD, p. 7).

TRUTH CAN BE a matter of the imagination on my homeworld too. I grew up with all of those television housewives. A great deal of my youth was spent watching women search for the correct laundry detergent while they glowed with victory at convincing their husbands to take out the trash. Such commercials portrayed an imaginative truth—no one could be *that* concerned with cleanliness.

I used to wonder—I still wonder—how some women could watch commercials and continue to view marriage as existence's culminating moment. Marriage was portrayed as life's "singular organic jewel." Pearls are made when an organism suffers: one grain of sand incessantly irritates the oyster. That's my conception of being a housewife—constant irritation coupled with an inability

138

to escape from a pesty metaphorical piece of sand.

Even though I'm single, I have felt my own version of these "solid," "round," "real" "pearls." In high school I didn't think much about "seas," but I was interested in attaining that perfect wave. Night after night I slept with hard round hair rollers irritating my scalp. Like the oyster, I suffered to create an aesthetically pleasing object.

Although I am sensitive about both this fact and other past "female" notions, I can't be characterized as a militant feminist who wishes to exclude marriage from her life. Ideally, I'd like to arrive at a compromise. For instance, I've noticed that after marriage some women "dull and go to dust" while others "grow brighter." It seems that those who don't crumble have a reason for living, a reason other than their husbands and children.

* * *

> *I [Genly] was in a parade.... Next come the lords and mayors and representatives.... If this is the Royal Music no wonder the kings of Karhide are all mad....King Argaven XV, in white tunic and shirt and breeches.... A goldfinger-ring is his only adornment and sign of office. Behind this group eight sturdy fellows bear the royal litter, rough with yellow sapphires, in which no king has ridden for centuries, a ceremonial relic of Very-Long-Ago.... Death walks behind the king (LDH pp. 8-9).*

The "parade" resembles a marriage ceremony. The king/bride is followed by a retinue, "lords and mayors and representatives" who allude to masculine power. Such power is quite apparent at a wedding where the bride's father gives her to a husband. The white clad, ringed king provides a further reason to recall matrimony.

After the ceremony a woman's wedding ring does become a sign of her office. She is now a wife, an individual entitled to all the respect and privileges coinciding with that position. Again, some women believe that marriage makes life complete.

The empty royal litter interests me. It is a relic from the past. The king/bride is now permitted to take charge of his own movement. Walking and abandoned custom brings a horrible practice to my mind: footbinding. As the following description shows, the similarity between this ancient tradition and the royal litter is striking:

The origins of Chinese footbinding...belong to that amorphous entity called antiquity.... The lady, unable to walk, remained properly invisible in her boudoir, an ornament, weak and small, a testimony to the wealth and privilege of the man who could afford to keep her—to keep her idle. Only on the rarest of occasions was she allowed outside of the incarcerating walls of her home and then only in a sedan chair behind heavy curtains.... The art of the shoe was basic to the sexual aesthetics of the bound foot.[4]

Le Guin's fairy tale like phrase, "Very-Long-Ago" brings the reality of "antiquity" to mind. A royal litter and bound feet both signify wealth and economic privilege. The litter "rough with yellow sapphires" bears some resemblance to the shoes which covered bound feet: jewels were sometimes sewn to these shoes.

An empty litter is a tangible object which can be linked to historical fact. Not so for the metaphysical image "death walks behind the king." This is indeed curious. Why should death be included in a ceremonial march? Does death belong at a wedding? Argaven's personality provides answers. This king who "was pregnant" (LHD p. 90) is an extremely feminine Gethenian. Unfortunately, for some women death—not marriage—proves to be the ultimate problem solver:

Death is our only remedy. We imagine heaven. There is no suffering there, we say. There is no sex there, we say. We mean there is no gender there. We dream that death will release us from suffering—from guilt sex and the body. We recognize the body as the source of our suffering. We dream of a death which will mean freedom from it because here on Earth, in our bodies, we are fragmented, anguished—either men or women, bound by the very fact of a particularized body to a role which is annihilating, totalitarian, which forbids us any real self-becoming or self-realization (WH p. 34).

* * *

...a stocky dark Karhider...wearing a heavy overtunic of green leather worked with gold...and a neck-chain of heavy silver links a hand broad—this person sweating heavily, replies, 'So it is'...the king begins to mortar the long joints of the keystone....The cement he uses is a pinkish color different from the rest of the mortarwork.... *(LHD pp. 10-11).*

Jewelry plays an important role in the first chapter; pearls, a gold ring, sapphires and now a silver neck chain. The chain differs from the other jewelry though. It is dainty, "feminine"; the bulky silver is obviously "masculine."

It is difficult for me to relate to this heavy neck chain. The adjective "heavy" is hardly ever used to describe women's jewelry. This word reminds me that I am not as free as a male. Literally, I am unable to secure a position involving mortar—heavy work; figuratively, I am not allowed to sweat. So it is.

Pink cement? Imagine a burly, sweaty male construction worker handling pink cement. The vision is as ironic as the idealized conception of a woman who never perspires.

* * *

*   *   *

> *He [Estraven] was a head shorter than I [Genly], and built
> more like a woman than a man, more fat than muscle; when
> we hauled together I had to shorten my pace to his, hold in
> my strength so as not to outpull him...There is a frailty
> about him [Genly]. He is all unprotected, exposed,
> vulnerable, even to his sexual organ which he must carry
> always outside himself; but he is strong....(LHD pp. 207,
> 216).*

Masculine strength images. I don't believe that it is easy for
women to forget the fact that men are physically stronger. Often,
when walking next to a man, it has been necessary for me to say,
"Slow down. You have bigger feet." Despite my mental work, mental
strength, and strength of character, my envy of men's physical
power lies beneath this remark's flippancy. If I were as strong as
most men, I would be that much less afraid to walk alone at night.

*   *   *

> *Cultural shock was nothing much compared to the
> biological shock I [Genly] suffered as a human male among
> human beings who were, five-sixths of the time,
> hermaphroditic neuters....Among my fellow prisoners I
> had also for the first time on Winter a certain feeling of
> being a man among women....I [Estraven] will be in
> kemmer in a day or so, and all strains will increase (LHD pp.
> 51, 169, 218).*

Readers have felt that Le Guin's Gethenians resemble men
instead of androgynous wholes: "I receive [frequent criticism] that
Gethenians seem like men, instead of menwomen."[5] I do not feel
that such criticism is entirely valid. The whole Gethenian society
must cope with a repetitious biological manifestation. This natural
occurrence is definitely feminine; young women and Gethenians
both cannot escape biological cycles.

There is also a value in creating a male envoy. The female is an
aberration in our phallocentric society. Genly, our masculine norm,
is an oddity on Gethen. Le Guin was "privately delighted at
watching not a man, but a manwoman, do all these 'masculine'
things, and do them with considerable skill and flair" (IGN p. 138). I
took pleasure in seeing a man as the social exception for a change. It
is not necessary for me to read a novel to view woman as The Other.
Genly's surname shows just how much differences can hurt.

*   *   *

> *Normal individuals have no predisposition to either sexual
> role in kemmer; they do not know whether they will be the
> male or the female, and have no choice in the matter....No*

> *physiological habit is established, and the mother of*
> *several children may be the father of several more . . . no one*
> is quite so thoroughly 'tied down' here as women, elsewhere,
> *are likely to be—psychologically or physically. Burden and*
> *privilege are shared out pretty equally; everybody has the*
> *same risk to run or choice to make. Therefore nobody here is*
> *quite so free as a free male anywhere else (LHD pp. 90, 91,*
> *93).*

I envy Gethenians. Unlike myself, they are sometimes free of pregnancy's biological specter. I will always be the female.

Often, I think about having children. After all, these are my prime childbearing years—years that will never come again. Yet I quickly dismiss these thoughts. I do not presently have the time to devote to raising a child. Children? I barely have enough time now to give to casual relationships.

This comment illustrates that professionalism is independent of gender. If I were a male, I would also spend large numbers of weekend evenings writing. But, when I compare myself to a successful friend of mine, it is quite evident that he is in a superior position. He is the father of four books, two children and numerous articles. He had his son when he was twenty-four, one year younger than my present age. Rather, his wife had his son. His wife carried the baby and cared for the baby; he finished his dissertation and took a job as an assistant professor. Since he is not bound to the domestic and biological burdens coinciding with children, he has the opportunity to devote himself fully to his career.

I am as free to pursue my career as he is—as long as I do not become a mother. Nobody will be *my* wife; nobody can take the time to have *my* children. Although academic success is of the utmost importance to me, when I hear of his achievements, I am more happy for him than envious of him. Yet, when I recently saw the latest pictures of his children, I felt a great deal of that aforementioned emotion: envy. He can enjoy a career and children; he has the best of both worlds. I had to make a choice, an obvious choice. Academe is not made for mothers.

A popular women's magazine states a wry corollary to my sentiments: "The one absolute alternative to the possibility of needing an abortion is to be born a man. An additional advantage of being born male is the time saved by not having to worry about becoming pregnant—which can be usefully spent becoming secretary of Health, Education, and Welfare and making policies designed to keep women busy worrying."[6] Again, men's saved time leads to professional success.

* * *

*I [Genly] suppose the most important thing, the heaviest
single factor in one's life, is whether one's born male or
female. In most societies, it determines one's expectations,
activities, outlook, ethics, manners—almost
everything....It's extremely hard to separate the innate
differences from the learned ones. Even where women
participate equally with men in the society, they still after
all do all the childbearing and most of the child-rearing....
A man wants his virility regarded, a woman wants her
femininity appreciated, however, indirect and subtle the
indications of regard and appreciation. On Winter they will
not exist. One is respected and judged only as a human
being. It is an appalling experience (LHD pp. 223, 94).*

Yes, being born female has had a social and biological influence
upon me. But I must say that so far, gender has not been "the most
important thing, the heaviest single factor" in my academic life.
Almost without exception, male instructors have taken my work
seriously. (I have not been taught by female professors in graduate
school.)

Work, my professional goals, take precedence over my
relationships with men. I want to be equal, and, if "equal" means
that I cannot have children in the near future, so be it. (It's a good
thing that the vast majority of women do not think like me—
enrollment levels would fall even lower.) Naturally, I do want my
femininity to be appreciated. Yet, I would not find it appalling to be
treated solely as a human being—I might welcome it.

* * *

*In such fortunate moments as I fall asleep I know beyond
doubt what the real center of my own life is, that time which
is past and lost and yet is permanent, the enduring moment,
the heart of warmth (LHD p. 227).*

I conclude this section of the essay with a strong response. I
think I am aware of the center of my life and I am trying to be happy
with it. Of course, I have sacrificed—sacrificed time. To date, my
entire adult life has revolved around the university. There have been
many times that are past and lost: social time, reproductive time.
But, I idealistically believe that eduational experience is lasting.
Unlike a party, unlike a child or even a spouse, my knowledge will
definitely stay with me as long as I live. A moment can only endure
on a printed page which transcends time in a way human relations

and children do not. The thought of creating such pages fills my heart with warmth. For me, private feminine personal cost coincides with personal gain and personal satisfaction.

The crew of Genly's ship established their own definition of time. The books I read—and the ones I intend to write—are my time machine. Like Genly, I must be patient.

* * *

Brass Tacks II: Institutional "Masculine" Public Achievement

> *This is a hard age we live in, an ungrateful age...he [Genly] does not and perhaps never will understand the foundations of power and the workings of government in that kingdom. No doubt this was all a matter of 'shifgrethor'—prestige, face, place the pride-relationship, the untranslatable and all-important principle of social authority in Karhide and all the civilizations of Gethen (LHD p. 14, 19).*

Here, I must deviate from the intensely personal to step back from myself, look at my associations and chuckle. I can't believe that it is possible to see so many things in terms of academic experience. For example, when I read "a hard age" an "ungrateful age" I think about the job market. I think about the truth: America can do without literature and literary critics.

Regardless, English departments are important to me. They definitely do have political "foundations of power"—an academic "shifgrethor" that is beyond an outsider's comprehension. As one critic has observed, "Universities were more like political organizations, microcosmic nations of a very special sort.... The appropriate training would have to be a special political training.... Life in academe is marked by periodic rituals of ascension and ordeal."[7] There most certainly is a hierarchy of social authority in any particular English department and in all the departments of academe.

* * *

> *I [Genly] was alone, with a stranger, inside the walls of a dark palace, in a strange snow-changed city, in the heart of the Ice Age of an alien world.... I've been cold ever since I came to this world.... Two years I had spent on this damned planet, and the third winter had begun before autumn was underway—months and months of unrelenting cold, sleet, ice, wind, rain, snow, cold, cold inside, cold outside, cold to the bone and the marrow of the*

bone (LHD pp. 23, 25, 128).

Buffalo, Buffalo, Buffalo. (Stop snickering—everyone always snickers when I mention Buffalo.) Well, how else did you expect me to react? Two years ago I came to this alien city. (I'm a New Yorker, hence, anything across the Hudson, is, by definition, alien.) No sooner did I unpack, then, plunk, the Great Blizzard of '77 fell down on my head. According to me, it hasn't stopped snowing since. So help me God, today is May 1 and there are flurries. I really did expect it to snow in Irvine California last summer.

* * *

I'm [Genly] not much taller than the Gethenian norm, but the difference is most noticeable in a crowd....more and more often I longed for anonymity, for sameness. I craved to be like everybody else...(LHD pp. 13-14).

Since I was twenty-three, when I first read a paper at a conference, the age difference separating the crowd from me was very noticeable. I was painfully aware of this difference; I am still aware of it. It seems that I'm always younger than everyone. I feel this most strongly when sitting in a restaurant conversing with people ten and twenty years my senior. Often, during such conversations, I want to be like everyone else, to somehow close my glaring experiential gaps.

For me, age is analogous to gender: it is another boundary to be rendered insignificant. I demand more than even Gethen.

* * *

Estraven, Lord of Estre in Kerm, by this order forfeits title of the Kingdom,...and is commanded to quit the Kingdom and all Domains of Karhide....No countryman of Karhide shall...speak to him or stay within his house or on his lands....Estraven's behavior...[was] that of a man once powerful and now fallen, who grasps at any chance to influence person or events—always less rationally, more desperately, as time passes and he knows himself sinking into powerless anonymity. I [Genly] agreed that this would explain Estraven's anxious, almost frantic manner. The anxiety had however infected me...I...felt a pang of pure pity for the man whom I had seen in yesterday's parade...a man at the prime of his career,...gone now, down, done (LHD pp. 33, 158-9, 44).

Here Estraven is reminiscent of the unfortunate assistant professor who is denied tenure. The following comment states that a person in this position is treated as an excluded, untouchable, castoff; the system does in fact resemble both India's social stratification and the terms of Estraven's exile:

But should the candidate fail the test of promotion...he is, though present, already a pariah.... And the pariah imagines himself as having lost substance. He is unseen in the halls, an ectoplasm floating into the office to obtain his mail. His social life changes, and he declines invitations, even to official functions.... Yet the pariah does not always go quietly and by degrees.... Certain pariahs have been known to go into the desert of student rumor and activisim, returning with a brand of ragged followers to storm the trible enclave (AT pp. 90-91).

As an undergraduate, I knew someone who behaved this way after his contract was terminated. I can still recall his facial expression as I helped him move his books out of the office, remove his name from the door. I watched him grow less rational, more withdrawn as he desperately clung to the idea that student support would sway the tenure committee's decision. This once popular, outspoken teacher became lonely and anonymous. I will never forget his situation and his anxiety. I experienced sympathy pains; I felt the pain of a departmental knife slowly turning in my back; I feel the pain now, again, as I recall the past. Thus, I had a secondhand encounter with academic agony before I ever experienced the ecstatic high of successful scholarly achievement.

The dismissed professor is removed from a department and collegial social gatherings; Genly's ship is not immediately allowed to land on Gethen. Academic and political failure, then, are analogous to being excluded from a place.

* * *

What next?... He [Estraven] had been saying, however indirectly, that I should get away from the city and the court.... The king had given me the freedom of the country; I [Genly] would avail myself of it. As they say in Ekumenical School, when action grows unprofitable, gather information; when information grows unprofitable, sleep. I was not sleepy (LHD p. 45).

I have had my low points too. After I completed my M.A., a professor of mine intimated that I should leave Ann Arbor, take a rest from academe. Armed with an unmarketable degree and a lack of teaching experience, I didn't have anywhere else to go. So, I stayed and became a bookstore clerk. This was futile. I couldn't make enough money to support myself and I was wasting my time.

My parents came to the rescue. They offered to support me if I agreed to spend my working hours reading and writing. So, under the sharp eye of my professor, I spent a year studying in the University of Michigan's library. The actions of clerking and job hunting were unprofitable; I gathered information. This activity still has not tired me.

A Tertium Quid: The Sharpest Projection of Them All

> For it seemed to me, [Genly] and I think to him, [Estraven] that it was from that sexual tension between us, admitted now and understood, but not assuaged, that the great and sudden assurance of friendship between us rose: a friendship so much needed by us both in our exile, and already so well proved in the days and nights of our bitter journey, that it might as well be called, now as later, love. But it was from the difference between us, not from the affinities and likenesses, but from the difference, that that love came: and it was itself the bridge, the only bridge, across what divided us. For us to meet sexually would be for us to meet onece more as aliens. We had touched, in the only way we could touch. We left it at that. I do not know if we were right (LHD p. 235).

A discussion of gender in *The Left Hand of Darkness* cannot afford to omit the question of Genly's and Estraven's mutual sexual attraction. Their resolution belongs in the middle ground between my personal "feminine" self and my "masculine" public world. Any further personal reactions to this passage are too deep to say directly.

Let me cope by reaching out to Marion Milner. Listen to her voice while mine is silenced. Her comment provides an illustrative example of the passage's point: "Did it mean that there are moments in which one does not have to decide which is one self and which is the other—moments of illusion, but illusions that are perhaps the essential root of a high morale and vital enthusiasm for living— moments which can perhaps be most often experienced in physical love combined with in-loveness, but also which need not always require bodily contact and physical sexual experience, but which can be imaginatively experienced in an infinite variety of contacts with the world?"[8] Genly and Estraven share a moment of "in-loveness" which omits bodily contact; instead of physical connection, a shared understanding of a harsh environment's physical reality binds the pair together. In the instance of their exclusion of erotic physicality, a sexually Janusian Gethenian undergoes an experiential, homospatial merger with a human male.[9]

Their metaphysical merger transcends sexuality and moves beyond stereotypes. In our society, as well as on Gethen, sexual intercourse does not necessarily coincide with the expression of the highest degree of human emotion. It is possible to sleep with someone, wake up, look at the person and see a stranger; it is possible to avoid sex and share a deep sense of mutually understanding concern. Genly and Estraven never become half of a divided whole, mere components of Shakespeare's "beast with two backs." They are complete unto themselves in regard to their relationship. Although they never become lovers, the two are comrades. And that is most important:

> ...it [LHD] turns the alien encounter into a consideration of human sexuality, and of the ways that their male and female attributes make men and women perpetually foreign to one another.... But above all it explores the way human beings relate to one another.... The fantastic displacement of human sexual mores is used by Le Guin to make her readers perceive that humans rely on sexual stereotyping for much of their identities.... The alien encounter has been subtly altered by Le Guin until it becomes the obvious metaphor for relations between the human sexes.... We *are* of two sexes, in some senses doomed to alien extremes, and we must make a special effort to see one another as humans who can work together and be friendly without always falling into sexually stereotyped patterns of behavior.[10]

Thus, the novel finally stresses human unity instead of the dichotomous nature of "masculine" and "feminine" sexual stereotypes. And, hence, the passage describing the protagonists' solution to their social quandary appropriately has a place in both my public and personal spheres of experience.

A Justification and Definition of Transactive Criticism: Or, One Reader Describes Herself and Her Reading

My particular re-creation of Le Guin's novel adheres to Norman N. Holland's insistence that "... it becomes useless and impossible to separate the act of reading from the creative personality of the reader" (5RR, p. 123). For the benefit of readers who might be unfamiliar with Holland's work—or, to reply to those who cannot abide transactive criticism—I digress from responding to LHD to explain and justify this critical methodology. It is useful to begin by referring the reader back to the quotations which appear at the start of this essay.

Denied? Avoided? I can certainly understand such tactics. If I respond to this novel by making it a part of my psychological process, if I react "in terms of [my] own 'lifestyle' (or 'character' or 'personality' or 'identity')" (5RR p. 8), then, quite simply, if I cast "professional avoidance techniques" to the winds, I must tell *you* about *me*. Although such self-revelation is far from easy for me, I have resolved to take the plunge. Nevertheless, like a swimmer who gingerly places her/ his big toe in a cool lake on a brisk morning, I had to acclimate slowly throughout the course of my work with Holland.

Like any responsible swimmer, I find myself resorting to the "buddy system." Holland is more adept and experienced than I in moving counter to strong professional currents. He has gone before:

I read this story ["The Purloined Letter"] when I was thirteen and I also had something to hide, something that is perfectly known to anyone who knows anything at all about thirteen-year-old boys. Most obvious, yet most carefully concealed.... It cost me something to admit to you that I masturbated, even thirty-six years ago and at an age when all boys do. It costs me nothing to say a little brass knob stands for the clitoris.[11]

Holland clearly does not feel that "face-saving was more important than honesty."

Thus, transactive criticism is personal and carries the potential of emotional cost. There is also a model of reading behind the idea of associating freely to texts. It is useful to mention Holland's description of this model:

I intend a criticism which takes as its subject matter, not the text in supposed isolation, as the New Criticism claimed it did, but the *transaction* between the reader and the text. In other words, I would like to see a criticism which frankly acknowledges, accepts, and uses the critic's role in his own experience.... Whenever we experience something ostensibly outside ourselves we do so by re-creating ourselves through that something.... Identity re-creates itself or, it is perhaps clearer to say, personal style creates itself.... People seek out in the literary work what they characteristically wish and fear, and they deal with it by whatever in the literary work they can adapt to make their characteristic ego strategies.... Indeed, the only way anyone can ever discover unity in text or identity in selves is by creating them from one's own inner style, for we are all caught up in the general principle that identity creates and re-creates itself as each of us discovers and achieves the world in his own mind.[12]

Although we psychologically achieve differing worlds, all people share basic similarities: everyone must eat, sleep and breathe. (Ah! unobjectionable biological examples.) The activities we hold in common bring an element of reassurance to the type of criticism` which acknowledges the critic's experiential role. In other words, Holland admitted an intensely personal activity. Did this information shock you? It shouldn't have. As he implies, his statement is not very surprising. Most everyone masturbates. Sometimes the personal can be blatantly obvious.

Here is one more illustration of this point: "Once I [Holland] could contemplate the death the poem describes as a comfortable pantheistic abstraction.... Now, however, I bring to the poem more experience of the losses and deteriorations of middle age."[13] These words do not reveal a jarring personal secret. If you never met the man, you could find his birthday in *The Directory of American Scholars*. What middle-aged individual has failed to contemplate old age, deterioration, and death?

Of course, I lean on Holland's professional authority to assuage the difficulty of explaining my own wild and woolly, the previously nonpublicly explored realm of my identity:

> In effect, we can read one another like music, hearing ourselves play our lives like variations on a melody, an identity theme which is, quite simply, our very essence.... All my acts perceptions and relationships are functions of my identity...for that is what identity is: my thematic sameness plus my variations on it. My relation to the poem includes both my emotions and my characteristic use of the critic's discipline. It is precisely because I feel emotion toward the poem that I can re-imagine it in my own characteristic use.... Identity theory enables me to understand the interaction of firm critical hypotheses with exciting shimmering fields of personal knowledge. This third phase is not a retreat to subjectivity. It is giving up the illusion that I can only understand reality (or a text) by keeping myself out" (LI pp. 230-231).

An explanation of my identity and its relationship to Le Guin's novel begins with the obvious: I am a female. This deceptively simple statement is fraught with contradictions to the stereotypical notions routinely evoked by the word "female." My point is clarified as I continue: I am a female who has finished my dissertation. I am a woman pursuing an academic career. Hence, "masculine" characteristics circumvent the "feminine." Le Guin's conception of these terms helps to explain my point: "... the driving linearity of the 'male,' the pushing forward to the limit, the logicality that admits no boundary—and the circularity of the 'female,' the valuing of patience, ripeness, practicality, livableness" (IGN, p. 135). I have been described as "driven"; I often push myself to my limit. For me, this behavior is logical. Predictably, I cannot tolerate the thought of going around in circles: making breakfast, washing dishes, two more meals, two more sets of dishes. I certainly would never spend all of my energy doing this for a family year after year—I don't have the patience. Youthful ripeness be damned; a baby would presently be a hindrance. Practicality? Anyone who has pursued a Ph. D. in English is definitely not practical. And, as far as livableness is concerned, I'm perfectly livable—with the sort of person who enjoys the incessant sound of a typewriter reverberating in his ears. Hence, like most career-oriented women, my identity lacks many stereotypically feminine aspects.

Holland is an observer who sees me in a similar light:

> I [Holland] am at a loss to find feminine images for you.... You are a professional. That's the only word I can use, although I know what Robin Lakoff says about calling a woman a professional. I mean it only in the sense I would call a Charles

Bronson gunslinger or a Toshiro Mifune samurai a professional—someone who is right on target with no wasted motion. You are a professional student to my professor. You are a professional professor to your students, yet you can learn from them. Learning and professing—that's *it*. And you are startled to see one of your Irvine profs swimming up to you.... Yet I feel you have said enough to tell me and the rest of us that there are other things in your life beside studenting and professing, but you say so, so very guardedly. I feel switched abruptly back to the academic track. Are you like me in having trouble finding a middle ground, a space that is not bound down to the paper chase of text and not deeply intimate, a *tertium quid*.[14]

Thus, I am a highly motivated, direct professional "masculine" person who sometimes falls in love. I could feel at home on Gethen.

This is not to say that I cannot be characterized by "feminine" images. These images are apparent in my relationship with Holland. I view him as an exemplar of "someone who is right on target with no wasted motion." I cannot help trying to learn from his example. I look up to him and see an academic hero—a perfect professorial father figure. But, unlike Holland, I cannot relate to the text in terms of middle age or the activities of male adolescence; I cannot avoid *my* own unique response, that of a twenty-five year old woman who is steeped in the ceremonines of the academic tribe.

I must also explain the structure of my re-creations. Again, I refer to Holland:

What does interpretation through the third phase of psychoanalysis look like? It could look like...a conscious in-mixing of the features of the poem with my own feelings of guilt and punishment, my personal achievement of generality and intimacy. It could look like that but it need not. There can be as many readings as there are readers to write them. Can be and should be. For criticism from the third phase of psychoanalysis risks intimacy in order to restore individuality. The best interpreters will speak from self-knowledge as well as from knowledge of literature. How to do this? That, the third phase tells us, we each will have to find for ourselves (LI p. 233).

I have found this out for myself. Like Le Guin, I wish to "define and understand the meaning of sexuality and the meaning of gender, in my life and in our society" (IGN p. 130). The structure I've chosen stems from a coupling of this wish with the novel's balance of "public achievement against personal cost," its concern for "public and private imperatives."[15]

A Threefold Conclusion: On *The Left Hand of Darkness*, Transactive Criticism—and Feminist Literary Theory

Le Guin has characterized LHD as an experiment: "It was a heuristic device, a thought experiment.... One of the essential functions of science fiction, I think, is precisely this kind of question-asking: reversals of an habitual way of thinking, metaphors for what our language has no words for as yet, experiments in the imagination.... I eliminated gender to find out what was left" (IGN pp. 132-33). Her experiment led me to further questioning: What will result when critics of both sexes create personal responses to the fictitious eradication of gender? One thing is certain: free and open self-expression is an integral aspect of the answer to this question.

Another question occurs to me. Although this essay has included a justification of transactive criticism, some readers may want to know why this theory is especially pertinent to LHD. Jeanne Murray Walker's recent essay on myth, exchange, and history in this novel helps me provide an explanation:

...the myths in LHD assert the impossibility of retreating from history and from human society. They insist that the goal of 'keeping to oneself' in a fixed, temporal place is an impossible fantasy, a fantasy that must be sacrificed to the demands of communal exchange in history. In her [Le Guin's] myths...the oppositions define human problems, particularly problems with exchange; their mediation creates or maintains community.... The novel thus locates significance not in some static, timeless place, but in history; and its myths reflect social ideals which continually—and with difficulty—emerge from that history.[16]

Like LHD, transactive criticism discourages the goal of keeping to oneself. And, both the novel and the theory articulate the history of individuals seeking solutions to inner and outer—or private and social—demands: LHD concerns a male envoy's desire to exchange the Ekumen's communal values for a genderless world's insistence upon nationalism; my transaction with the novel reveals a refusal to exchange my individualistic career goals for my society's prevailing antifeminist notions. This dominant theme is evident throughout my response. Just as the Gethenians lack gender consequences or limit sexuality to kemmer, I am saying that by becoming a professional, I elude or localize the consequences of gender in our society. I seek a mediation between the implications of "female" and the definition of "professional."

A solution to this human problem is emerging—with difficulty— at this time in American history. In this essay, a female critic's transaction with a female writer's work calls attention to the problem's consequences. The essay, then, illustrates a reason for my hope that feminist critics will not completely dismiss the theories generated by the male critical establishment as they strive to create a new feminist criticism. After all, I have articulated my personal feminine statement by combining my thoughts with a man's critical notion and a woman's creative vision. This statement has acquainted me with a truth which is very familiar to Holland and Genly: "to be close with another person, you must unseal yourself in a world of perhaps indifference or perhaps intrusion. Either way, you must risk yourself, but it is worth it, because you can gain both intimacy and the safety of a larger being" (LI p. 233).

Notes

* I place such words within quotation marks when referring to their stereotypical meanings.

[1]Murray M. Schwartz, "Where Is Literature?," *College English,* 36 (1975), 756.

[2]Norman N. Holland, *5 Readers Reading* (New Haven: Yale University Press, 1975), p. 28. Hereafter referred to by 5RR and page number.

[3]Ursula K. Le Guin, *The Left Hand of Darkness* (New York: Ace Books, 1969), p. 20. Hereafter referred to by LHD and page number.

[4]Andrea Dworkin, *Women Hating* (New York: E.P. Dutton, 1974), pp. 95-105. Hereafter referred to by WH and page number.

[5]Ursula K. Le Guin, "Is Gender Necessary?," in *Aurora: Beyond Equality,* ed. Susan Janice Anderson and Vonda N. McIntyre (Greenwich, Conn.: Fawcett, 1976), p. 135. Hereafter referred to by IGN and page number.

[6]Jane O'Reilly, "The Way We Live Now: Okay Mr. Califano, Consider the Alternatives to Abortion," *Ms.,* May 1978, p. 76.

[7]Hazard Adams, *The Academic Tribes* (New York: Liveright, 1976), pp. 2, 77. Hereafter referred to by AT and page number.

[8]Marion Milner, *On Not Being Able To Paint,* 2nd ed. (New York: International Universities Press, 1957), p. 29.

[9]Albert Rothenberg describes Janusian thinking as "the capacity to conceive and utilize two or more opposite or contradictory ideas, concepts, or images simultaneously." "The Process of Janusian Thinking in Creativity," *Archives of General Psychiatry,* 24 (1971), 195. Thus, Gethenians are a Janusian combination of the sexual oppositions existing between men and women. Rothenberg defines Homospatial thinking as consisting of "actively conceiving two or more discrete entites occupying the same space, a conception leading to the articulation of new identities." Further, "as a creative process, the major function of Homospatial thinking is unification and integration of Janusian thoughts, and unification of diverse other aspects of the product being created.... Homospatial thinking, when it functions together with Janusian thinking, serves to integrate the specific opposites and antitheses and fuse the encapsulated domain." "Homospatial Thinking In Creativity," *Archives of General Psychiatry,* 33 (1976), 17, 26. Genly and Estraven meet on the ice in Homospatial mental unity.

[10]Robert Scholes and Eric S. Rabkin, *Science Fiction: History Science Vision* (New York: Oxford University Press, 1977), pp. 226-30.

[11]Norman N. Holland, "Re-Covering 'The Purloined Letter': Reading as a Personal Transaction," Lecture, Department of Comparative Literature, University of Toronto, 24 February 1977. Hereafter referred to by PL and page number.

[12]Norman N. Holland, "Transactive Criticsm: Re-creation Through Identity," *Criticism,* 18 (1976), 334, 352.

[13]Norman N. Holland, "Literary Interpretation and Three Phases of Psychoanalysis," *Critical Inquiry,* 3 (1976), 22. Hereafter referred to by LI and page number.

[14]Norman N. Holland, mimeographed response, English Graduate Seminar, SUNY/Buffalo, Fall 1977.

[15]John Huntington states, "LHD balances public achievement against personal cost, and Le Guin, dismissing neither, maintains the dialectical tension between them.... In all her work Le Guin probes in various ways for the point at which the public and the private imperatives intersect, for the act that will allow them to be unified, if only momentarily.... LHD stands apart from Le Guin's other works hovering in its extraordinary balance and its commitment to both of the rival imperatives.... LHD renders a basic allegiance to private humane values without denying the degree to which public institutional values influence and limit private ones." "Public

and Private Imperatives in Le Guin's Novels," *Science-Fiction Studies,* 7(1975), 240.

[16]Jeanne Murray Walker, "Myth, Exchange and History in *The Left Hand of Darkness,*" *Science-Fiction Studies* 6 (1979), 187.

VI Fiction and Other Art Forms

Edward Whetmore

A Female Captain's Enterprise: The Implications of *Star Trek*'s "Turnabout Intruder"

CRITICISM OF TELEVISION content has often come from individuals who are steeped in the written word. With some relish, they apply literary aesthetic criteria and judge the medium to be woefully deficient. Thus, by definition, the content of electronic media must "fall short." The very measuring devices are derived from a print tradition in many ways alien to television.

McLuhan reminds us that "in the name of progress our official culture is striving to make the new media do the work of the old."[1] This "official culture" is comprised of both network programmers and their critics. The networks supply programming with content borrowed from literature, while the critics evaluate TV in terms derived from that same tradition. Fair enough? Perhaps, but does this really afford us an understanding of the intricate relationship between media content and audience?

A second body of research has evolved from those in the social sciences. Borrowing techniques from psychology and sociology, it analyzes TV content in terms of its empirically *measurable* effects on the audience. While these techniques provide valuable information, they leave us unable to authoritatively discuss the *total* impact of TV. There are too many scientific constraints to adequately approach such a rapidly changing and volatile medium.

The bulk of material attempting to understand television's role in the sex role socialization process exemplifies this point. Busby[2] reviewed over 100 studies in the area. Most involved television ads since these provide a larger "N" for the social scientists. Typically, they found that 90.1% of all doctors in ads are men, while 58% of all women in ads are housewives. While this information has been useful in pointing up some problems in TV content, it does not address the larger question of television programs and their characters, and, significantly, the relationships that develop between the audience and these characters. Busby concluded that content analysis was not enough. This was the same conclusion that guided Whetmore's "Androgyny and Sex Role Perception in

Television Situation Comedies."[3] The study analyzed specific reactions to character sex role stereotyping, comparing them with individual sex role self-assessments.

Even this more sophisticated approach employed methodology that necessitated ignoring a number of crucial variables. Character motivation, development and behavior have largely been omitted because they are virtually unmeasurable, too "subtle" to consider. This leaves us back where we started—with the literary tradition. Busby notes that "since the same cultural influences have influenced writers, producers, directors and publishers, it is not surprising to find a similarity of sex role imagery across media."[4] More importantly, since television borrowed so heavily from literature, we find it now overtly reinforces stereotypic notions about masculine and feminine behavior.

The present article proposes a third approach to understanding television content: an examination of character behavior in a social science context which lacks the "aesthetic" criteria borrowed from literary criticism. Though this approach is hardly revolutionary, it does enable us to focus on a single show or character, and discuss that character's social impact without being confined by methodology requiring a greater formality.

Science fiction purists often shudder when *Star Trek* is mentioned. It is true that the program was not really science fiction in the literary sense. It was science fiction in the television sense. Yet, few TV shows borrowed more heavily from literature. Hark's *Quotations and Allusions in Star Trek*[5] lists over 100 specific instances of such "borrowing" with material ranging from Ovid to Shakespeare.

Much has been made of the pioneering role of *Star Trek*'s women. There were some steps forward given the medium's commercial constraints and the attitudes of the mid 1960s. The ship's communication officer was female as were a number of guest commanders. (Usually this provided romantic interest for the Captain or Spock.) There were also a large number of professional women: geologists, psychologists, biologists, etc. Most interesting of these was Dr. Janet Lester (her field of expertise was never revealed) in "Turnabout Intruder."[6] Dr. Lester once had an unhappy love affair with Kirk at the space academy. Her ambition to become a star ship captain interfered with their romance. She tells him: "Your world of star ship captains does not admit women.... It's not fair."

To remedy this situation she traps Kirk, and, using some equipment discovered on another planet, switches bodies with him. Now, as the mind of Lester in Kirk's body, she attempts to quash the captain's essence. Revealing her motives she cries, "It's better to be dead than to live alone in the body of a woman."

Before she can finish, she hears McCoy and Spock returning and is forced to take Kirk, now imprisoned in the Lester body, back to the ship. There, complications ensue. Finally, after the mutiny trial, the horrible truth surfaces. Kirk explains Lester's motives: she wanted the exchange "to get the power that she craved—to get the position she doesn't merit by temperament or training ... and most of all, she wanted to murder James Kirk, a man who once loved her. But her intense hatred of her own womanhood made [his] life with her impossible."

We must examine what is implicit in these remarks. Because Lester is a woman, she cannot be a spaceship captain. Is it her individual "temperament" that is referred to, or the "temperament" of all stereotypic "flighty and unreliable" women? Is she being punished for this "intense hatred of her own womanhood?" The answers to these questions are important because any single *Star Trek* episode has probably reached a greater single audience than all science fiction texts combined.

Once again the audience learns that women are not suitable for command; they have little of Spock's precious "logic." Dr. Lester in Kirk's body isn't Kirk because sex role goes beyond biology. During the course of the episode she breaks down; she cannot handle Kirk's duties; the pressures of the captaincy prove to be too much. Her ultimate undoing comes when she orders the execution of Spock, McCoy and Scotty. In the end, she is a small child banging her fist on the bridge and crying, "Why won't anyone follow my orders?"

After all is restored to normal Kirk muses, "I didn't want to destroy her ... her life could have been as rich as ... any woman's." But how rich can a woman's life be on television given the constraints of these roles? It's no wonder Lester went mad.

Yet, there is more to this than lesson giving. Despite her shortcomings, Janet Lester is presented as a character deserving pity. In the final scene she sobs and we are told that she "will be cared for." Apparently she will never be punished.

Somehow, we also tolerate her motives and understand her frustrations. This understanding is probably not universal, but has much to do with the viewer's own social perspectives and political feelings about feminism. Despite its almost medieval notion of "a woman's place," it is easy to walk away from "Turnabout Intruder" thinking that it advocates feminism. For some, it certainly must create a sympathetic feeling for the sex role limitations that will apparently continue to constrain women—even in the future time of *Star Trek*.

This is the key to moving toward a new understanding of TV content. There must be a way to approach an audience as individuals, finding the subtle and often subconscious conclusions they draw from these dramas. In a now famous study, Vidmar and Rokeach[7] learned that some members of the mass audience identified directly with Archie Bunker, supporting his rightest and racist views. Others continued to watch the show because they found Bunker an objectionable character and enjoyed watching him being ridiculed week after week. So it is with episodes like "Turnabout Intruder" which may elicit a similar dichotomous response toward feminism.

Before condemning commercial TV content as sexist and/or irrelevant, we should have sound evaluative criteria. At this point we do not. By dismissing the content of television (as we do when we examine it in literary terms), we neglect the awesome power of this medium and its magic hold over the viewer. After all, commercials picturing women as mindless housewives in search of a male to tell them what detergent to use may have done more to stir the collective conscience of women than anything else.

Star Trek will be with us long after Asimov has been forgotten; the show's images will probably exert greater influence on future social norms than any other work in the history of science fiction. Although this may not be what we would like, this is the way it is.

To understand all of this we must examine relationships between program and audience, with a view toward the audience as a critical consumer. The work that Katz, Blumer and Gurevitch have done in this area seems promising.[8] Horace Newcomb[9] has successfully incorporated some of these ideas in his work, though he often tends to see TV in literary terms.

A more useful examination involves *what the audience wants* from television. The audience does not exist in a political vacuum and it approaches the medium with some predetermined social and political values. However, for those under thirty, these values were largely shaped by television itself.

A careful examination of audience motives and demands will yield the most useful data in understanding the power of television. Schramm and others[10] found "the obstinate audience" would not "fall over" according to the bullet theory. It was not possible, in many instances, to predict audience reaction to mass media content.

This brief plea for new approaches to analysis of television content raises a number of questions and answers very few. The author would prefer to think of that as a plus. After all, there are so many "strange new worlds" out there where we can "boldly go where no man (or woman) has gone before!"

Star Trek is one of television's most popular and successful programs. To view its portrayal of women is to view our ambivalent attitudes toward female stereotypes. To understand *Star Trek* is to understand our hopes and fears about the future since television so forcefully reflects our culture and our destiny as a civilization.

Notes

[1]Marshall McLuhan, *The Medium is the Massage* (New York: Bantam Books, 1967), p. 81.

[2]Linda Busby, "Sex Role Research on the Mass Media," *Journal of Communications*, 25, No. 4 (1975), pp. 107-131.

[3]Edward Jay Whetmore, "Androgyny and Sex Role Perception in Television Situation Comedies," Univ. of Oregon, Eugene, OR. (Unpublished doctoral dissertation.)

[4]Busby, p. 127.

[5]Ina Rae Hark, *The Lord of the Rings* and *Star Trek*, Northwestern University, unpublished paper.

[6]"Turnabout Intruder" was first aired April 3, 1969 as the final show of *Star Trek*'s third and final season.

[7]Neil Vidmar and Milton Rokeach, "Archie Bunker's Bigotry," in *Mass Media and Society*, ed. Alan Welles (Palo Alto, CA: Mayfield Publishing, 1975), pp. 381-390.

[8]Elihu Katz, Jay G. Blumer and Michael Gurevitch, "Uses and Gratification Research," *Public Opinion Quarterly*, 37, No. 4 (1974), pp. 509-523.

[9]Horace Newcomb, *TV: The Most Popular Art* (Garden City: NY: Anchor Books, 1974).

[10]Wilbur Schramm, and Donald F. Roberts, *The Process and Effects of Mass Communication* (Urbana: Univ. of Illinois Press, 1971), pp. 8-11.

Arthur Asa Berger

A Personal Response to Whetmore's "A Female Captain's Enterprise"

SO, WHETMORE—you're looking for a third way. Bravo. I feel the same way you do about the various literary elitists who snub their noses at television and popular culture in general. It may be true that most of the programming on television is crap, but most everything in every field is crap. As soon as you realize that more than 49% of the people are below-average you can understand why this is the case. But most of the mediocre novels that get published die quietly and that is that. Television is there for everyone to see and get off some cheap shots at.

You don't like the sociologues either—and neither do I. Not that some of what they do isn't occasionally useful. I've always felt we are training legions of social scientists who are loaded with technique but have no imagination. Thus they produce accurate but trivial stuff, in part because they are limited to counting what is countable and that is not always interesting or useful. Also, much of this kind of research is directed at audiences and neglects television *programs* per se, which do not lend themselves yet to quantification.

And so you propose a third way—focusing upon a given program or a given character as a means of freeing yourself to talk about a "character's social impact without being confined by methodology requiring greater formality." A good idea but not an original one. And I'm not sure that "social impact" is what you mean. Rather, I think, you want to be able to talk about the values and beliefs and ideologies reflected in a given character or program. Social impact brings you back to audiences, N's and null or dull hypotheses.

I think a bit more grounding and context would have made your analysis of your episode stronger. You could have placed Janet Lester's activities within a more general framework of fascination in the series with identity; the matter of identity seems to be a pervasive subject in *Star Trek*, so that Janet Lester's "transmogrification" or whatever you call it takes on added dimensions. She may also be seen in terms of a general kind of ambivalence toward women in the series—they are talented, professional, competent, at times powerful (when they come from other galaxies, etc.) and often murderous. You can never be sure whether they will thrill you, kill you—or both. And that might explain why Janet Lester and all women have to be "contained" somehow.

All this leads me to suggest you add a couple of techniques to your repertoire. You might find psychoanalytical techniques useful in making sense of some things and profounding your understanding of the programs you wish to analyze. And you might also add a touch of structuralism/semiotics which will help you see how meaning is generated in a television program. Finally, what about aesthetic matters such as lighting, kinds of shots, sound effects and color? All this ought to be taken into consideration. I'm not sure, now, whether Janet's self-hatred was caused by disappointed love, penis envy, depression, menstrual cramps, destructive self-images of women in our society, or some combination of the above. If I knew more I could understand her relevance to feminism better.

So—keep pushing forward in your explorations of characters, episodes, television and society. You're off to a good start and are on the right trek.

Jeffrey Berman
Where's All the Fiction
in Science Fiction?

WHERE'S ALL THE fiction in science fiction? The question is
admittedly ambiguous, and lest it cause undue alarm, I had better
reassure you that I am not attacking the quality of science fiction or
its validity as an art form. Nor am I challenging the marital
compatibility of science and art. Rather, my question is this: how do
science fiction writers imagine the role of the artist? Which
characters in science fiction find themselves engaged in the act of
writing and reading, and therefore sensitive to the literary
imagination? What kinds of poems and novels appear in the science
fiction now being written? In short, how do science fiction writers
imagine their future colleagues?

The paradox of science fiction is that while it is a speculative
literature, it has neglected to speculate about the nature of literature.
Science fiction writers have imagined subjects ranging from
telepathy to telekinesis to teleportation, but they have largely
ignored one of the most basic questions—the nature of art in other
galaxies and ages. Science fiction has made astonishing
predictions, including Jules Verne's prophecies of advanced forms
of travel, and H.G.Well's prediction of the atomic bomb. Can the
science fiction writer similarly forecast the shape of future art,
including its new forms, themes, techniques and audience? Unless it
can, this young genre, so revolutionary in its predictions of scientific
achievements, will become reactionary in its vision of art.

Surprisingly, few critics have explored these questions. The
anthology edited by Reginald Bretnor, *Science Fiction: Today and
Tomorrow*, typifies this omission. James Gunn comes the closest in
discussing the portrayal of art in science fiction. "Man, says the
science fiction main current, must be tough and aggressive, but his
glory is that he can temper his toughness and aggressiveness with
an appreciation for beauty, with artistic creativity, with self-
sacrifice, with a capacity for love. And that paradox is what it
means to be truly human."[1] Yet he does not elaborate on the
depiction of art in science fiction, nor on how the appreciation for
beauty may change in the future.

164

The absence of this investigation of art becomes more conspicuous when science fiction is compared to more traditional twentieth-century literature, which has remained preoccupied with the creative process. There are, it is true, a few writers—Borges, Barth, Barthelme—who in their experimental fictions explore the artist's role in society. They tend to parody the creative act, to suggest both the difficulty of artistic originality and the sense of exhaustion perceived by the contemporary writer. As Edward A. Sklepowich has perceptively noted about *What Entropy Means to Me,* George Alec Effinger "exemplifies the interesting turn taken by much of the most provocative science fiction and fantasy. Rather than fabricating more convincing worlds with startling yet believable inventions or transporting the reader to fantasy-land with minimal attention to the illogicality of the move, many science fiction and fantasy writers are emphasizing the fictive aspects of their material and method."[2] These writers, however, represent a recent development in science fiction; they are not part of the "mainstream," to use James Gunn's image.

There are several reasons for the few artist figures who appear in science fiction. It has remained more devoted to technology than to science, and more interested in science than in art. Science fiction writers tend to exalt or despise technology and science, and to view them as the boon or bane of civilization. They don't perceive the artist as having the same power. Indeed, few writers believe that future survival may depend upon the artist as well as the technician or scientist.

Moreover, the genre characteristics of science fiction limit an exploration of art. The emphasis placed upon ideas instead of character development tends to exaggerate the importance of action and plot. Consequently, characters have little time for the meditation necessary for the creation of art. Few heroes or heroines in science fiction appear interested in literature, though their creators, of course, are writers themselves. And when an artist shows up in a science fiction story, too often his art is merely asserted rather than demonstrated. "Telling," as we know, is inferior to "showing."

Thus the forbidden, or ignored, subject of science fiction is neither sex nor death, but art. Since our focus is on images of women in science fiction, we may raise the following questions. What will the female artist be like in the future, and will she differ from her male counterpart? Does the contemporary female science fiction writer imagine her artists to be alienated from or integrated into society? What new art forms does the female science fiction writer envision? What type of individual will be creating art in other worlds? Will she be, for instance, a cyborg—a creature part human, part machine—and if so, will her art be organic or mechanical? Will there be, as there is now, a dichotomy between serious and popular literature? Or will science fiction help narrow the gap?

*   *   *

Pamela Sargent's two excellent anthologies of science fiction written by women, *Women of Wonder* and *More Women of Wonder*,[3] offer a starting point for our discussion. In Kate Wilhelm's "Baby, You Were Great," art is less important for its own sake than for the vicarious sexual pleasure it conveys to a passive audience. Anne Beaumont is a glamorous actress with an electronic implant, which allows her audience to experience her tempestuous emotions as she acts out her soap opera stories. Technological advances have rendered obsolete television cameras and other primitive equipment:

> The gimmick was fairly simple. A person fitted with electrodes in his brain could transmit his emotions, which in turn could be broadcast and picked up by the helmets to be felt by the audience. No words or thoughts went out, only basic emotions... fear, love, anger, hatred.... That, tied in with a camera showing what the person saw, with a voice dubbed in, and you were the person having the experience, with one important difference, you could turn it off if it got to be too much. The 'actor' couldn't (*Women of Wonder*, p. 148).

Those helmets are not sold but rented, for a fee of one dollar per month. With over thirty-seven million subscribers, the broadcasts have an international audience. There are no boundaries between Anne Beaumont's life and art: she involuntarily broadcasts her stories all day, except when she is asleep. Nor is there a structure or unifying vision to her art, apart from loose editing around a melodramatic story line. Art becomes a masturbatory sensation for a voyeuristic audience, with the artist or actress gratifying the viewer's private fantasies. As the title suggests, "Baby, You Were Great" satirizes the present day exploitation of women in Hollywood and elsewhere, and it projects this X-rated art into the future.

A more positive vision of art appears in another story by Kate Wilhelm called "The Funeral." The story describes how an uneducated youth named Carla turns to writing as an escape from a repressive society. As the novelette opens, Carla is told by a cheerless teacher to meditate upon and record the dying "words of wisdom" of Madame Westfall, a political revolutionary whose funeral is being eulogized. Madame Westfall was a writer, though her writings are characterized by propagandistic themes and platitudinous expressions. An example of her literary art: "Maturity brings grace, beauty, wisdom, happiness. Immaturity means ugliness, unfinished beings with potential only, wholly dependent upon and subservient to the mature citizens" (*More Women of Wonder*, p. 179).

Carla is precisely one of these immature and unfinished beings in the beginning of the story, entirely dependent upon her unenlightened teachers for guidance. Her fascination for the notebook and pen, given to her to record Madame Westfall's trite observations of life, reflects her own developing appreciation of the significance of writing. "She turned the blank pages of the notebook, felt the paper between her fingers, tore a tiny corner off one of the back pages, examined it closely, the jagged edge, the texture of the fragment; she tasted it. She studied the pen just as minutely; it had a pointed, smooth end, and it wrote black. She made a line, stopped to admire it, and crossed it with another line" (*More Women of Wonder*, p. 184).

Although Kate Wilhelm asserts rather than demonstrates Carla's notebook writings, they are identified with the principle of freedom from an intolerable society. Writing enables Carla to express her unverbalized longings, to define her identity. Herein lies the power of art for her: it creates her individuality amidst a monolithic society, and provides her with the pleasure long absent from her life. Art proves to be both a moral and aesthetic experience. "She wrote her life story, and then made up other things to say. She wrote her name over and over, and wept because she had no last name. She wrote nonsense words and rhymed them with other nonsense words."

The themes of Carla's writing are traditional and humanistic, attesting to imperishable human values. Appropriately, she finds herself increasingly estranged from her world. Along with the girl named Lisa whom she befriends, she escapes into a hidden cave wherein she continues to write. It is unclear whether their escape will be successful. They remain cut off from food and water, growing weaker by the day. The elegiac ending of "The Funeral" parallels Carla's lyrical art, but the ambiguity of the title raises the question of whose funeral is being described, Madame Westfall's or Carla's. As the story ends, Carla imperceptibly drifts off into hallucination, her imagination awakened by a literary art that has moved her toward an unknown world.

She wrote of the golden light through the green-black pine trees and of birds' songs and moss underfoot. She wrote of Lisa lying peacefully now at the far end of the cave amidst riches that neither of them could ever have comprehended. When she could no longer write, she drifted in and out of the golden light in the forest, listening to the birds' songs, hearing the raucous laughter that now sounded so beautiful (*More Women of Wonder*, p. 213).

Kate Wilhelm thus portrays antithetical visions of female artists in her science fiction. "Baby, You Were Great" evokes the image of escapist art, in which Anne Beaumont's self-imprisonment and exploitation as a sex object betray her society's moral hollowness. By contrast, "The Funeral" identifies art as an intensification and crystallization of life, with Carla achieving a self-discovery denied to those who do not know the meaning of lyrical and autobiographical art. Despite the suggestion of the impossibility of Carla's escape, "The Funeral" reveals a more affirmative attitude toward art. There is nothing funereal about the tone of the story. Nor must the artist supply the answers to the problems besetting society. Whereas the technician, scientist, and engineer are called upon to solve social problems, the artist's task is different. Chekhov makes a distinction between "the solution of the problem and a correct presentation of the problem." "Only the latter is obligatory," he adds.

Yet the presentation of these problems often places the artist in a vulnerable position. A persistent theme in science fiction has been the subversive power of literature, and the suspicion of an inverse relationship between technological and artistic progress. In *Brave New World* Huxley foreshadows the assault upon the spoken word and written image. He also demonstrates how an advanced totalitarian state successfully defuses the power of literature. In the infant nurseries, technicians use neo-Pavlovian conditioning to associate books and flowers with punishment. As the infants touch the books, which are "opened invitingly ... at some gaily coloured image of beast or fish or bird," they suffer an electrical shock. The Director of the nurseries lectures his students: "They'll grow up with what the psychologists used to call an 'instinctive' hatred of books and flowers. Reflexes unalterably conditioned. They'll be safe from books and botany all their lives."[4]

The Director proves correct in his estimation of the dangers of literature to the monolithic society, which values social conformity and a drug-induced euphoria over the expansion of knowledge and the intensification of a spiritual consciousness. Indeed, Huxley structures his novel around the contrast between the brave new world and the brave new word. John the Savage's moral education begins when he accidentally comes across *The Complete Works of William Shakespeare,* which he later cites with professorial expertise. Huxley ridicules the opiate art read in the dystopian state by contrasting it to Shakespearean art, associated with the mysteries of passion and suffering. Helmholtz Watson, whose "mental excess" endows him with authorial omniscience, articulates the objections to language and literature. "Words can be like X-rays, if you use them properly—they'll go through anything.

You read and you're pierced. That's one of the things I try to teach my students—how to write piercingly. But what on earth's the good of being pierced by an article about a Community Sing, or the latest improvement in scent organs?"[5]

Yevgeny Zamyatin similarly reveals the antagonistic relationship between literary art and dystopian values in his bitterly satirical novel *We*. Like Huxley, he identifies Shakespeare and Dostoevsky with the "right to be happy"—the impassioned awareness of the pleasure and pain of life, and the right to choose one's existence. These ideas are repugnant to a political state which thrives upon the depersonalization of its collective citizenry. Zamyatin also realizes that the destruction of the human imagination requires the banning of all serious art. The self-deceived narrator of *We*—the nameless D-503 who inhabits the futuristic technological nightmare called United State—rejoices in the passing of the old tradition of world literature. "Fortunately, the antediluvian ages of all those Shakespeares and Dostoyevskys, or whatever you call them, are gone...."[6] Not only has the State replaced this "reactionary" tradition with "progressive" art, but the creative process itself has changed. Contemplation, discipline, and skill no longer are necessary for the creation of music. "Simply by turning this handle, any of you can produce up to three sonatas an hour. Yet think how much effort this had cost your forebears! They were able to create only by whipping themselves up to fits of 'inspiration'—an unknown form of epilepsy."[7]

In contrast to the mad art of the past, contemporary music epitomizes mathematical rationality to the State. Moreover, the Institute of State Poets and Writers has democratized the art of poetry. "Today, poetry is no longer the idle, impudent whistling of a nightingale; poetry is civic service, poetry is useful." How useful? D-503 sings this hymn of praise:

Our poets no longer soar in the empyrean; they have come down to earth; they stride beside us to the stern mechanical March of the Music Plant. Their lyre encompasses the morning scraping of electric toothbrushes and the dread crackle of the sparks in the Benefactor's Machine; the majestic echoes of the Hymn to the One State and the intimate tinkle of the gleaming crystal chamberpot....[8]

Significantly, Zamyatin's fear of the subjection of the arts to governmental control also appears in Ursula Le Guin's *The Dispossessed*. And while Anarres, Shevek's bleak homeland, does not elicit the horror and contempt the reader feels in *We*, it too produces largely inferior art. Two reasons for the absence of major art in Anarres include their repudiation of suffering, from which perhaps most great art springs, and their distrust of "egoizing," the sinful glorification of the self. "An Odonian's goal is positive, not negative. Suffering is dysfunctional, except as a bodily warning against danger. Psychologically and socially it's merely destructive."[9] Judged by the criterion of its art, an accurate reflection of a civilization's values and achievement, Anarres is an ambiguous utopia. Learning centers teach the skills necessary for the practice of art, including training in singing, dancing and the use of the lathe; yet the heavy emphasis upon the pragmatic—as in arts and crafts—results in the sacrifice of more abstract and imaginative art forms. Only drama seems to be flourishing, the genre which comes closest to being public, social art. Predictably, Anarres frowns upon satirical drama and dissonant music, which are perceived to be subversive. Both Zamyatin and Le Guin imply that the greatest service an artist can perform in a conformist age is the creation of nonconformist art. Paradoxically, the dissonant rhythms of the artist may reveal an organic harmony.

Ursula Le Guin celebrates the oral tradition of literature in her acclaimed novel *The Left Hand of Darkness*. Most of the critical attention on the novel has centered around the absence of sex roles among the Gethenians, who are sexually neuter except for a brief period of activity called "kemmer," when they assume male or female roles. But apart from ambisexuality, the novelist explores the contrast between two galactic cultures and literary traditions. The novel opens with Genly Ai apologizing for the storylike quality of the report he is sending home:

I'll make my report as if I told a story, for I was taught as a child on my homeworld that Truth is a matter of the imagination. The soundest fact may fail or prevail in the style of its telling: like that singular organic jewel of our seas, which grows brighter as one woman wears it and, worn by another, dulls and goes to dust. Facts are no more solid, coherent, round, and real than pearls are. But both are sensitive.[10]

Genly Ai's language here may reveal a faint Dickensian echo of *Hard Times*, in which Gradgrind's utilitarian suspicion of art manifests itself in his demand for facts. "Now, what I want is Facts. Teach these boys and girls nothing but Facts. Facts alone are wanted in life." But Genly Ai's literary self-consciousness derives less from an ambivalence toward the imagination than from the Mindspeech practiced in his native Ekumer. In contrast to the characteristic paraverbal speech of the Ekumen, the glacial Gethenians are versed in the oral-literature tradition. They are all expert storytellers. Toward the end of the novel, Estraven narrates to a group of strangers the tale of the arduous crossing of the Ice with Genly Ai. "He told it as only a person of an oral-literature tradition can tell a story, notes Genly Ai,

so that it became a saga, full of traditional locutions and even episodes, yet exact and vivid, from the sulphurous fire and dark of the pass between Drumner and Dremegole to the screaming gusts from the mountain-gaps that swept the Bay of Guthen; with comic interludes, such as his fall into the crevasse, and mystical ones, when he spoke of the sounds and silences of the Ice, of the shadowless weather, of the night's darkness.[11]

Even Genly Ai, who has lived through these adventures, remains spellbound by his friend's story. *The Left Hand of Darkness* closes with Estraven's son imploring Genly Ai to narrate the details of his father's death; and Ursula Le Guin pays tribute to the oral and written tradition of literature, whose unbroken continuity reveals an infinitude of stories. " 'Will you tell us how he died?—Will you tell us about the other worlds out among the stars—the other kinds of men, the other lives?' "

Which stories and poems are mentioned in science fiction? The characters in Josephine Saxton's "The Power of Time" engage in a discussion of Russian literature, and the reference to *Crime and Punishment* indicates the frequency with which Dostoevsky appears in science fiction. There is also an allusion to the twentieth-century literary scene: "authors like John Barth and Donald Barthelme, the poems of Sonya Dorman and Nabokov's entry into the world of science fiction" (*More Women of Wonder*, p. 158). Miltonic lines appear in Joan D. Vinge's "Tin Soldier": "Attired with stars we shall forever sit, triumphing over Death, and Chance, and thee, O time" (*More Women of Wonder*, p. 232). The cyborg in "Tin Soldier" refers to *Anderson's Fairy Tales*, from which he discovers a parallel to his own life. Wordsworth's poetry is still read: "Though inland far we be, our souls have sight of that immortal sea which brought us hither."

Music echoes through Anne McCaffrey's "The Ship Who Sang." Helva, a female cyborg, is the brain of a spaceship. Early in her career she reveals an unusual talent for music. While performing her duties, she would absent-mindedly croon, producing an eerie but pleasing sound. Although these sounds emanate from a microphone instead of a mouth, Helva acquires a cosmic reputation for her singing. Her hum "had a curious vibrancy, a warm, dulcet quality even in its aimless chromatic wanderings" (*Women of Wonder*, p. 85). In a music appreciation course she studies classics ranging from the familiar old masters—*Tristan und Isolde, Candide, Oklahoma, Nozze di Figarro*; to the "atomic-age singers," Birgit Nilsson, Bob Dylan, Geraldine Page; to other forms of music literally out of this world: "the curious rhythmic progressions of the Venusians, Capellan visual chromatics, the sonic concerti of the Altairians and Reticulan croons."

Surrealistic art emerges from Leigh Brackett's hypnotic story

"The Lake of the Gone Forever." The lake magically re-creates from its black waters the images of those individuals who have died. Peering into its infinite depths, Rand Conway witnesses the pictorial re-creation of his dead father. "Slowly, slowly, the image of his father took shape in the substance of the lake, a ghostly picture painted with a brush of cold firs against the utter dark" (*More Women of Wonder*, p. 98). Neither a reflection nor a projection of the son's memories of his father, the images testify to the immortality of the human spirit and the ability of art to transcend time. There are also Conradian echoes in the story, as the language suggests. "Conway knew that his father and the pale-haired lovely girl had stood where he stood now on the brink of the Lake and looked down as he was looking, that their images might be forever graven into the heart of the strange darkness below."

Of all the contemporary female science fiction writers, Joanna Russ is perhaps the most appreciative of the myth-making process and the creation of illusions. Her characters delight in the art of spinning narrations, and they are expert in the oral and written tradition of literature. Part of her achievement as a writer is that she preserves the value of storytelling in her fictions: she cannot and will not imagine a world without art.

In "Nobody's Home," technological advances have transformed Jannina's civilization into a utopia, and the citizens pride themselves on the superiority of their world to what they call the "bad old days." But amidst the technological glitter and the easiness of things, Jannina remains aware of the "bitter stuff under the surface of life." Nor is it nostalgia alone which causes her to feel a loss of the past. She asks a friend to tell her a story, which turns out to be an ancient creation myth whose theme emphasizes the irresolvable problems of time, suffering and death. Hearing the story, Jannina bursts into tears. Indeed, the content of the creation myth coincides with the title and meaning of "Nobody's Home": the transiency of life precludes a permanent home, and without a moral consciousness, one remains a "nobody," oblivious to painful yet potentially ennobling truths.

However gloomy their themes, these myths and stories assume a wondrous importance in Joanna Russ's works. She ends another story with the exuberant narrator whetting our appetites for the future exploits of the heroine Alyx. "She was to become a classic, in time. But that's another story."[12]

This love for literature appears in another story by Joanna Russ—one of her best—called "The Second Inquisition." The first person narrator is a sixteen year old girl searching for escape from a harsh parental homelife and a cheerless American town set in 1925. Spending the summer with the family is a mysterious visitor, a six-foot four inch female with "hair that was reddish black but so rough that it looked like the things my mother used for scouring pots and pans." In its dreamlike imagery and deliberate blurring of reality and illusion, "The Second Inquisition" has a Jamesian ambiguity suggestive of *The Turn of the Screw*. And like James's novella, whose "story *won't* tell,... not in any literal, vulgar way," "The Second Inquisition" maintains the ambiguity over the mysterious visitor's identity. Is she a human being whom the impressionable youth has mythologized into a larger than life figure? Or is she a visitor from another universe?

"The Second Inquisition" may also be interpreted as an allegory of the power of imaginative literature. The story opens with the narrator watching the visitor reading a novel. "I am reading a very stupid book," the visitor observes; "You will take it away from me, yes?" When the reticent youth refuses, the visitor repeats the command. " 'You must,' she said, 'or it will poison me, sure as God,' and from her lap she plucked up *The Green Hat: A Romance*, gold letters on green binding, last year's best seller which I had to swear never to read...." (*More Women of Wonder*, pp. 106-107). As attuned to the dangers of inferior literature as to the Morlocks who come later to destroy her, she wages a war against literary philistinism reminiscent of Pope's *The Dunciad*. Yet Joanna Russ implies that even mediocre literature may stimulate the imagination and enrich an otherwise dull existence. Despite her parents' warnings, the narrator reads the forbidden book and finds herself transported to a fantastic world that contrasts the impoverishment of her own. Her father scolds her for reading the novel, rightly interpreting the illicit act as her quest for liberation.

Just as the carefully constructed plot of "The Second Inquisition" confuses the boundaries between art and life, its literary allusiveness heightens the narrator's entanglement of fiction and fact. Seeing a copy of *The Time Machine* lying on the visitor's bed, the narrator fabricates a dialogue between the two women. " 'Are you reading Wells?' I would say then, leaning against the door jamb. 'I think that's funny. Nobody in this town reads anything; they just think about social life. I read a lot, however. I would like to learn a great deal' " (pp. 113-114). Continuing her imaginary dialogue, she tells of how after reading *The Time Machine* she would ask people whether they were Eloi or Morlocks. She imagines the visitor echoing her own preference for the fierce Morlocks, and she invests the visitor's life with high drama:

'You are always right,' she would say, "and you know the rest of it, too. You know what murderers we are and how terribly we live. We are waiting for the big bang when everything falls over and even the Morlocks will be destroyed; meanwhile I stay here waiting for the signal and I leave messages clipped to the frame of your mother's amateur oil painting of Main Street because it will be in a museum some day and my friends can find it; meanwhile I read *The Time Machine* (*More Women of Wonder*, pp. 114-115).

Literature comes alive for the narrator as she experiences a bewildering sequence of events that shatters the tedium of her life. Following the visitor's orders, she participates in the murder of a sinister alien, and she becomes entranced with a love affair between the visitor and a thickset garage mechanic named "Bogalusa Joe." Later in the story, the youth's parents are inexplicably immobilized, rendered "motionless as zombies." The science fiction element intensifies. The invasion of the Morlocks testifies to the power of *The Time Machine*, from which they emerge with terrifying realism. The uncertainty surrounding the visitor also inheres within the Morlocks. Are they part of the fictional world of H.G. Wells's story, or have they actualized into existence? Monstrous seal-people accompany the Morlocks, and "The Second Inquisition" assumes a nightmarish quality as the visitor engages in a hideous battle with a creature who slashes open her eye. Ironically, of all the crimes the Morlocks accuse the visitor of having committed, the worst offense is being an artist. " 'Damn your sketches!' shouted the Morlock she had fought with, completely losing control of himself. 'We are at war; Trans-Temp is at our heels; do you think we have time for dilettantism?...We are fighting for the freedom of fifty billions of people, not for your scribbles" (p. 142). Before the Morlock leaves with the visitor, through the window from which they have entered, he warns the narrator: "Do not try to impress anyone with stories." Hearing her parents shout at her, the narrator awakens from a faint.

"The Second Inquisition" ends plaintively, with the saddened adolescent unable to rediscover, except for a brief reunion, the mysterious visitor. Yet the teenager's curiosity has been aroused by this vision. For she has encountered—or created—a woman of paradoxical contrasts: an Amazonian warrior with a refined literary sensibility, an individial committed to the contradictory worlds of external reality and internal consciousness, a time traveler who dwells outside of history.

"The Second Inquisition" may achieve in time the high position in science fiction that *The Turn of the Screw* holds among the great supernatural tales of Gothic literature. Interestingly, both stories lend themselves to a psychoanalytic approach and yield similar conclusions. Just as *The Turn of the Screw* may be interpreted as the governess' elaborate sexual hallucination, with Peter Quint personifying her repressed erotic desires, "The Second Inquisition" dramatizes the mysterious visitor as a projection of the narrator's sexual fantasies. A Freudian analysis of the story reveals the daughter's submerged hostility toward her parents, and their apparent death as a consequence of her murderous feelings—the omnipotence of thought. The parents magically spring back to life after she awakens from a fainting spell, itself caused by an anticipated parental argument over her awakening sexuality. The chronology of the plot makes this clear:

I came down one morning to ask my mother whether I couldn't have a jumper taken up at the hem because the magazines said it was all right for young girls. I expected a fight over it. I couldn't find my mother in the hall or the kitchen so I tried the living room, but before I had got halfway through the living room arch, someone said, 'Stop there,' and I saw both my parents sitting on two chairs near the front door, both with their hands in their laps, both staring straight ahead, motionless as zombies (*More Women of Wonder*, pp. 136-137).

The youth and the visitor maintain a secret sharer relationship throughout the story. The ambiguity arises not over the visitor's realness, as in James's ghost story, but in whether she is a human or superhuman figure. The youth's fascination with the visitor's body, especially the "long, hard, unladylike legs"; the voyeuristic imagery that pervades the story, both in her repeated acts of staring and the omnipresence of mirrors; and her identification with "Bogalusa Joe," whose rough masculine sexuality coincides with the visitor's—all hint at the narrator's greater interest in the female body, and perhaps her unconscious preference for homosexual love. Even as the youth appears horrified by their lovemaking, she is fascinated by his entry into the mysterious woman. "She leaned back against the cushions of the swing and seemed to spread her feet in the invisible grass; she let her head and arms fall back onto the cushion. Without saying a word, he lifted her skirt far above her knees and put his hand between her legs. There was a great deal more of the same business and I watched it all, from the first twistings to the stabbings, the noises, the life-and-death battle in the dark" (p. 136).

Literature proves to be for the narrator not only a substitute gratification but also, more importantly, a method to express her deepest fears and desires. The mirror from which the visitor appears symbolizes the artist's ability to create the unseen reality; the visitor embodies the power of fiction to transform fantasies into reality. At the end of the story, the youth cannot live divorced from the literary world, and she turns to the mirror to invoke another vision to penetrate her life. "I wanted something to come out of the mirror and strike me dead. If I could not have a protector, I wanted a monster, a mutation, a horror, a murderous disease, anything! anything at all to accompany me downstairs so that I would not have to go down alone" (pp. 147-148). The visitor's departure leaves the youth bereft of spirit. She has, in the final words of "The Second Inquistion," "No more stories."

"No more stories": must we accept this gloomy answer to the opening question of "Where's all the fiction in science fiction?" Despite the conclusion that science fiction has insufficiently explored the act of reading and the role of the artist in imaginary times and worlds, a few contemporary writers, like Joanna Russ, are investigating these questions. And she continues to write about the emerging female artist in her novel *The Female Man*, with its spoof of literary critics and its final invocation to the muse: "Go, little book...." All of this is reassuring. If we ever find ourselves confronted with the necessity to choose to live in one out of many universes, the decision may depend upon the fiction it has wrought. We are, finally, what we read.

Notes

I am indebted to Kathleen Roberts for her help with this essay.

[1] James Gunn, "Science Fiction and the Mainstream," Reginald Bretnor, ed., *Science Fiction: Today and Tomorrow* (Baltimore: Penguin, 1974), p. 193.

[2] Edward A. Sklepowich, "The Fictive Quest: Effinger's *What Entropy Means to Me*," *Extrapolation*, Vol. 18 (No. 2, May 1977), p. 108.

[3] Pamela Sargent, ed., *Women of Wonder* (New York: Vintage Books, 1975); Pamela Sargent, ed., *More Women of Wonder* (New York: Vintage Books, 1976). All references are to these editions.

[4] Aldous Huxley, *Brave New World* (New York: Bantam, 1968), p. 14.

[5] Huxley, p. 47.

[6] Yevgeny Zamyatin, *We*, translated by Mirra Ginsburg (New York: Bantam, 1972), p. 43.

[7] Zamyatin, p. 17.

[8] Zamyatin, pp. 68-69.

[9] Ursula K. Le Guin, *The Dispossessed* (New York: Avon, 1975), p. 49.

[10] Ursula K. Le Guin, *The Left Hand of Darkness* (New York: Ace Books, 1969), p. 7.

[11] *The Left Hand of Darkness*, p. 260.

[12] Joanna Russ, *Alyx* (Boston: Gregg Press, 1976), p. 48.

VII Bibliography

The Future Females:
A Selected Checklist through 1979

Roger C. Schlobin

All items in the following checklist of women science-fiction writers are cited by first edition only, unless otherwise indicated. Series and their reading orders are noted. Anthologies, which have been restricted to those that feature women writers exclusively, are designated by asterisks.

Readers interested in the excellent fantasy written by women should consult this author's *The Literature of Fantasy: A Comprehensive, Annotated Bibliography of Modern Fantasy Fiction* (New York: Garland, 1979).

[Abrahamson, Christine]. Cristabel, pseud. *The Golden Olive.* New York: Curtis, 1972.

_____ *The Mortal Immortals.* New York: Walker, 1971.

Arch, E.L. See Rachel Payes

Adam, Ruth. *War on Saturday Week.* Philadelphia: J.B. Lippencott, 1937.

Asquith, Cynthia. *This Mortal Coil.* Sauk City, WI: Arkham House, 1947.

[Austin, Mary]. Stairs, Gordon, pseud. *Outland.* London: Murray, 1910 [2nd ed. as Mary Austin].

Barnett, Ada. *The Man on the Other Side.* London: Allen and Unwin, 1921.

Bauman, Carolyn Busey. *The Woman Who Would Not Die.* New York: Signet, 1969.

Beauclerk, Helen. *The Love of a Foolish Angel.* London: Collins, 1929.

[Bennett, Gertrude Barrows]. Stevens, Francis, pseud. *The Citadel of Fear.* New York: Popular Library, 1970.

_____ *Claimed.* New York: Avalon, 1966.

_____ *The Heads of Cerberus.* Reading, PA: Polaris Press, 1952.

Bennett, Margot. *The Furious Masters.* London: Eyre and Spottswoode, 1968.

_____*The Long Way Back.* London: Bodley Head, 1954.

Blodgett, Mabel. *At the Queen's Mercy.* Boston: Lamson, Wolffe, 1897.

Borden, Mary. *Jehovah's Day.* London: Heinemann, 1929.

Bowen, Marjorie. *Kecksies and Other Twilight Tales.* Sauk City, WI: Arkham House, 1976.

Brackett, Leigh. *Alpha Centauri—or Die!* New York: Ace, 1963.

_____ *The Best of Leigh Brackett.* Ed. Edmund Hamilton. Garden City, NY: Nelson Doubleday [Science Fiction Book Club], 1977.

_____ *The Big Jump.* New York: Ace, 1955. Bound with Philip K. Dick's *The Solar Lottery.*

_____ *The Book of Skaith: The Adventures of Eric John Stark.* Garden City, NY: Nelson Doubleday [Science Fiction Book Club], 1976. Contains *The Ginger Star* (1974), *The Hounds of Skaith* (1974), and *The Reavers of Skaith* (1976).

_____ *The Coming of the Terrans.* New York: Ace, 1967.

_____ *The Galactic Breed* Bound with Robert Moore Williams' *Conquest of the Space Sea.* Abr. ed. of *The Starmen* (see below).

_____*The Galactic Breed.* New York: Ace, 1955. Bound with Robert Moore Williams' *Conquest of the Space Sea.* Abr. ed. of *The Starmen* (see below).

179

_____ *The Hounds of Skaith*. New York: Ballentine, 1974 [Eric Stark #4].
_____ *The Long Tomorrow*. Garden City, NY: Doubleday, 1955.
_____ *The Nemesis From Terra*. New York: Ace, 1961. Bound with Robert
  Silverberg's *Collision Course*.
_____ *People of the Talisman* [and] *The Secret of Sinharat*. New York: Ace [double],
  1964 [Eric Stark #1 and 2].
_____ *Shadow Over Mars*. Manchester: World Distributors, 1951.
_____ *The Reavers of Skaith*. New York: Ballantine, 1976 [Eric Stark #5].
_____ *The Starmen*. New York: Gnome, 1952. Abr. ed. as *The Galactic Breed* (see
  above). Later title: *The Starmen of Llyrdis* (1976).
_____ *The Sword of Rhiannon*. New York: Ace, 1953. Bound with Robert E. Howard's
  Conan the Conqueror.
Bradley, Marion Zimmer. *The Brass Dragon*. New York: Ace, 1969. Bound with John
  Rackham's *Ipomoea*.
_____ *The Door Through Space*. New York: Ace, 1961. Bound with A. Bertram
  Chandler's *Rendezvous on a Lost World*.
_____ *Falcons of Narabedla* [and] *The Dark Intruder and Other Stories*. New York:
  Ace [double], 1964.
_____ *Hunters of the Red Moon*. New York: DAW, 1973. Sequel: *The Survivors*.
_____ *Ruins of Isis*. Norfork, VA: Downing, 1978.
_____ *Seven From the Stars*. New York: Ace, 1962. Bound with Keith Laumer's
  Worlds of the Imperium.
_____ *The Survivors*. New York: DAW, 1979. With Paul Edwin Zimmer. Sequel to
  Hunters of the Red Moon.
Darkover Series (reading order approximate)
_____ *Darkover Landfall*. New York: DAW, 1972.
_____ *The Shattered Chain: A Darkover Novel*. New York: DAW, 1976.
_____ *The Spell Sword*. New York: DAW, 1974.
_____ *The Winds of Darkover*. New York: Ace, 1971. Bound with John Rackham's
  The Anything Tree.
_____ *The Bloody Sun*. New York: Ace, 1964. Rev. ed. New York: Ace, 1979.
_____ *The Heritage of Hastur*. New York: DAW, 1975.
_____ *The Sword of Aldones* [and] *The Planet Savers*. New York: Ace [double], 1962.
_____ *The World Wreakers*. New York: Ace, 1971.
_____ *The Forbidden Tower*. New York: DAW, 1977.
_____ *Starqueen*. New York: DAW, 1978.
Bridge, Ann. See Mary Dolling O'Malley
[Briggs, Phyllis]. Briggs, Philip, pseud. *Escape From Gravity*. London:
  Lutterworth, 1955.
Brook-Rose, Christine. *Out*. London: Joseph, 1964.
_____ *Such*. London: Joseph, 1966.
Brown, Rosel George. *Earthblood*. Garden City, NY: Doubleday, 1966. With
  Keith Laumer.
_____ *A Handful of Time*. New York: Ballantine, 1963.
Sibyl Sue Brown Books
_____ *Sibyl Sue Brown*. Garden City, NY: Doubleday, 1966.
_____ *The Waters of Centaurus*. Garden City, NY: Doubleday, 1970.
Butler, Octavia E. *Kindred*. Garden City, NY: Doubleday, 1979.
_____ *Mind of My Mind*. Garden City, NY: Doubleday, 1977.
_____ *Patternmaster*. Garden City, NY: Doubleday, 1976.
_____ *Survivor*. Garden City, NY: Doubleday, 1978.
Calisher, Hortense. *Journal from Ellipsia*. Boston: Little, Brown, 1965.
Carroll, Gladys Hasty. *Man on the Mountain*. Boston: Little, Brown, 1969.
Carter, Mary. *The Minutes of the Night*. Boston: Little, Brown, 1965.
Charnas, Suzy McKee. *Motherlines*. New York: Berkley/Putnam, 1978.

_____ *Walk to the End of the World.* New York: Ballantine, 1974.
[Cherry, Carolyn Janice]. Cherryh, C.J., pseud. *Brothers of the Earth.* Garden City, NY: Nelson Doubleday [Science Fiction Book Club], 1976.
_____ *Hestia.* New York: DAW, 1979.
_____ *Hunter of Worlds.* Garden City, NY: Nelson Doubleday [Science Fiction Book Club], 1977.
Morgaine Series
_____ *Gate of Ivrel.* New York: DAW, 1976.
_____ *Well of Shiuan.* New York: DAW, 1978.
_____ *Fires of Azeroth.* New York: DAW, 1979.
Faded Sun Series
_____ *The Faded Sun: Kesrith.* Garden City, NY: Nelson Doubleday [Science Fiction Book Club], 1978.
_____ *The Faded Sun: Shon'jir.* Garden City, NY: Doubleday [Science Fiction Book Club], 1978.
_____ *The Faded Sun: Kutath.* Garden City, NY: Nelson Doubleday [Science Fiction Book Club], 1979.
Chetwynd, Bridget. *Future Imperfect.* London: Hutchinson, 1946.
Cicellis, Kay. *The Day the Fish Came Out.* New York: Bantam, 1967.
Clayton, Jo. The Diadem Series.
_____ *Diadem for the Stars.* New York: DAW, 1977.
_____ *Lamarchos.* New York: DAW, 1978.
_____ *Irsud.* New York: DAW, 1978.
_____ *Maeve: A Novel of the Diadem.* New York: DAW, 1979.
Clingerman, Mildred. *A Cupful of Space.* New York: Ballantine, 1961.
Cormack, Maribelle. *The Star-Crossed Woman.* London: Harrap, 1961.
Cory, Howard L. See Julie Ann Jardine
Coulson, Juanita. *Crisis on Cheiron.* New York: Ace, 1967. Bound with E.C. Tubb's *The Winds of Gath.*
_____ *The Singing Stones.* New York: Ace, 1968. Bound with E.C. Tubb's *Derai.*
_____ *Space Trap.* New York: Laser, 1976.
_____ *Unto the Next Generation.* New York: Lancer, 1975.
Cristabel. See Christine Abrahamsen
De Ford, Miriam Allen. *Elsewhere, Elsewhen, Elsehow....*New York: Walker, 1971.
_____ *Xenogenesis.* New York: Ballantine, 1969.
[De Reyna, Diane Detzer]. Lukens, Adam, pseud. *Alien World.* New York: Avalon, 1963.
_____ *Conquest of Life.* New York: Avalon, 1960.
_____ *Eevalu.* New York: Avalon, 1963.
_____ *The Glass Cage.* New York: Avalon, 1962.
_____ *Planet of Fear.* New York: Avalon, 1968.
_____ de Reyna, Jorge, pseud. *Return to the Starships.* New York: Avalon, 1968.
_____ Lukens, Adam, pseud. *Sons of the Wolf.* New York: Avalon, 1961.
_____ *The World Within.* New York: Avalon, 1962.
Dixon, Marjorie. *The Forbidden Island.* London: Hart-Davis, 1960.
Doney, Nina M. *My Life on Eight Planets, or a Glimpse of Other Worlds.* Auburn, NY: Doney & Cashill, 1928.
Dubois, Theodora. *Solution T-25.* Garden City, NY: Doubleday, 1951.
Duke, Madelaine. *The Business of Bomfog.* London: Heinemann, 1964.
_____ *Claret, Sandwiches and Sin.* London: Heinemann, 1967.
[Edmonds, Helen]. Kavan, Anna, pseud. *Ice.* London: Owen, 1967.
Elgin, Suzette H. The Coyote Jones Series.
_____ *The Communipaths.* New York: Ace, 1970. Bound with Louis Tremble's *The Noblest Experiment in the Galaxy.*

_____ *Furthest.* New York: Ace, 1971.

_____ *At the Seventh Level.* New York: DAW, 1972.

_____ *Star-Anchored, Star-Angered.* Garden City, NY: Doubleday, 1979.

Emshwiller, Carol. *Joy in our Cause.* New York: Harper, 1974.

Engdahl, Sylvia Louise. *Beyond the Tomorrow Mountains.* New York: Atheneum, 1973 [Noren #2].

_____ *Enchantress of the Stars.* New York: Atheneum, 1970 [Elana #1].

_____ *The Far Side of Evil.* New York: Atheneum, 1971 [Elana #2].

_____ *The Star Shall Abide.* New York: Atheneum, 1972 [Noren #1]. Later title: *Heritage of the Star (1973).*

Eisenstein, Phyllis. *Shadow of Earth.* New York: DAW, 1979.

Farca, Marie C. *Complex Man.* Garden City, NY: Doubleday, 1973.

_____ *Earth.* Garden City, NY: Doubleday, 1972 [Sequel: to the *Complex Man*].

Fontana, D[orothy] C. *The Questor Tapes.* New York: Ballantine, 1974.

Forrest, Maryann. *Here (Away From It All).* London: Joseph, 1969.

Frankau, Pamela. *The Bridge.* New York: Harper, 1957.

Freedman, Nancy. *The Immortals.* New York: St. Martin's, 1976.

_____ *Joshua, Son of None.* New York: Delacorte, 1973.

Friedberg, Gertrude. *The Revolving Boy.* Garden City, NY: Doubleday, 1966.

Garby, Lee Hawkins. *The Skylark of Space: The Tale of the First Inter-Stellar Cruise.* Providence: Buffalo, 1946. With Edward E. "Doc" Smith.

Gaskell, Jane. See Jane Lynch.

Gillon, Diana. *The Unsleep.* London: Barrie, 1961. With Meir Gillon.

Gilman, Charlotte Perkins. Utopia Trilogy.

_____ *Moving the Mountain.* New York: Charlton, 1911.

_____ *Herland.* New York: Pantheon, 1979 [originally serialized in *The Forerunner,* 1915].

_____ *Ourland* [1916]. As of 1979, had not appeared in separate book form.

Gotlieb, Phyllis. *Sunburst.* Greenwich, CT: Fawcett, 1964.

Griffith, Mary. *Three Hundred Years Hence.* Philadelphia: Prime, 1950.

Harris, Clare Winger. *Away from the Here and Now.* Philadelphia: Dorrance, 1947.

Hawkes, Jacquetta. *Providence Island.* London: Chatto & Windus, 1959.

_____ *Fables.* London: Cresset, 1953. Later title: *A Woman As Great As the World and Other Fables* (1953).

Henderson, Zenna. *The Anything Box.* Garden City, NY: Doubleday, 1965.

_____ *Holding Wonder.* Garden City, NY: Doubleday, 1971.

_____ *The People: No Different Flesh.* London: Gollancz, 1966 [The People #2].

_____ *Pilgrimage: The Book of the People.* Garden City, NY: Doubleday, 1961 [The People #1].

[Hoffman, Shirley Lee]. Hoffman, Lee, pseud. *Always the Black Knight.* New York: Avon, 1970.

_____ *Change Song.* Garden City, NY: Doubleday, 1972.

Holland, Cecelia. *Floating Worlds.* New York: Knopf, 1976.

Holly, J. Hunter. See Joan Carol Holly.

[Holly, Joan Carol]. Holly, J. Hunter, pseud. *The Assassination Affair.* New York: Ace, 1967.

_____ *The Dark Enemy.* New York: Avalon, 1965.

_____ *The Dark Planet.* New York: Avalon, 1962.

_____ *Encounter.* New York: Avalon, 1959.

_____ *The Gray Aliens.* New York: Avalon, 1963.

_____ *The Green Planet.* New York: Avalon, 1960.

_____ *Keeper.* New York: Laser, 1976.

_____ *The Mind Traders*. New York: Avalon, 1966.

_____ *The Running Man*. New York: Avalon, 1963.

_____ *Shepard*. New York: Laser, 1977.

Hughes, Monica. *Crisis on Conshelf Ten*. New York: Atheneum, 1977.

Hull, Edna Mayne. *Out of the Unknown*. Alhambra, CA: Fantasy Publishing, 1948. With A.E. Van Vogt.

_____ *Planets for Sale*. New York: Fell, 1954.

_____ *The Winged Man*. Garden City, NY: Doubleday, 1966. With A.E. Van Vogt.

Hunger, Anna. *The Man Who Lived Forever*. New York: Ace, 1956. With Walter R. DeWitt. Later title: *Year 3097* (1958). Bound with Jerry Sohl's *The Mars Monopoly*.

Hunt, Laura Shellabarger. *Ultra: A Story of Pre-Natal Influence*. Los Angeles: Times-Mirror, 1923.

[Jameson, Margaret]. Lamb, William, pseud. *The World Ends*. London: J.M. Dent, 1937.

[Jardine, Julie Ann]. Cory, Howard L., pseud. *The Mind Monsters*. New York: Ace, 1966. With Jack Jardine. Bound with Philip K. Dick's *The Unteleported Man*.

Jeppson, J.O. *The Second Experiment*. Boston: Houghton, Mifflin, 1974.

Johnston, Mary. *Sweet Rocket*. New York: Harper, 1920.

Judd, Cyril. See Judith Merril

Kavan, Anna. See Helen Edmonds.

*Kidd, Virginia, ed. *Millennial Women: Tales for Tomorrow*. New York: Delacorte, 1978.

Kimberly, Gail. *Flyer*. New York: Popular Library, 1975.

Kreisheimer, H.C. *The Whooping Crane*. New York: Pageant, 1955.

Lane, Mary Bradley. *Mizora*, 1890. Rpt. Boston: G.K. Hall, 1975.

*Laurence, Alice, ed. *Cassandra Rising*. New York: Doubleday, 1978.

Lawrence, Josephine. *Not a Cloud in the Sky*. New York: Harcourt, Brace & world, 1964.

Lawrence, Louise. *The Power of the Stars*. London: Collins, 1972.

Lawrence, Margery. See A.E. Towle

Le Guin, Ursula K., *City of Illusions*. New York: Ace, 1967 [Hainish #3].

_____ *The Dispossessed*. New York: Harper, 1974.

_____ *The Lathe of Heaven*. New York: Scribner, 1971.

_____ *The Left Hand of Darkness*. New York: Ace, 1969.

_____ *Planet of Exile*. New York: Ace, 1966. Bound with Thomas M. Disch's *Mankind Under the Leash* [Hainish #2].

_____ *Rocannon's World*. New York: Ace, 1966. Bound with Avram Davidson's *The Kar-Chee Reign* [Hainish #1].

_____ *The Wind's Twelve Quarters*. New York: Harper, 1975.

_____ *The Word for World is Forest*. New York: Berkley/Putnam, 1976.

Lee, Tanith. *Don't Bite the Sun*. New York: DAW, 1976.

_____ *Drinking Sapphire Wine*. New York: DAW, 1977.

_____ *Electric Forest*. Garden City, NY: Nelson Doubleday [Science Fiction Book Club], 1979.

Lessing, Doris. *The Memoirs of a Survivor*. London: Octagon, 1974.

_____ *Shikasta*. New York: Knopf, 1979.

Lightner, Alice M. *The Day of the Drones*. New York: Norton, 1969.

_____ *Doctor to the Galaxy*. New York: Norton, 1965.

_____ *The Galactic Troubadours*. New York: Norton, 1965.

_____ *The Planet Poachers*. New York: Putnam, 1965 [Rock #2].

_____ *The Rock of Three Planets*. New York: Putnam, 1963 [Rock #1].

_____ *The Space Ark*. New York: Putnam, 1968 [Rock #3].

_____ *Star Dog*. New York: McGraw-Hill, 1973.

Livingston, Marjorie. *Muted Strings*. London: Dakers, 1946.

[Lynch, Jane]. Gaskell, Jane, pseud. *A Sweet Sweet Summer*. London: Holder & Stoughton, 1969.

McCaffrey, Anne. *Decision at Doona*. New York: Ballantine, 1969.

———. *Get Off the Unicorn*. New York: Ballantine, 1977.

———. *Restoree*. New York: Ballantine, 1967.

———. *The Ship Who Sang*. New York: Walker, 1969.

———. *To Ride Pegasus*. New York: Ballantine, 1973.

Dragonriders of Pern Series: Adult

———. *Dragonflight*. New York: Ballantine, 1968.

———. *Dragonquest*. New York: Ballantine, 1971.

———. *The White Dragon*. New York: Ballantine, 1978. The first portion of this novel first appeared in book form as *A Time When*. Cambridge, MA: New England Science Fiction Association, 1975.

The Dragonriders of Pern Series: Juvenile

———. *Dragonsong*. New York: Atheneum, 1976.

———. *Dragonsinger*. New York: Atheneum, 1977.

———. *Dragondrums*. New York: Atheneum, 1979.

MacClennan, Phyllis. *Turned Loose on Irdra*. Garden City, NY: Doubleday, 1970.

McCloy, Helen. *Through a Glass, Darkly*. New York: Random House, 1950.

McIntyre, Vonda. *Dreamsnake*. New York: Houghton Mifflin, 1978.

———. *The Exile Waiting*. Garden City, NY: Nelson Doubleday [Science Fiction Book Club], 1975.

———. *Fireflood and Other Stories*. New York: Houghton Mifflin, 1979.

*McIntyre, Vonda N., and Susan Janice Anderson, eds. *Aurora: Beyond Equality*. New York: Fawcett, 1976.

MacLean, Katherine. *Cosmic Checkmate*. New York: Ace, 1962. With Charles V. de Vet. Bound with Robert Moore Williams' *King of the Fourth Planet*.

———. *Dark Wings*. New York: Atheneum, 1979. With Carl West.

———. *The Diploids*. New York: Avon, 1962.

———. *The Man in the Bird Cage*. New York: Ace, 1971.

———. *Missing Man*. New York: Putnam, 1975.

———. *Trouble With Treaties*. Tacoma, WA: Lanthorne Press, 1975.

Maddux, Rachel. *The Green Kingdom*. New York: Simon & Schuster, 1957.

Mannes, Marya. *They*. New York: Doubleday, 1968.

Martel, Suzanne. *The City Underground*. Trans. Norah Smaridge. New York: Viking, 1964.

Maxwell, Ann. *Change*. New York: Popular Library, 1975.

———. *A Dead God Dancing*. New York: Avon, 1979.

———. *The Singer Enigma*. New York: Popular Library, 1976.

Merril, Judith. *The Best of Judith Merril*. New York: Warner, 1976.

———. *Daughters of Earth*. London: Gollancz, 1968.

———. Judd, Cyril, pseud. *Gunner Cade*. Simon & Schuster, 1952. With C.M. Kornbluth.

———. *Out of Bounds*. New York: Pyramid, 1960.

———. Judd, Cyril, Pseud. *Outpost Mars*. New York: Abelard, 1952. With C.M. Kornbluth. Rev. ed. *Sin in Space* (1961).

———. *Shadow on the Hearth*. Garden City, NY: Doubleday, 1950. Rev. ed. *Sin in Space* (1961).

———. *The Tomorrow People*. New York: Pyramid, 1960.

Mitchison, Naomi Haldane. *Memoirs of a Spacewoman*. London: Gollancz, 1962.

———. *Solution Three*. New York: Warner, 1975.

Moore, C[atherine] L. *The Best of C.L. Moore.* Garden City, NY: Nelson

Doubleday [Science Fiction Book Club], 1975.

____ *Beyond Earth's Gates.* New York: Ace, 1954. With Henry Kuttner. Bound with Andre Norton's *Daybreak—2250 A.D.*

____ *Doomsday Morning.* Garden City, NY: Doubleday, 1957.

____ *Earth's Last Citadel.* New York: Ace, 1964. With Henry Kuttner.

____ *Fury.* New York: Grosset & Dunlap, 1950. With Henry Kuttner. Later title: *Destination Infinity* (1958).

____ *Judgment Night.* New York: Gnome, 1952.

____ Padgett, Lewis, pseud. *Mutant.* New York: Gnome, 1953. With Henry Kuttner.

____ *No Boundaries.* New York: Ballantine, 1955. With Henry Kuttner.

____ *Northwest of Earth.* New York: Gnome, 1954.

____ *Shambleau and Others.* New York: Gnome, 1953.

____ *Well of the Worlds.* New York: Galaxy, 1953. With Henry Kuttner.

Morris, Janet E. The Silistra Series.

____ *High Couch of Silistra (Returning Creation).* New York: Bantam, 1977.

____ *The Golden Sword.* New York: Bantam, 1977.

____ *Wind from the Abyss.* New York: Bantam, 1978.

____ *The Carnelian Throne.* New York: Bantam, 1979.

Murray, Jacqueline. *Daughter of Atlantis.* London: Regency, n.d.

[Neeper, Carolyn]. Neeper, Gary, pseud. *A Place Beyond Man.* New York: Scribner's, 1975.

Norris, Kathleen. *Through a Glass Darkly.* New York: Doubleday, 1957.

North, Andrew. See Andre Norton.

Norton, Andre. *Android at Arms.* New York: Harcourt Brace Jovanovich, 1971.

____ *The Beast Master.* New York: Harcourt, Brace, 1959 [Holsteen Storm #1].

____ *Breed to Come.* New York: Viking, 1972.

____ *Catseye.* New York: Harcourt, Brace & World, 1961.

____ *The Crossroads of Time.* New York: Ace, 1956 [Blake Walker #1]. Bound with Gordon Dickson's *Mankind on the Run.*

____ *Dark Piper.* New York: Harcourt, Brace & World, 1968.

____ *The Defiant Agents.* Cleveland: World, 1962 [Time War #3].

____ *Eye of the Monster.* New York: Ace, 1962. Bound with Norton's *Sea Siege.*

____ *Galactic Derelict.* Cleveland: World, 1959 [Time War #2].

____ *Here Abide Monsters.* New York: Atheneum, 1973.

____ *Ice Crown.* New York: Viking, 1970.

____ *Iron Cage.* New York: Viking, 1974.

____ *Judgment on Janus.* New York: Harcourt, Brace & World, 1963 [Janus #1].

____ *Key Out of Time.* Cleveland: World, 1963 [Time War #4].

____ *Knave of Dreams.* New York: Viking, 1975.

____ *Lord of Thunder.* New York: Harcourt, Brace & World, 1962 [Holsteen Storm #2].

____ *Merlin's Mirror.* New York: DAW, 1975.

____ *Night of Masks.* New York: Harcourt, Brace & World, 1964.

____ *Operation Time Search.* New York: Harcourt, Brace & World, 1967.

____ *Ordeal in Otherwhere.* Cleveland: World, 1964 [Shann Lantee #2].

____ *Perilous Dreams.* New York: DAW, 1976.

____ North, Andrew, pseud. *Plague Ship.* New York: Gnome, 1956 [Solar Queen #2].

____ *Postmarked the Stars.* New York: Harcourt, Brace & World, 1969 [Solar Queen #4].

____ *Quest Crosstime.* New York: Viking, 1965 [Blake Walker #2]. Later title: *Crosstime Agent* (1975).

____ North, Andrew, pseud. *Sargasso of Space.* New York: Gnome, 1955 [Solar Queen #1].

_____ *Sea Siege*. New York: Harcourt, Brace, 1957.

_____ *Secret of the Lost Race*. New York: Ace, 1959. Bound with Jerry Sohl's *One Against Herculum*.

_____ *The Sioux Spaceman*. New York: Ace, 1960. Bound with Richard Wilson's *The Day the Town Took Off*.

_____ *Star Born*. Cleveland: World, 1957 [Astra #2].

_____ *Star Gate*. New York: Harcourt, Brace, 1958.

_____ *Star Guard*. New York: Harcourt, Brace, 1955.

_____ *Star Hunter*. New York: Ace, 1961. Bound with Norton's *Beast Master*.

_____ *Star Man's Son 2250 A.D.* New York: Harcourt, Brace, 1952. Later title: *Daybreak 2250 A.D.* (1954).

_____ *Star Rangers*. New York: Harcourt, Brace, 1953.

_____ *The Stars are Ours!* Cleveland: World, 1954 [Astra #1].

_____ *Storm Over Warlock*. Cleveland: World, 1960 [Shann Lantee #1].

_____ *The Time Traders*. Cleveland: World, 1958 [Time War #1].

_____ *Uncharted Stars*. New York: Viking, 1969 [Zero Stone #2].

_____ *Victory on Janus*. New York: Harcourt, Brace & World, 1966 [Janus #2].

_____ North, Andrew, pseud. *Voodoo Planet*. New York: Ace, 1969 [Solar Queen #1].

_____ *The X Factor*. New York: Harcourt, Brace & World, 1965.

_____ *Zero Stone*. New York: Viking, 1968 [Zero Stone #1].
York:Viking, 1968 [Zero Stone#1].

[O'Malley, Mary Dolling]. Bridge, Ann, pseud. *And Then You Came*. New York: Macmillan, 1949.

Padgett, Lewis. See C.L. Moore

[Payes, Rachel]. Arch, E.L., pseud. *Bridge to Yesterday*. New York: Avalon, 1963.

_____ *The Deathstone*. New York: Avalon, 1964.

_____ *The Double-Minded Man*. New York: Avalon, 1966.

_____ *First Immortals*. New York: Avalon, 1965.

_____ *Forbidden Island*. New York: Berkley, 1973 [as Rachel Payes].

_____ *The Man With Three Eyes*. New York: Avalon, 1967.

_____ *Planet of Death*. New York: Avalon, 1964.

Philmus, Lois C. *A Funny Thing Happened on the Way to the Moon*. New York: Spartan, 1966.

Piercy, Marge. *Woman on the Edge of Time*. New York: Knopf, 1976.

_____ *Woman on the Edge of Time*. New York: Knopf, 1976.

Piserchia, Doris. *A Billion Days of Earth*. New York: Bantam, 1976.

_____ *Earthchild*. New York: Bantam, 1974.

_____ *Mister Justice*. New York: Ace, 1973.

_____ *Spaceling*. Garden City, NY: Nelson Doubleday [Science Fiction Book Club], 1978.

_____ *Star Rider*. New York: Bantam, 1974.

Putney, Susan K. *Against Arcturus*. New York: Ace, 1972. Bound with Dean Koontz's *Time Thieves*.

Rand, Ayn. *Anthem*. London: Cassell, 1938.

_____ *Atlas Shrugged*. New York: Random House, 1957.

Randall, Florence Engel. *Haldane Station*. New York: Harcourt Brace Jovanovich, 1973.

Randall, Marta. *A City in the North*. New York: Warner, 1976.

_____ *Journey*. New York: Pocket Books, 1978 [sequel: *Dangerous Games,* 1980].

[Reed, Lillian Craig]. Reed, Kit, pseud. *Armed Camps*. London: Faber & Faber, 1969.

_____ *Mister Da V. and Other Stories*. London: Faber & Faber, 1967.

Reynolds, Pamela. *Earth Times Two*. New York: Lothrop, 1970.

Ricci, Barbara G. *The Year of the Rats.* New York: Walker, 1973.
Richmond, Leigh (with Walt Richmond). *Gallagher's Glacier* [and] *Positive Charge.* New York: Ace [double], 1970.
_____ *The Lost Millennium.* New York: Ace, 1967. Bound with A. Bertram Chandler's *The Road to the Rim.* Later title: *Siva* (1979).
_____ *The Probability Corner.* New York: Ace, 1977.
_____ *Shock Wave.* New York: Ace, 1967. Bound with Frederick L. Shaw, Jr.'s *Envoy to the Dog Star.*
Roberts, Jane. *The Rebellers.* New York: Ace, 1963. Bound with John Brunner's *Listen! The Stars!*
Robinson, Jeanne. *Stardance.* New York: Dial, 1979. With Spider Robinson.
Romano, Deane. *Flight from Time One.* New York: Walker, 1972.
Roy, Lillian Elizabeth. *The Prince of Atlantis.* New York: Educational, 1929.
Russ, Joanna. *Alyx.* Boston: Gregg, 1976. Includes *Picnic on Paradise.*
_____ *And Chaos Died.* New York: Ace, 1970.
_____ *The Female Man.* New York: Bantam, 1975.
_____ *Picnic On Paradise.* New York: Ace, 1968.
_____ *The Two of Them.* New York: Berkley/Putnam, 1978.
_____ *We Who Are About To....* New York: Dell, 1977.
St. Clair, Margaret. *Agent of the Unknown.* New York: Ace, 1956. Bound with Philip K. Dick's *The World Jones Made.*
_____ *The Dancers of Noyo.* New York: Ace, 1973.
_____ *The Dolphins of Altair.* New York: Dell, 1967.
_____ *The Games of Neith.* New York: Ace, 1960.
_____ *The Green Queen.* New York: Ace, 1956. Bound with Calvert McClay's *3 Thousand Years.*
_____ *Message from Eocene.* New York: Ace, 1964. Bound with St. Clair's *Three Worlds of Futurity.*
_____ *Sign of the Labrys.* New York: Bantam, 1963.
_____ *Three Worlds of Futurity.* New York: Ace, 1964. Bound with St. Clair's *Message from Eocene.*
*Salmonson, Jessica Amanda, ed. *Amazons!* New York: DAW, 1979.
Sargent, Pamela. *Cloned Lives.* New York: Fawcett, 1976.
_____ *Starshadows.* New York: Ace, 1977.
_____ *The Sudden Star.* New York: Fawcett, 1979.
*Sargent, Pamela, ed. *Women of Wonder: Science Fiction Stories by Women about Women.* New York: Vintage, 1975.
*_____ *More Women of Wonder: Science Fiction Novelettes by Women about Women.* New York: Vintage, 1976.
*_____ *The New Women of Wonder: New Science Fiction Stories by Women about Women.* New York: Vintage, 1978.
Saxton, Josephine. *Group Feast.* Garden City, NY: Doubleday, 1971.
_____ *Vector for Seven.* Garden City, NY: Doubleday, 1970.
Sewell, Elizabeth. *The Dividing of Time.* London: Chatto & Windus, 1951.
[Sheldon, Alice]. Tiptree, James, Jr., pseud. *Star Songs for an Old Primate.* New York: Ballantine, 1978.
_____ *Ten Thousand Light Years from Home.* New York: Ace, 1973.
_____ *Up the Walls of the World.* New York: Berkeley, 1978.
_____ *Warm Worlds and Otherwise.* New York: Ballantine, 1975.
Sheehan, Carolyn. *Magnifi-Cat.* Garden City, NY: Doubleday, 1972. With Edmund Sheehan.
Shelley, Mary Wollstonecraft. *Frankenstein or the Modern Prometheus.* London: Hughes, 1818.
Sherburne, Zoa. The Girl Who Knew Tomorrow. New York: Morrow, 1970.

Shiras, Wilmar H. *Children of the Atom.* New York: Gnome, 1953.
Sky, Kathleen. *Birthright.* New York: Laser, 1975.
———. *Ice Prison.* New York: Laser, 1976.
Smith, Evelyn E. *The Perfect Planet.* New York: Avalon, 1962.
———. *Unpopular Planet.* New York: Dell, 1975.
Smith, Suzy. *The Power of the Mind.* Radnor, PA: Chilton, 1975.
Spotswood, Clair Myers. *The Unpredictable Adventure: A Comedy of Women's Independence.* Garden City, NY: Doubleday, 1935.
Stairs, Gordon. See Mary Austin.
Staton, Mary. *From the Legend of Biel.* New York: Ace, 1975.
Stevens, Francis. See Gertrude Barrows Bennett.
Stone, Leslie F. *Out of the Void.* New York: Avalon, 1967.
———. *When the Sun Went Down.* New York: Stellar, 1929.
Sudak, Eudice. *X.* New York: Lancer, 1963.
Susann, Jacqueline. *Yargo.* New York: Bantam, 1979.
Sutton, Jean (with Jeff Sutton). *Alien from the Stars.* New York: Putnam, 1970.
———. *The Beyond.* New York: Putnam, 1967.
———. *Lord of the Stars.* New York: Putnam, 1969.
———. *The Programmed Man.* New York: Putnam, 1968.
Thayer, Tiffany. *Doctor Arnoldi.* New York: Messner, 1934.
Tiptree, James, Jr. See Alice Sheldon.
Tonks, Angela. *Mind Out of Time.* New York: Knopf, 1959.
[Towle, A.E]. Lawrence, Margery, pseud. *The Tomorrow of Yesterday.* London: Hale, 1966.
Uttley, Alison. *A Traveller in Time.* London: Faber & Faber, 1939.
Vassos, Ruth. *Ultimo: An Imaginative Narration of Life Under the Earth...* New York: Dutton, 1930. With John Vassos.
Verseau, Dominique. *Yolanda, The Girl from Erosphere.* New York: Dell, 1975.
Vinge, Joan D. *Eyes of Amber and Other Stories.* New York: NAL/Signet, 1979.
———. *Fireship.* New York: Dell, 1978.
———. *The Outcasts of Heaven Belt.* New York: NAL/Signet, 1978.
Von Harbou, Thea. *The Girl in the Moon.* London: Reader's Library, 1930. Title change: *The Rocket to the Moon* (1930).
———. *Metropolis.* London: Reader's Library, 1927.
.Waller, Louise. *Take Me to Your Leader.* New York: Putnam, 1961. With Leslie Waller.
Weaver, Henrietta. *Flame and the Shadow-Eater.* New York: Holt, 1917.
Weiss, Sara. *Journeys to the Planet Mars or our Mission to Ento.....* 2nd. ed. Rochester: Austin, 1905.
Wetherell, June. *Blueprint for Yesterday.* New York: Walker, 1971.
White, Jane. *Comet.* New York: Harper, 1976 [1st American edition].
Whitell, Evelyn. *Shekinah.* Los Angeles: DeVorss, 1937.
Wilder, Cherry. *The Luck of Brin's Five.* New York: Atheneum, 1977.
Wilhelm, Kate. *Abyss: Two Novellas.* Garden City, NY: Doubleday, 1971.
———. *City of Cain.* Boston: Little, Brown, 1974.
———. *The Clewiston Test.* New York: Farrar, 1976.
———. *The Clone.* New York: Berkley, 1965. With Theodore L. Thomas.
———. *The Downstairs Room.* Garden City, NY: Doubleday, 1968.
———. *The Infinity Box.* New York: Harper & Row, 1975.
———. *Juniper Time.* New York: Harper & Row, 1979.
———. *The Killer Thing.* Garden City, NY: Doubleday, 1967.
———. *Let The Fire Fall.* New York: Doubleday, 1969.
———. *The Mile-Long Spaceship.* New York: Berkley, 1963. Later title: *Andover and the Android* (1966).
———. *The Nevermore Affair.* Garden City, NY: Doubleday, 1966.

_____ *Somerset Dreams and Other Fictions.* New York: Harper & Row, 1978.

_____ *Where Late the Sweet Birds Sang.* New York: Harper & Row, 1976.

_____ *Year of the Cloud.* Garden City, NY: Doubleday, 1970. With Ted Thomas.

Wobig, Ellen. *The Youth Monopoly.* New York: Ace, 1968. Bound with Lan Wright's *Pictures of Pavanne.*

Wrightson, Patricia. *Down to Earth.* New York: Harcourt, Brace & World, 1965.

_____ *The Nargun and the Stars.* London: Hutchinson, 1973.

Yarbro, Chelsea Quinn, *Cautionary Tales.* Garden City, NY: Doubleday, 1978.

_____ *False Dawn.* Garden City, NY: Doubleday, 1978.

_____ *The Palace.* New York: St. Martin's, 1979.

_____ *The Time of the Four Horsemen.* New York: Ace, 1976.

Zerwick, Chloe. *The Cassiopeia Affair.* Garden City, NY: Doubleday, 1968. With Harrison Brown.

Contributors

Marleen S. Barr first thought of editing a critical anthology about women and science fiction when she chaired a panel on the subject at the 1978 Popular Culture Association Conference. Three of the essays in this book were presented at that session. She is also the editor of *The Diary of Deborah Norris Logan*.

Arthur Asa Berger is a member of San Francisco State University's Broadcast Communication Arts Department. He recently edited *Television as an Instrument of Terror* and *Film in Society*.

Jeffrey Berman, Associate Professor of English at SUNY Albany, is the author of *Joseph Conrad: Writing as Rescue*. He is completing *The Shrinking Vision*, a book on the characterization of the psychoanalyst in literature.

Suzy Mckee Charnas is the author of *Walk To The End of The World, Motherlines* and *The Vampire Tapestry*. Her "Scorched Supper on New Niger" recently appeared in *New Voices 3. August 1980* is her next full-length work.

Norman N. Holland is the McNulty Professor of English at SUNY Buffalo. He is currently writing a book on human identity.

Anne Hudson Jones is an Assistant Professor of Literature and Medicine at the University of Texas Institute for the Medical Humanities in Galveston. She organized a special session on Feminist Science Fiction for MLA in 1977. Currently, she is completing a book on Kate Wilhelm.

Susan Kress joined the Skidmore College English Department after completing her Ph.D. at Cambridge University. Her interests include fictional theory and women's studies.

James D. Merritt, Professor of English. Brooklyn College, has written *Ronald Firbank* and *The Pre-Raphaelite Poem* in addition to many articles about nineteenth and twentieth century literature.

Carol Pearson chairs the Women's Studies Program at the University of Maryland. She is the editor (with Katherine Pope) of *Who Am I This Time?: Female Portraits in British and American Literature*.

Eric S. Rabkin, Professor of English and Director of the Collegiate Institute for Values and Science at the University of Michigan, has recently published *Arthur C. Clarke*.

Joanna Russ is currently a member of the University of Washington's English Department. *The Two of Them* is her latest novel.

Scott Sanders, Associate Professor of English, Indiana University, is the author of *D.H. Lawrence: The World of the Five Major Novels.* His articles on science fiction have appeared in *New Boston Review* and *Science-Fiction Studies.*

Lyman Tower Sargent, Chairman of the Political Science Department, University of Missouri-St. Louis, is the author of many articles on utopian literature and *British and American Utopias: A Bibliography.*

Roger C. Schlobin of the Department of English at the North Central Campus of Purdue University, is one of the most active science fiction bibliographers now at work. He is the editor of *The Garland Press Reprint Series of Science Fiction and Fantasy* and *The Reader's Guides to Contemporary Science Fiction Authors.*

Robert Scholes is Professor of English at Brown University. *Fabulation and Metafiction* is his most recent book.

Edward Jay Whetmore is Associate Professor of Communication Arts at the University of San Francisco. His *Mediamerica: Form, Content and Consequence of Mass Communication* and *The Magic Medium: Radio In America* were published a short time ago.